PUBLISHING

Kaplan Publishing are constantly finding new ways to make a difference to your studies and our exciting online resources really do offer something different to ACCA students looking for exam success.

THIS COMPLETE TEXT COMES WITH FREE EN-gage ONLINE RESOURCES SO THAT YOU CAN STUDY ANYTIME, ANYWHERE

Having purchased this Complete Text, you have access to the following online study materials:

- An online version of the Text which allows you to click in and out of the expandable content and view the answers to the Test Your Understanding exercises
- Fixed Online Tests with instant answers
- Test History and Results to allow you to track your performance
- Interim Assessments including Questions and Answers

How to access your online resources

- **Kaplan Financial students** will already have a Kaplan EN-gage account and these extra resources will be available to you online. You do not need to register again, as this process was completed when you enrolled. If you are having problems accessing online materials, please ask your course administrator.
- **If you purchased through Kaplan Flexible Learning or via the Kaplan Publishing website** you will automatically receive an e-mail invitation to Kaplan EN-gage online. Please register your details using this e-mail to gain access to your content. If you do not receive the e-mail or book content, please contact Kaplan Flexible Learning.
- **If you are already a registered Kaplan EN-gage user** go to www.EN-gage.co.uk and log in. Select the 'add a book' feature and enter the ISBN number of this book and the unique pass key at the bottom of this card. Then click 'finished' or 'add another book'. You may add as many books as you have purchased from this screen.
- **If you are a new Kaplan EN-gage user** register at www.EN-gage.co.uk and click on the link contained in the e-mail we sent you to activate your account. Then select the 'add a book' feature, enter the ISBN number of this book and the unique pass key at the bottom of this card. Then click 'finished' or 'add another book'.

Your Code and Information
This code can only be used once for the registration of one book online. This registration will expire when the final sittings for the examinations covered by this book have taken place. Please allow one hour from the time you submitted your book details for us to process your request.

LKIR-ImMP-J3dv-LTgh

Please be aware that this code is case-sensitive and you will need to include the dashes within the passcode, but not when entering the ISBN. For further technical support, please visit www.EN-gage.co.uk

ACCA

Paper F4 ENG

Corporate and Business Law

Complete Text

British library cataloguing-in-publication data

A catalogue record for this book is available from the British Library.

Published by:
Kaplan Publishing UK
Unit 2 The Business Centre
Molly Millars Lane
Wokingham
Berkshire
RG41 2QZ

ISBN 978-0-85732-132-9

© Kaplan Financial Limited, 2010

Printed in the UK by CPI William Clowes, Beccles NR34 7TL.

Acknowledgements

We are grateful to the Association of Chartered Certified Accountants and the Chartered Institute of Management Accountants for permission to reproduce past examination questions. The answers have been prepared by Kaplan Publishing.

Contents

chapter

Introduction

How to Use the Materials

These Kaplan Publishing learning materials have been carefully designed to make your learning experience as easy as possible and to give you the best chances of success in your examinations.

The product range contains a number of features to help you in the study process. They include:

(1) Detailed study guide and syllabus objectives

(2) Description of the examination

(3) Study skills and revision guidance

(4) Complete text or essential text

(5) Question practice

The sections on the study guide, the syllabus objectives, the examination and study skills should all be read before you commence your studies. They are designed to familiarise you with the nature and content of the examination and give you tips on how to best to approach your learning.

The **complete text or essential text** comprises the main learning materials and gives guidance as to the importance of topics and where other related resources can be found. Each chapter includes:

- The **learning objectives** contained in each chapter, which have been carefully mapped to the examining body's own syllabus learning objectives or outcomes. You should use these to check you have a clear understanding of all the topics on which you might be assessed in the examination.

- The **chapter diagram** provides a visual reference for the content in the chapter, giving an overview of the topics and how they link together.

- The **content** for each topic area commences with a brief explanation or definition to put the topic into context before covering the topic in detail. You should follow your studying of the content with a review of the illustration/s. These are worked examples which will help you to understand better how to apply the content for the topic.

- **Test your understanding** sections provide an opportunity to assess your understanding of the key topics by applying what you have learned to short questions. Answers can be found at the back of each chapter.

- **Summary diagrams** complete each chapter to show the important links between topics and the overall content of the paper. These diagrams should be used to check that you have covered and understood the core topics before moving on.

- **Question practice** is provided at the back of each text.

Icon Explanations

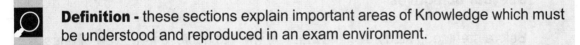

Definition - these sections explain important areas of Knowledge which must be understood and reproduced in an exam environment.

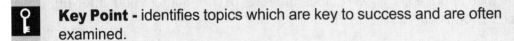

Key Point - identifies topics which are key to success and are often examined.

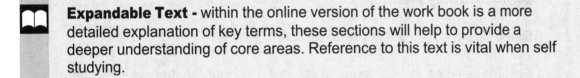

Expandable Text - within the online version of the work book is a more detailed explanation of key terms, these sections will help to provide a deeper understanding of core areas. Reference to this text is vital when self studying.

Test Your Understanding - following key points and definitions are exercises which give the opportunity to assess the understanding of these core areas. Within the work book the answers to these sections are left blank, explanations to the questions can be found within the online version which can be hidden or shown on screen to enable repetition of activities.

Illustration - to help develop an understanding of topics and the test your understanding exercises the illustrative examples can be used.

Exclamation Mark - this symbol signifies a topic which can be more difficult to understand, when reviewing these areas care should be taken.

On-line subscribers

Our on-line resources are designed to increase the flexibility of your learning materials and provide you with immediate feedback on how your studies are progressing.

If you are subscribed to our on-line resources you will find:

(1) On-line referenceware: reproduces your Complete or Essential Text on-line, giving you anytime, anywhere access.

(2) On-line testing: provides you with additional on-line objective testing so you can practice what you have learned further.

(3) On-line performance management: immediate access to your on-line testing results. Review your performance by key topics and chart your achievement through the course relative to your peer group.

Ask your local customer services staff if you are not already a subscriber and wish to join.

Study skills and revision guidance

This section aims to give guidance on how to study for your ACCA exams and to give ideas on how to improve your existing study techniques.

Preparing to study

Set your objectives

Before starting to study decide what you want to achieve - the type of pass you wish to obtain. This will decide the level of commitment and time you need to dedicate to your studies.

Devise a study plan

Determine which times of the week you will study.

Split these times into sessions of at least one hour for study of new material. Any shorter periods could be used for revision or practice.

Put the times you plan to study onto a study plan for the weeks from now until the exam and set yourself targets for each period of study - in your sessions make sure you cover the course, course assignments and revision.

If you are studying for more than one paper at a time, try to vary your subjects as this can help you to keep interested and see subjects as part of wider knowledge.

When working through your course, compare your progress with your plan and, if necessary, re-plan your work (perhaps including extra sessions) or, if you are ahead, do some extra revision/practice questions.

Effective studying

Active reading

You are not expected to learn the text by rote, rather, you must understand what you are reading and be able to use it to pass the exam and develop good practice. A good technique to use is SQ3Rs - Survey, Question, Read, Recall, Review:

(1) **Survey the chapter** - look at the headings and read the introduction, summary and objectives, so as to get an overview of what the chapter deals with.

(2) **Question** - whilst undertaking the survey, ask yourself the questions that you hope the chapter will answer for you.

(3) **Read** through the chapter thoroughly, answering the questions and making sure you can meet the objectives. Attempt the exercises and activities in the text, and work through all the examples.

(4) **Recall** - at the end of each section and at the end of the chapter, try to recall the main ideas of the section/chapter without referring to the text. This is best done after a short break of a couple of minutes after the reading stage.

(5) **Review** - check that your recall notes are correct.

You may also find it helpful to re-read the chapter to try to see the topic(s) it deals with as a whole.

Note-taking

Taking notes is a useful way of learning, but do not simply copy out the text. The notes must:

- be in your own words
- be concise
- cover the key points
- be well-organised
- be modified as you study further chapters in this text or in related ones.

Trying to summarise a chapter without referring to the text can be a useful way of determining which areas you know and which you don't.

Three ways of taking notes:

Summarise the key points of a chapter.

Make linear notes - a list of headings, divided up with subheadings listing the key points. If you use linear notes, you can use different colours to highlight key points and keep topic areas together. Use plenty of space to make your notes easy to use.

Try a diagrammatic form - the most common of which is a mind-map. To make a mind-map, put the main heading in the centre of the paper and put a circle around it. Then draw short lines radiating from this to the main sub-headings, which again have circles around them. Then continue the process from the sub-headings to sub-sub-headings, advantages, disadvantages, etc.

Highlighting and underlining

You may find it useful to underline or highlight key points in your study text - but do be selective. You may also wish to make notes in the margins.

Revision

The best approach to revision is to revise the course as you work through it. Also try to leave four to six weeks before the exam for final revision. Make sure you cover the whole syllabus and pay special attention to those areas where your knowledge is weak. Here are some recommendations:

Read through the text and your notes again and condense your notes into key phrases. It may help to put key revision points onto index cards to look at when you have a few minutes to spare.

Review any assignments you have completed and look at where you lost marks - put more work into those areas where you were weak.

Practise exam standard questions under timed conditions. If you are short of time, list the points that you would cover in your answer and then read the model answer, but do try to complete at least a few questions under exam conditions.

Also practise producing answer plans and comparing them to the model answer.

If you are stuck on a topic find somebody (a tutor) to explain it to you.

Read good newspapers and professional journals, especially ACCA's Student Accountant - this can give you an advantage in the exam.

Ensure you know the structure of the exam - how many questions and of what type you will be expected to answer. During your revision attempt all the different styles of questions you may be asked.

Further reading

You can find further reading and technical articles under the student section of ACCA's website.

Paper introduction

Paper background

The aim of ACCA Paper F4 (ENG), **Corporate and Business Law**, is to develop knowledge and skills in the understanding of the general legal framework, and of specific legal areas relating to business, recognising the need to seek further specialist legal advice where necessary.

Objectives of the syllabus

- Identify the essential elements of the legal system including the main sources of law.

- Recognise and apply the appropriate legal rules relating to the law of obligations.

- Explain and apply the law relating to employment relationships.

- Distinguish between alternative forms and constitutions of business organisations.

- Recognise and compare types of capital and the financing of companies.

- Describe and explain how companies are managed, administered and regulated.

- Recognise the legal implications relating to companies in difficulty or in crisis.

- Demonstrate an understanding of governance and ethical issues relating to business.

Core areas of the syllabus

- Essential elements of the legal system.

- The law of obligations.

- Employment law.

- The formation and constitution of business organisations.

- Capital and the financing of companies.

- Management, administration and regulation of companies.

- Legal implications relating to companies in difficulty or in crisis.

- Governance and ethical issues relating to business.

Syllabus objectives

1   We have reproduced the ACCA's syllabus below, showing where the objectives are explored within this book. Within the chapters, we have broken down the extensive information found in the syllabus into easily digestible and relevant sections, called **Content Objectives**. These correspond to the objectives at the beginning of each chapter.

Syllabus learning objective Chapter reference

1A ESSENTIAL ELEMENTS OF THE LEGAL SYSTEM

21 Court structure

(a) Define law and distinguish types of law.[2]	1
(b) Explain the structure and operation of the courts and tribunals systems.[2]	1

2 Sources of law

(a) Explain what is meant by case law and precedent within the context of the hierarchy of the courts.[2]	1
(b) Explain legislation and evaluate delegated legislation.[2]	1
(c) Illustrate the rules and presumptions used by the courts in interpreting statutes.[2]	1

3 Human rights

(a) Identify the concept of human rights as expressed in the Human Rights Act 1998.[2]	1
(b) Explain the impact of human rights law on statutory interpretation.[2]	1
(c) Explain the impact of human rights law on the common law.[2]	1

B THE LAW OF OBLIGATIONS

1 Formation of contract

(a) Analyse the nature of a simple contract.[2]	2
(b) Explain the meaning of offer and distinguish it from invitations to treat.[2]	2
(c) Explain the meaning and consequence of acceptance.[2]	2
(d) Explain the need for consideration.[2]	2
(e) Analyse the doctrine of privity.[2]	2
(f) Distinguish the presumptions relating to intention to create legal relations.[2]	2

2 Content of contracts

(a) Distinguish terms from mere representations.[2]	2
(b) Define the various contractual terms.[2]	2
(c) Explain the effect of exclusion clauses and evaluate their control.[2]	2

3 Breach of contract and remedies

(a) Explain the meaning and effect of breach of contract.[2]	2
(b) Explain the rules relating to the award of damages.[2]	2
(c) Analyse the equitable remedies for breach of contract.[2]	2

2   Fraudulent behaviour

(a) Recognise the nature and legal control over insider dealing. 13 [2]

(b) Recognise the nature and legal control over money laundering.[2]   13

(c) Discuss potential criminal activity in the operation, management and winding up of companies.[2]   13

(d) Distinguish between fraudulent and wrongful trading.[2]   13

The superscript numbers in square brackets indicate the intellectual depth at which the subject area could be assessed within the examination. Level 1 (knowledge and comprehension) broadly equates with the Knowledge module, Level 2 (application and analysis) with the Skills module and Level 3 (synthesis and evaluation) with the Professional level. However, lower level skills can continue to be assessed as you progress through each module and level.

The examination

Examination format

	Number of marks
Seven 10-mark questions (Knowledge)	70
Three 10-mark questions (Application)	30
	———
	100

Total time allowed: 3 hours

On-line subscribers

Study skills and revision guidance

Preparing to study

Effective studying

Revision

Further reading

Paper introduction

Objectives of the syllabus

KAPLAN PUBLISHING

Core areas of the syllabus

Syllabus objectives

The examination

Examination format

English legal system

Chapter learning objectives

Upon completion of this chapter you will be able to:

- explain the difference between civil and criminal law
- explain the structure and operation of the civil courts and tribunal systems
- explain the meaning of judicial precedent, ratio decidend and obiter dicta
- illustrate how the doctrine of judicial precedent works in relation to the civil courts
- explain how legislation is made and the doctrine of sovereignty
- set out the rules and presumptions used by the courts in interpreting statutes
- identify the concept of human rights as expressed in the Human Rights Act 1998 (HRA 1998)
- explain the impact of human rights law on statutory interpretation
- explain the impact of human rights law on the common law.

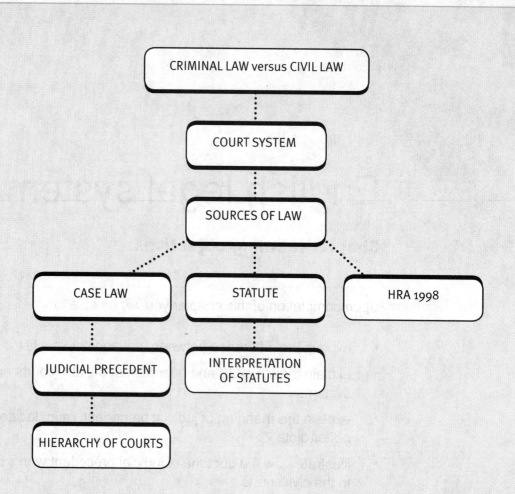

1 Criminal law versus civil law

Criminal law	Civil law
Criminal law relates to conduct of which the State disapproves and which it seeks to control.	Civil law is a form of private law and involves the relationships between individual citizens.
Purpose - the enforcement of particular forms of behaviour by the State, which acts to ensure compliance.	**Purpose** - to settle disputes between individuals and to provide remedies.
In criminal law the case is brought by the **State** in the name of the Crown. A criminal case will be reported as Regina v ..., where Regina means the latin for 'queen'.	In civil law the case is brought by the **claimant**, who is seeking a remedy. The case will be referred to by the names of the parties involved in the dispute, such as Brown v Smith.
Burden of proof – guilt must be shown **beyond reasonable doubt** (high standard of proof).	**Burden of proof** – liability must be shown on the **balance of probabilities** (lower standard of proof).
Object – to regulate society by the threat of punishment.	**Object** – usually financial compensation to put the claimant in the position he would have been in had the wrong not occurred.
If found guilty the criminal court will sentence the accused and it may fine him or impose a period of imprisonment. If innocent the accused will be acquitted.	The civil court will order the defendant to pay damages or it may order some other remedy, e.g. specific performance or injunction.

Test your understanding 1

(1) **Which one of the following statements is correct?**

   A   The aim of the criminal law is to regulate behaviour within society by the threat of punishment.

   B   The aim of the criminal law is to punish offenders.

   C   The aim of the criminal law is to provide a means whereby injured persons may obtain compensation.

   D   The aim of the criminal law is to ensure that the will of the majority is imposed upon the minority.

2 The court system

The main English civil courts

The following diagram shows the main civil courts. The term 'first instance' refers to the court in which the case is first heard. Appeals are heard in a different court. The arrows show the way a case will progress through the court system.

Supreme Court (previously House of Lords)
Five Law Lords hear appeals from Court of Appeal
and exceptionally from High Court

Court of Appeal (civil division)
Three Lords Justices of Appeal hear appeals from the
High Court and County courts

County court	High Court of Justice
First instance civil claims in contract, tort, landlord and tenant, probate and insolvency. One district judge hears small claims. The hearing is informal and no costs are awarded. One circuit judge hears most fast-track, and some multitrack, cases.	One High Court judge in first instance. Queen's Bench Division (QBD) hears first instance cases of contract and tort. Chancery Division (ChD) deals with land law, trusts, company law, partnership law, insolvency, etc. It hears appeals from County courts on probate and insolvency. Family Division hears matrimonial cases.

Magistrates' court

Jurisdiction is mainly criminal (see section on criminal courts) but does have civil jurisdiction in family matters such as contact orders, adoption, and maintenance. There are also powers of recovery of council tax arrears and charges for water, gas and electricity.

The House of Lords was replaced by the Supreme Court on 1 October 2009. This new court has assumed the judicial functions of the House of Lords. The Law Lords that used to sit in the House of Lords now sit as twelve Justices of the Supreme Court, with a President at its head.

KAPLAN PUBLISHING

The Supreme Court was established by the Constitutional Reform Act 2005. It was felt that there needed to be a separation of powers between the judicial functions of the House of Lords (to decide issues in relation to the law) and the legislative functions of the House of Lords (to make the law) to give assurance of the independence of the judges.

The Supreme Court is now in a separate building from the House of Lords and has its own appointment system, staff and budget.

The three-track system

When a claim is received, it will be allocated to one of three tracks for the hearing.

(1)   The small claims track – deals with simple claims valued at no more than £5,000, an informal court.

(2)   The fast-track – deals with moderately valued claims of between £5,000 and £15,000, expected to last no more than one day.

(3)   The multitrack – deals with claims of over £15,000 and/or complex claims.

Note: the County court deals with all cases allocated to the small claims track, the majority of fast track and some multi track cases. All other claims are dealt with by the High Court.

Other civil courts

European Court of Justice (ECJ)	European Court of Human Rights (ECtHR)
ECJ deals with actions between the EU institutions and the member states. It is the ultimate authority on the interpretation of European law. ECJ is therefore superior to the House of Lords. Cases are referred to the ECJ by national courts.	The final court of appeal in relation to matters concerning HRA 1998. Proceedings in the English courts must have been exhausted before ECtHR will hear a case.
No appeal.	No appeal.

The main English criminal courts

SUPREME COURT
Five Justices of Supreme Court hear appeals from the Court of Appeal and exceptionally from High Court.

COURT OF APPEAL (Criminal division)
Three Lord Justice of Appeal hear appeals from the Crown Court.

CROWN COURT
Presided over by a judge whose role is to decide questions of law and impose the punishment.

Case will be heard before a jury whose role is to decide questions of fact i.e. whether defendant is guilty of the offence.

MAGISTRATES COURT
Court of first instance. Deals with criminal cases in various ways:
- Summary offences – decides whether defendant is guilty of the offence and imposes the penalty. Penalties are less in the Magistrates court.
- Indictable offences where there is to be trial by jury. Magistrates will conduct committal proceedings to make sure the defendant has a case to answer.

Presided over by either:
- Lay Magistrates. The bench usually consists of three.
- Stipendiary Magistrate sitting alone.

Appeals on questions of fact go to the Crown Court.

Appeals on questions of law go to the High Court.

HIGH COURT (Queens Bench Division)
Three judges preside.

Hears appeals from Magistrates Court on points of law.

Appeals go directly to the Supreme Court.

Tribunals

Tribunals are also an important part of the English legal system and are an alternative to using the court system to settle a dispute.

In the past, tribunals had been created on an ad hoc basis to perform various judicial functions, for example Employment Tribunals and Asylum and Immigration Tribunals. The tribunals' members were a mixture of judges, lawyers, experts and laypeople, and were regulated by various government departments and bodies. Though these tribunals were supervised by and had rights of appeal within the UK court system, a reform was recommended to create a unified and simplified structure which was better integrated into the courts system.

The Tribunals, Courts and Enforcement Act 2007

The Act made various reforms with regards to tribunals in particular the structure of tribunals.

Section 1 of the Act recognises legally qualified members of tribunals as members of the judiciary of the United Kingdom who are guaranteed continued judicial independence.

Section 3 of the Act creates two new tribunals to which existing jurisdictions will be transferred, a First-tier Tribunal and an Upper Tribunal.

The First-tier Tribunal is divided into six chambers:

- General Regulatory Chamber
- Social Entitlement Chamber
- Health, Education and Social Care Chamber
- War Pensions and Armed Forces Compensation Chamber
- Tax Chamber
- The Immigration and Asylum Chamber.

The main functions of the Upper Tribunal are to

- take over hearing appeals to the courts, and similar bodies from the decisions of local tribunals
- decide certain cases that do not go through the First-tier Tribunal
- exercise powers of judicial review in certain circumstances ; and
- deal with enforcement of decisions, directions and orders made by tribunals.

There is a right of appeal to the Court of Appeal of England and Wales.

Some tribunals will still lie outside the new system.

Employment tribunals

Employment tribunals are established to hear disputes between an employee and their employer on certain statutory employment matters, such as unfair dismissal (see **Chapter 4**).

Employment tribunals are composed of one employment judge, plus two expert laymen who are drawn from panels representing both sides of the industry.

Appeals are to the employment appeal tribunal (EAT) and can only be made on a point of law.

The EAT is composed of one High Court judge, plus two or four expert laymen.

Court v Tribunal

	Court	Tribunal
Expertise	Case may not be heard by a specialist in that particular area of law.	Case will be heard by someone who has expertise in that area.
Speed	A slower process.	A much quicker process.
Cost	Legal aid maybe available, but if not can be an expensive process.	Legal aid is not available (except for land tribunals and EAT's) but can be a much cheaper procedure.
Proceedings	Strict rules relating to evidence, pleading and procedure.	Much less formal and can be less intimidating.
Decisions	Are bound by the doctrine of judicial precedent, therefore make consistent decisions.	Not bound by the doctrine of judicial precedent, therefore risk of making inconsistent decisions.

3 Sources of law

Overview

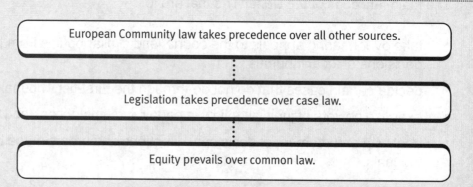

European Community law takes precedence over all other sources.

Legislation takes precedence over case law.

Equity prevails over common law.

Case law

Throughout this text you will find examples of cases which have come before the courts. These cases are not simply examples of the way in which the law is applied; they also illustrate the way in which the law is made. The examiner expects you to learn the cases and to include them in your answers.

Case law can be subdivided into:

* common law

* equity.

KAPLAN PUBLISHING

Common law:

- developed from local customs
- introduced the system of precedent (see below)
- the only remedy is damages
- may be rigid and inflexible.

Equity:

- developed as a petition by a party who felt the common law had led to injustice
- it is more flexible than the common law
- it introduced new discretionary remedies, e.g. injunctions and specific performance
- it is concerned with fairness and therefore will not be granted if there is undue delay in bringing the case or if the petitioner has himself acted unfairly, or where there is no mutuality (both parties should be able to bring a case).

Doctrine of judicial precedent

The system, adopted by the judges, of following the decisions in previous cases is called the doctrine of judicial precedent.

- Some precedents are **binding** (meaning they **must** be followed in later cases).
- Others are merely **persuasive** (meaning that a judge in a later case **may** choose to follow it but he is not bound to do so).

There are three factors to be considered in deciding whether a precedent is binding or persuasive:

- the hierarchy of the courts
- ratio decidendi and obiter dicta
- the material facts of the case.

The hierarchy of the courts

As a general rule, the precedents of higher courts bind lower courts, but not vice versa.

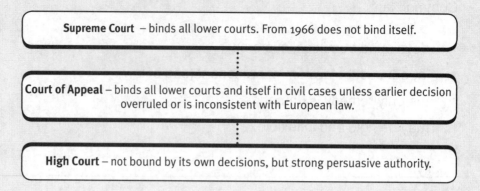

Supreme Court – binds all lower courts. From 1966 does not bind itself.

Court of Appeal – binds all lower courts and itself in civil cases unless earlier decision overruled or is inconsistent with European law.

High Court – not bound by its own decisions, but strong persuasive authority.

Ratio decidendi and obiter dicta

The ratio decidendi is the legal reason for the decision. It is capable of forming the binding precedent. It is a statement of law which is carried down to later decisions.

Obiter dicta are statements which are not part of the ratio, they are other statements made by the judges such as hypothetical situations or wide legal principles. They are persuasive rather than binding. This means that the judge can take the statement into account (and usually will) when reaching his decision, but he does not have to follow it.

Facts of the case

In order for a precedent to be binding on a judge in a later case, the material facts of the two cases must be the same. If they are significantly different, the precedent will be persuasive rather than binding.

When is a precedent not binding?

A precedent is not binding where it:

- has been overruled by a higher court.
- has been overruled by statute.
- was made without proper care (per incuriam).
- can be distinguished from the earlier case, i.e. the material facts differ.

Advantages and disadvantages of judicial precedent

Advantages

- Reaching decisions as a result of the doctrine of precedent makes the system consistent. It becomes easier to predict the result of litigation.
- It allows the English legal system to be flexible. Decisions can be adapted and extended to reflect changes in society.

KAPLAN PUBLISHING

- The law is clear. As it is only the ratio decidendi that is followed it is easy to see what law is being applied.

- Decisions arise from actual events, therefore the system is practical.

Disadvantages

- The law is very complex because there is a vast number of cases, and inconsistencies can arise. The same judgement may contain differing, and even conflicting, arguments making the precedent hard to understand and even harder to apply.

- The law can become rigid, leading to inflexibility and loss of development.

- Case law is reactive rather than proactive. Rather than dealing with issues in advance and stating the law, a case is considered and a decision made once a particular situation has arisen.

Test your understanding 2

(1) **Which one of the following statements about the law of equity is untrue?**

    A   Equitable remedies may only be awarded at the discretion of the court.

    B   Equity originally developed as a result of individual appeals to the King being delegated to the Lord Chancellor.

    C   Equitable remedies include damages, injunctions and decrees of specific performance.

    D   Equity will prevail in a case of conflict between it and the common law.

(2) **Which part of a case decided by the courts is binding on lower courts dealing with the same material facts?**

    A   Obiter dicta.

    B   The decision of the judge.

    C   The ratio decidendi.

    D   All of the above.

(3) **Which one of the following is the highest court in England?**

    A   The Court of Appeal.

    B   The Supreme Court.

    C   The High Court.

    D   The Crown Court.

(4) **Which one of the following statements is untrue?**

    A   Decisions of the Supreme Court (formerly the House of Lords) bind all lower courts.

    B   The Supreme Court (formerly the House of Lords) is not bound by its own decisions.

    C   Decisions of the Supreme Court (formerly the House of Lords) override statute.

    D   Appeals can be made from the Supreme Court (formerly the House of Lords) to the ECJ.

KAPLAN PUBLISHING

4 Legislation

Types of legislation

Legislation falls into two categories:

- Acts of Parliament
- delegated legislation.

Acts of Parliament

Parliament consists of:

- the House of Commons
- the House of Lords
- the Monarch.

In order to become an Act of Parliament, a Bill must go through the following stages in both Houses:

- first reading - the name of the Bill and the its proposer is read out
- second reading - debate takes place on the principles of the Bill and it is then voted upon
- committee stage - a smaller number of MP's consider the wording of the Bill. This stage can last several months depending on the contentiousness of the Bill
- report stage - the Bill as amended by the Committee is reported back to the full House
- third reading - the Bill is read for the final time.

At the end of this process in both Houses, the Bill must receive the Royal Assent.

Note that an Act does not necessarily come into force immediately. Its provisions may take effect on a piece-meal basis. An example is the Companies Act 2006.

Doctrine of sovereignty of Parliament

Parliament is sovereign. This means that, in theory, it is only Parliament that can make new law and it can make any law it wishes. However it cannot pass an Act which can never be repealed.

The courts cannot question the validity of an Act. However, they must refuse to apply an Act that contravenes EC law.

Delegated legislation

Delegated legislation is made on behalf of Parliament. It consists of:

- statutory instruments: made by Government Ministers using powers delegated by Parliament

- bye-laws: made by local authorities

- Orders in Council: made by the Privy Council in the name of the Monarch on the advice of the Prime Minister.

Delegated legislation has a number of advantages:

- It saves Parliamentary time.

- It may benefit from access to technical expertise, thus leaving Parliament free to consider and debate the underlying principles.

- Flexibility – it is quick and easy to make and to change.

However, it also has a number of disadvantages:

- Its volume and lack of publicity means that it can be difficult to keep up with the changes introduced.

- It is criticised as being undemocratic as it is made without recourse to the elected House of Commons.

There are a number of means of controlling delegated legislation:

- **Parliamentary** – Since 1973 there has been a Joint Select Committee on Statutory Instruments, whose function it is to scrutinise all statutory instruments. They have the power to draw the instrument to the attention of both Houses on any number of grounds, but cannot do so on a ground which relates to the actual merits of the instrument or the policy it is pursuing.

- **Judicial** – The courts can challenge the validity of delegated legislation through the process of judicial review. It can be challenged on the grounds that the person making it has acted ultra vires, by exceeding their powers. If successful the court will declare it void and unenforceable.

- **Human Rights Act 1998** – Delegated legislation is secondary legislation, therefore it can be declared invalid by the courts if it is incompatible with HRA 1998.

Test your understanding 3

(1) **Which of the following statements is correct?**

I   In the event of a conflict between equity and the common law, the common law prevails.

II   An Act of Parliament can overrule any common law or equitable rule.

A   (I) only.

B   (II) only.

C   Neither (I) nor (II).

D   Both (I) and (II).

(2) **Which of the following is NOT a form of delegated legislation?**

A   Orders in Council.

B   Statutory instruments.

C   Local authority bye-laws.

D   Acts of Parliament.

5 Rules of statutory interpretation

Introduction

The process by which judges assign meanings to ambiguous words or phrases in statutes is called the interpretation of statutes.

Judges can use certain aids, rules and presumptions to help them assign a meaning to a word.

Aids to interpretation

The courts can use the following aids to help them interpret a statute:

- the legislation itself (i.e. its definition section).

- judicial precedents.

- the Interpretation Act 1978 - the Act defines certain terms frequently found in legislation. The Act also states that 'unless a specific intention to the contrary exists, the use in a statute of masculine gender terminology also inlcudes the feminine, and vice versa'.

- the Oxford English Dictionary.

- Hansard (to see what was said in Parliament when the Bill was being debated). In **Pepper v Hart (1992)** the House of Lords established the principle that when primary legislation is ambiguous then, under certain circumstances, the court may refer to statements made in the House of Commons or House of Lords in an attempt to interpret the meaning of the legislation.

- sources of EC law. Since the United Kingdom joined the EC in 1972 they agreed to conform with existing and future EC law. One of the many sources of EC law is a Directive which generally addresses the member states and requires that the states take action within an indentified time period to change their own law. When in doubt courts may look to the Directive for guidance on interpretation.

- Human Rights Act 1998 (see **section 6**).

Literal rule

Words must be given their ordinary dictionary meaning, even if this produces an undesirable outcome.

Fisher v Bell (1961) – Under the Restriction of Offensive Weapons Act 1959 it was a criminal offence to 'offer for sale' a flick knife. A shopkeeper who displayed one in his shop window was held not guilty as the court chose to follow the contract law meaning of the word 'offer'.

Golden rule

Where the literal rule gives more than one meaning or provides an absurd result, the golden rule is used to ensure that preference is given to the meaning that does not result in the provision being an absurdity.

Adler v George (1964)

Facts: a conviction was challenged on the basis of what appeared to be a miswording in the Official Secrets Act (1920). This Act made it an offence to obstruct a member of the armed forces `in the vicinity of' particular locations, but not actually `in' those locations. The defendant was actually inside an Air Force base at the time of the incident, which he claimed was beyond the literal scope of the act.

Held: The words 'in the vicinity of' a prohibited place in the Official Secrets Act were held to cover the acts of the defendant which took place 'within' a prohibited place.

Mischief rule

Used to interpret a statute in a way which provides a remedy for the mischief the statute was enacted to prevent.

Gorris v Scott (1874)

Facts: The Contagious Diseases (Animals) Act 1869 provided that any ship carrying animals should contain them in pens. The defendant neglected his duty, and some of the claimant's sheep were washed overboard and lost.

Held: Since the purpose of the statute was to prevent the spread of contagious disease, and not to guard against the danger of the property being washed overboard, the claim failed.

Purposive Rule

This is a more modern approach. Here the court is not just looking to see what the gap was in the old law, it is making a decision as to what they felt Parliament meant to achieve.

Gardiner v Sevenoaks RDC (1950)

Facts: The purpose of an Act was to provide for the safe storage of film wherever it might be stored on 'premises'. The claimant argued that 'premises' did not include a cave and so the Act had no application to this case.

Held: The purpose of the Act was to protect the safety of persons working in all places where film was stored. If film was stored in a cave, the word 'premises' included the cave.

Eiusdem generis

General words mean the same kind of thing as the specific words they follow.

Powell v Kempton Park Racecourse Co (1899)

Facts: Section 1 of the Betting Act 1853 prohibited betting in a 'house, office, room or other place'. The issue was whether a ring at a racecourse was an 'other place' for the purposes of this statute.

Held: The Lords decided that if the eiusdem generis rule was applied, the specific words such as 'room' and 'office' that preceded the general phrase 'or other place' created a class of indoor places. As a ring on a racecourse was outside it would not fall within this category. Therefore the Act did not apply to restrict gambling here.

Expressio unius exclusio alterius

Where a statute seeks to establish a list of what is covered by its provisions, then anything not expressly included in that list is specifically excluded.

Presumptions

There are presumptions which will generally apply unless the legislation specifically states otherwise, for example:

- A statute will not bind the Crown.

- A statute cannot conflict with international law. An Act should therefore be interpreted as giving effect to international obligations.

- A statute does not have any retrospective effect.

- A statute does not alter the common law.

- A statute does not exclude the jurisdiction of the court.

- Legislation does not extend beyond the territorial jurisdiction of the UK.

6 Human Right Act 1998

What is its purpose?	HRA 1998 incorporates the European Convention for the Protection of Human Rights and Fundamental Freedoms 1950 into UK domestic law.
Which rights are covered?	The most important are: • the right to life • the right to liberty and security • the right to a fair trial • the right to freedom of thought, conscience and religion • freedom of expression • freedom of assembly • prohibition of discrimination • the right to free elections.
What is Convention law?	Convention law means the Convention and the decisions of the ECtHR.
How does it affect judicial interpretation?	UK courts must take Convention law into account when deciding a question that has arisen in connection with a Convention right.

KAPLAN PUBLISHING

How does it affect judicial interpretation?	UK courts must take Convention law into account when deciding a question that has arisen in connection with a Convention right.
Any impact on the doctrine of precedent?	Judges will not be bound by a previous interpretation of existing legislation where it did not take into account Convention rights. Note that the ECtHR is free to depart from its own previous decisions. In **Stafford v UK (2002)** the court overruled its previous decision in **Wynne v UK (1994)**. It held that the Home Secretary's role in fixing the minimum tariff for a person convicted of murder was a sentencing exercise and not merely an administrative implementation of the sentence. It was therefore incompatible with the convention.
What if legislation is incompatible with the Convention?	Any existing legislation must be interpreted so it is compatible with the rights under the Convention. If a court feels that legislation is incompatible with the Covention and it cannot interpret it in such a way to make it compatible, then it may make a **declaration of incompatibility**. However, the declaration does not make the legislation invalid. It is left to Parliament to remedy the situation through new legislation. However, the courts do have the power to declare secondary legislation (e.g. statutory instruments) to be invalid.
What is derogation?	A derogation is a provision which allows for all or part of a legal measure to be applied differently, or not at all by public·authorities. However, where rights have been derogated the public authority can mitigate its actions by demonstrating a legitimate need to derogate and that the derogation was proportionate to the need. For example, the UK may choose not to enforce a specific provision in the HRA due to circumstances such as the threat of terrorism.

Bellinger v Bellinger (2003)

Facts: The House of Lords had to consider whether or not a male to female transsexual could be treated as a female under the Matrimonial Causes Act 1973.

Held: The court was unable to interpret the Act to allow the transsexual to be considered female. It did however issue a declaration of incompatibility.

The **Gender Recognition Act 2004** addressed the issue in **Bellinger v Bellinger (2003)**. The purpose of the Act is to provide transsexual people with legal recognition in their acquired gender. This is an example of the passing of a statute to put right a perceived unfair outcome of a case.

Mendoza v Ghaidan (2003)

Facts: The Rent Act 1977 allows a spouse to inherit a statutory tenancy. In **Fitzpatrick v Sterling Housing Association Limited (1999)**, the House of Lords had declined to allow same-sex partners to inherit statutory tenancies on the grounds that they could not be considered to be the wife or husband of the deceased.

Held: The Court of Appeal held that the Rent Act, as the House of Lords had construed it in the **Fitzpatrick** case, was incompatible with the Convention on the grounds of its discriminatory treatment of surviving same-sex partners. The Court held that the incompatibility could be remedied by reading the words 'as his or her wife or husband' as meaning 'as if they were his or her wife or husband'.

The above case is an example of how the judges used the Golden Rule to interpret statute.

7 Chapter summary

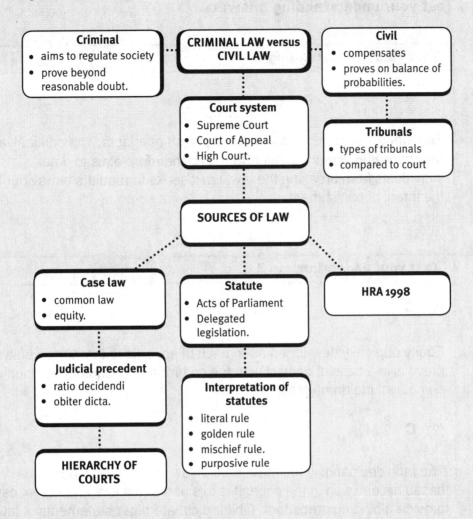

Test your understanding answers

Test your understanding 1

(1) A

The **aim** of the criminal law is not to punish offenders. The criminal law threatens punishment to offenders, and therefore aims to deter individuals from breaking the law, i.e. it seeks to regulate behaviour by the threat of punishment.

Test your understanding 2

(1) C

Equity originally developed as a result of appeals to the King. Equity prevails in a case of conflict with the common law. Equitable remedies do not include damages.

(2) C

The ratio decidendi is the statement of law on which the judge has based his decision in the case. It is this part of the judgement that can provide a binding precedent. Obiter dicta are other statements of law made by the judge which did not form a basis for the decision in the case, and do not create a binding precedent.

(3) B

The Supreme Court (formerly the House of Lords) is the highest court in England.

(4) C

Decisions of the Supreme Court are binding on all lower courts. However, the Supreme Court is not bound by its own decisions. Statute overrides decisions of the Supreme Court. Appeals can be made from the Supreme Court to the ECJ.

KAPLAN PUBLISHING

Test your understanding 3

(1) **B**

Equity is a body of discretionary rules devised by the court on the basis of fairness to remedy defects in the common law. It is therefore incorrect to say that common law prevails over equity. However, statement (ii) is correct. The effect of a new statute is to overrule any common law or equity rule that is inconsistent with the provisions of the new statute.

(2) **D**

Orders in Council, statutory instruments and local authority bye-laws are all examples of delegated legislation. Acts of Parliament are not.

2

Contract law

Chapter learning objectives

Upon completion of this chapter you will be able to:

- explain the essential elements of a contract
- explain what is and is not an offer
- explain the meaning and consequence of acceptance
- explain the meaning of consideration
- explain the doctrine of privity and the main exceptions
- distinguish the presumptions relating to the intention to create legal relations
- distinguish terms from mere representations
- define the various contractual terms
- explain the effect of exclusions and evaluate their control
- explain the meaning and effect of breach of contract
- explain the rules relating to the award of damages
- analyse the equitable remedies for breach of contract.

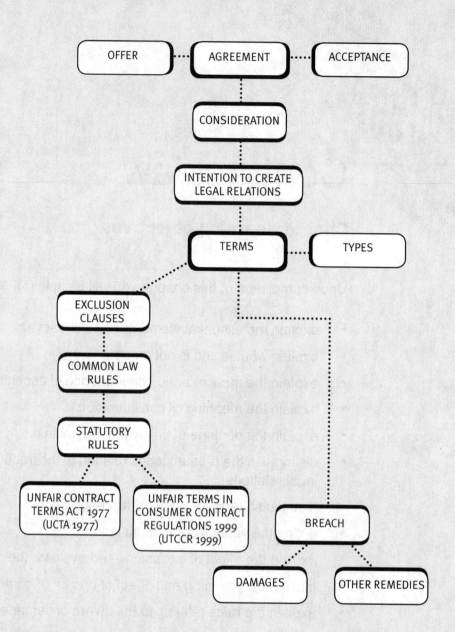

1 Essential elements of a valid contract

The following elements are needed to form a valid contract:

- **Agreement**, i.e. offer and acceptance.
- **Consideration.**
- **Intention to create legal relations.**
- **Capacity and Legality**

Form of the contract

General rule

A contract can be in any form - **simple contract**. It may be written, or oral, or inferred from the conduct of the parties. Most contracts are simple contracts.

Exceptions

Some contracts must be made in a particular form such as writing.

Contracts for the sale of land must be in writing.

Specialty contracts

Conveyances of land and leases for three years or more must be by deed – these are known as specialty contracts. Such contracts must be in writing, signed, witnessed and delivered (i.e. intended to take effect).

The limitation period for a contract made by deed is 12 years. For all other contracts, the limitation period is six years.

Test your understanding 1

(1) **Which of the following statements is/are correct?**

   I   If an agreement is stated to be 'binding in honour only', the parties have decided that the agreement should not have contractual force.

   II   If an agreement is not in writing, the parties are presumed to have intended that it should not be legally enforceable.

   A   (I) only.

   B   (II) only.

   C   Neither (I) nor (II).

(2) **The vast majority of contracts are 'simple'. What is the meaning of the word 'simple' in this context?**

   A   The terms of the contract are set out in writing.

   B   The contract does not need to be in any particular form to be binding.

   C   The contract contains fewer than ten provisions.

   D   The contract is not supported by consideration.

(3) **What is the limitation period for a contract that is made by deed?**

A   5 years.

B   6 years.

C   12 years.

D   30 years.

(4) The law of contract is of special importance in providing a legal framework within which businesses can operate.

Which one of the following statements is correct?

A   A contract need not necessarily be in writing.

B   A contract is valid even when one party does not intend the agreement to be legally binding.

C   A contract comes under the remit of criminal law rather than civil law.

D   A contract can be entered into validly by all adult persons.

2 Offer

What is an offer?

An offer is a definite and unequivocal statement of willingness to be bound on specified terms without further negotiations.

An offer can be in any form – oral, written or by conduct. However, it is not effective until it has been communicated to the offeree. For example, if a reward is offered for the return of a lost item, it cannot be claimed by someone who did not know of the reward before they returned the item.

An offer can be made to a particular person, to a class of persons or even to the whole world - **Carlill v Carbolic Smoke Ball Co (1893)**.

What is not an offer?

(1)   An invitation to treat is not an offer.

An invitation to treat means an invitation to the other party to make an offer; e.g. 'we may be prepared to sell' – **Gibson v Manchester City Council (1979)**. An invitation to treat cannot be accepted to form a valid contract.

Examples of invitations to treat:

Most advertisements

General rule - an advertisement is an invitation to treat, not an offer, as shown in:

Partridge v Crittenden (1968)

Facts: The defendant put the following advertisement in a magazine: 'Bramblefinch cocks and hens, 25s each'.

Held: This was an invitation to treat and not an offer. The advertisement stated that the birds were for sale, not that the seller would sell to all comers.

Exception to an advertisement not being an offer

Note, however, that it would be an offer if no further negotiations were intended or expected. This is the position in **Carlill v Carbolic Smoke Ball Co (1893)**, where the advertisers made it clear that they would pay money to anyone complying with the terms of the advertisement.

Carlill v Carbolic Smoke Ball Co (1893)

Facts: The manufacturers of a medicinal 'smoke ball' advertised in a newspaper that anyone who bought and used the ball properly and nevertheless contracted influenza would be paid a £100 reward. Mrs Carlill used the ball as directed and did catch influenza. The defendant claimed that there was no enforceable contract because Mrs Carlill had never notified the company that she accepted its offer

Held: The court rejected the defendants argument on the basis that the wording of the advert was such that Mrs Carlill needed only to comply with the terms of the offer and there was no further negotiations intended. Once Mrs Carlill had satisfied the conditions she was entitled to enforcement of the contract. Furthermore, weight was placed on the £1000 bank deposit that claimed to 'show their sincerity in the matter' in showing that the advertisement was not just a mere 'puff'.

Shop window displays

Fisher v Bell (1961)

Facts: The Restriction of Offensive Weapons Act 1959 creates a criminal offence of 'offering for sale' certain offensive weapons. A shopkeeper was prosecuted under this statute for displaying a flick knife in his shop window, and thus 'offering it for sale'.

Held: A window display was not an offer of sale, but only an invitation to treat. So the display did not infringe the law.

Goods on shop shelves

Pharmaceutical Society of Great Britain v Boots Cash Chemists (1953)

Facts: Statute requires that the sale of certain pharmaceuticals must be carried out under the supervision of a qualified pharmacist. Boots operated a store where the drugs were displayed on a self-service basis and the customers paid at a cash desk for the goods they had selected. A pharmacist was present at the cash desk but not at the shelves where the goods were displayed with a price tag. The Pharmaceutical Society claimed that the statute was being contravened.

Held: The display of goods in a shop was not an offer, but an invitation to treat. It was the customer who made the offer and Boots could either accept or reject this offer at the cash desk (in the presence of the qualified pharmacist). The act constituting the acceptance is the ringing up of the price on the till by the cashier and at that moment a binding contract of sale is made.

Expandable text

Tenders

A **tender** arises where one party issues a statement asking interested parties to submit the terms on which they are willing to carry out work or supply goods. The person inviting the tender is simply making an invitation to treat. The person submitting a tender is the offeror and the other party is free to accept or reject the offer as they please.

The effect of acceptance depends upon the wording of the invitation to tender. If the invitation states that the potential purchaser **will require** a certain quantity of goods, acceptance of a tender will form a contract and they will be in breach if they fail to order the stated quantity from the person submitting the tender.

If, on the other hand, the invitation states only that the potential purchaser **may require** goods, acceptance gives rise only to a standing offer. In this situation there is no compulsion on the purchaser to take any goods, but they must not deal with any other supplier. Each order forms a separate contract and the supplier must deliver any goods required within the time stated in the tender. The supplier can revoke the standing offer, but they must supply any goods already ordered **(Great Northern Railway v Witham (1873))**.

(2) A **mere statement of selling price** in response to a request for information is not an offer.

Harvey v Facey (1893)

Facts: The defendant (F) was in negotiations with the regarding the sale of his store. The claimant (H) sent the defendant a telegram stating: "Will you sell us Bumper Hall Pen? Telegraph lowest cash price- answer paid." On the same day, F sent H a reply by telegram stating: "Lowest price for Bumper Hall Pen £900." H sent F another telegram agreeing to purchase the property at the asking price. F refused to sell and H sued for specific performance and an injunction to prevent the new buyer from taking the property.

Held: The court held that by replying to H's question regarding the lowest price of the property, F did not make an affirmative answer to the first question regarding his willingness to sell. The defendant's response to the query was simply a statement of information. It was not an offer capable of being accepted by the claimant.

(3) A **mere statement of intention to sell** is not an offer.

Harris v Nickerson (1873)

Facts: The defendant placed an advertisement in London papers that certain items, including some office furniture would be placed up for auction over three days. The claimant obtained a commission to buy the office furniture and expended time and expense to travel to bid for the office furniture. On the third day, the lots for the office furniture were withdrawn. The claimant sued for loss of time and expense.

Held: An advertisement that goods will be put up for auction does not constitute an offer to any person that the goods will actually be put up, and that the advertiser is therefore free to withdraw the goods from the auction at any time prior to the auction.

Termination of an offer

Once an offer has been terminated, it cannot be accepted. An offer can be terminated by:

- revocation
- rejection
- lapse.

Revocation

Revocation by the offeror can be made at any time before acceptance, even if the offeror has agreed to keep the offer open.

Routledge v Grant (1828)

Facts: G offered to buy R's horse and stated that the offer would remain open for six weeks. However, before the six-week period had elapsed, G withdrew the offer.

Held: G was entitled to withdraw the offer at any time before acceptance.

The revocation must be communicated to the offeree, i.e. it must be brought to his actual notice.

Byrne v Leon Van Tienhoven (1880)

Facts: An offer was posted on 1 October. It reached the claimant on 11 October. The claimant immediately cabled his acceptance. In the meantime, the defendant had changed his mind and posted a letter of revocation on 8 October. The revocation was received by the claimant after he had cabled his acceptance.

Held: The revocation did not take effect as it was not communicated to the claimant prior to his acceptance. The contract was therefore binding.

The revocation can be communicated by the offeror or a reliable third party.

Dickinson v Dodds (1876)

Facts: The defendant agreed to keep an offer open for two days. However, in the meantime the defendant sold the property to a third party. The offeree was told of the sale by a third party, but then attempted to accept the original offer.

Held: This was a reasonable way of communicating revocation. The offer was therefore properly revoked and could not be accepted.

There are two exceptions to the above rules on revocation:

• If the offeree pays the offeror to keep the offer open, any revocation will amount to a breach of that collateral contract. The offeree could claim damages for the loss of the opportunity to accept the offer, although he could not accept the offer itself.

- In the case of a unilateral/option contract, the offeror cannot revoke his offer once the offeree has begun to perform the acts which would amount to acceptance.

Errington v Errington (1952)

Facts: A father offered to transfer his house to his son if the son paid the mortgage. The son began to pay the mortgage but, when the father died, his personal representatives wanted to withdraw the offer.

Held: The offer could not be withdrawn because the son, by paying some of the instalments, had started acceptance.

Rejection

Rejection by the offeree may be outright or by means of a counter-offer. A counter-offer is an offer made in response to an offer.

Hyde v Wrench (1840)

Facts: Wrench offered to sell Hyde a farm for £1,000. Hyde made a counter-offer, by offering £950. Wrench rejected this. Later Hyde came back and said that he now accepted the original offer of £1,000. Wrench rejected it.

Held: Hyde could no longer accept the original offer. It had been terminated by the counter-offer and was no longer capable of acceptance. His 'acceptance' was merely a fresh offer which Wrench was free to turn down.

Note that a mere request for further details does not constitute a counter-offer.

Stevenson v McLean (1880)

Facts: M offered, in writing, to sell a quantity of iron to S at a given price. S replied querying delivery times, but before receiving a reply sent a further letter accepting the offer. This acceptance crossed in the post with a letter of revocation from M to S. M refused to supply the iron to S, arguing that S's query was a counter-offer.

Held: M could not treat the query as a counter-offer. S had not intended to prejudice M's position, just to establish the boundaries of the deal. Therefore M's offer was still open when S wrote accepting it.

Lapse

An offer will lapse on:

- the death of the offeror (unless the offeree accepts in ignorance of the death)

- the death of the offeree
- after the expiry of a fixed time (if any) or after a reasonable time. What is a reasonable time may depend on the subject matter of the contract.

Ramsgate Victoria Hotel Co v Montefiore (1866)

Facts: The defendant applied to the company to buy some shares in June and paid a deposit. He didn't hear anything until November when the company sent him a letter of allotment as acceptance and a request for the balance. By this time the defendant had changed his mind and no longer wanted the shares.

Held: The offer was for a reasonable time only and since five months had passed since the offer had been made the offer was deemed to have lapsed. The defendant was not bound to buy the shares. Their value could have changed dramatically in such a long period.

If the goods are perishable the time for lapse will be very short.

Test your understanding 2

(1) **What is the legal effect of the following statement in a newspaper?**

'For sale. Computer, monitor and laser printer. Good condition. £500.'

A The statement is an offer for sale.

B The statement is a 'mere puff or boast'.

C The statement has no legal effect.

D The statement is an invitation to treat.

(2) Simon offers to sell his car to Tony for £600. Tony is unsure but, as he is leaving the pub, asks Simon if he can tell him by 9am the next day. Simon agrees. Later that night Tony meets Rick, a reliable mutual friend, who tells him that Simon has decided to keep the car. Tony visits Simon at 8.30am and accepts the offer.

Is there a contract?

A Yes, because the revocation has not been communicated.

B No, because revocation can be communicated by a reliable third party.

C Yes, because Simon has agreed to keep the offer open.

D No, because the promise to keep the offer open was gratuitous.

3 Acceptance

What is acceptance?

Acceptance is the unqualified and unconditional assent to all the terms of the offer.

It can be oral, written or by conduct – **Carlill v Carbolic Smoke Ball (1893)**.

The offeror can stipulate a particular mode of acceptance. However, if he merely requests a mode, the offeree is not limited to that mode.

Communication

As a general rule, acceptance is not effective until it is communicated to the offeror.

Entores v Miles Far Eastern (1955)

Facts: The claimants, who were based in London, made an offer by telex to the defendants in Amsterdam. The defendants accepted by telex. The point at issue was where the acceptance had taken place, i.e. in Amsterdam at the time the defendants sent the telex or in London when it was received. It can be important to know which country the contract was concluded in as different countries have different legal rules.

Held: Acceptance is not effective until it is communicated. Therefore the contract was made in London.

The following conclusions can be drawn from the **Entores** case:

- If a fax, telex or telephone message is received during normal business hours, that is when it is communicated even though it might not be read until later.

- If a fax, telex or telephone message is received outside normal business hours, it is deemed to be communicated when the business next opens.

Note, in addition, that the offeror can expressly or impliedly dispense with the need for communication – **Carlill v Carbolic Smoke Ball (1893)**. However, he cannot stipulate that silence is acceptance.

Felthouse v Bindley (1863)

Facts: The claimant was interested in buying a horse and had discussed with his nephew the purchase of a horse belonging to him. The claimant wrote to his nephew and stated in this letter that he assumed the horse was his for £30.15 if he did not receive a response from his nephew. The nephew did not reply, and instructed the defendant, an auctioneer he had engaged to conduct a sale of his farming stock, to withhold the horse from the auction. By mistake, the defendant allowed the horse to be put up and sold. The claimant sued the defendant for damages.

Held: An acceptance of offer will not give rise to a binding agreement unless it is expressly communicated to the individual who makes the offer. Although the nephew had the intent to sell his horse to the claimant at the offered price, he did not communicate this intention to his uncle, or do anything to bind himself. Since property was not vested in the claimant, he had no right to bring action against the defendant.

The postal rule

The postal rule is an exception to the rule that acceptance must be communicated.

The postal rule states that acceptance is complete as soon as the letter is posted.

Adams v Lindsell (1818)

Facts: The case involved two parties in the sale of wool. On 2 September, the defendants wrote to the claimants offering to sell them certain fleeces of wool and requiring an answer in the course of post. The defendants, misdirected the letter so that the claimants didn't receive it until 5 September. The claimants posted their acceptance on the same day but it was not received until 9 September. Meanwhile, on 8 September, the defendants, not having received an answer by 7 September as they had expected, sold the wool to someone else.

Held: The question for the court was whether a contract of sale had been entered into before 8 September when the wool was sold to the third party. If the acceptance was effective when it arrived at the address or when the defendant saw it, then no contract would have been made and the sale to the third party would amount to revocation of the offer. However, the court held that the offer had been accepted as soon as the letter had been posted. The defendant was therefore liable in breach of contract.

However, the postal rule only applies if:

* the letter is properly stamped, addressed and posted, and

- post is a reasonable method of communication.

It applies even if the letter is never received by the offeror.

Household Fire Insurance v Grant (1879)

Facts: G applied for shares in HFI. HFI posted a share allotment letter to G, accepting his offer. The letter was not received.

Held: Once the letter was posted, HFI could not recall it. They had accepted G's offer to take shares.

However, the postal rule does not apply if the offeror states that he must actually receive the acceptance – **Holwell Securities v Hughes (1974)**.

Test your understanding 3

(1) On 1 September, Seller Ltd sent a fax to Buyer Ltd offering to sell a machine at a price of £10,000, and stating that Buyer Ltd must accept by 10 September. On 3 September, Buyer Ltd sent a fax to Seller Ltd asking 'Will you accept payment over three months?'.

On 5 September, Seller Ltd sold the machine to New Ltd, and on 6 September received a second fax from Buyer Ltd accepting the offer and offering to make immediate payment.

Which one of the following is correct?

A There is no contract between Seller Ltd and Buyer Ltd because the offer was withdrawn on 5 September when the machine was sold to New Ltd.

B There is no contract between Seller Ltd and Buyer Ltd because Buyer Ltd's fax of 3 September amounted to a counter-offer which destroyed Seller Ltd's original offer.

C Seller Ltd and Buyer Ltd contracted on 3 September.

D Seller Ltd and Buyer Ltd contracted on 6 September.

(2) A Ltd placed the following advertisement in a local newspaper:

'We are able to offer for sale a number of portable colour television sets at the specially reduced price of £5.90. Order now while stocks last.'

The advertisement contained a mistake in that the television sets should have been priced at £59.00. B Ltd immediately placed an order for 100 television sets.

Which one of the following statements is correct?

A B Ltd has accepted an offer and is contractually entitled to the 100 television sets.

B A Ltd can refuse to supply B Ltd as the advertisement is not an offer, but an invitation to treat.

C A Ltd can only refuse to sell the television sets to B Ltd if it has sold all its stock.

D As B Ltd has not yet paid for the television sets, the company has no contractual right to them.

(3) Alf sends a letter to Bert on 1 January offering to buy Bert's antique Ming vase for £1,000. On the same day Bert sends a letter to Alf offering to sell to Alf the same antique Ming vase for £1,000.

Alf now changes his mind and wishes to know the likely legal position.

A There is a valid contract; Alf and Bert have reached agreement and waived the need for acceptance.

B Both have made offers on the same terms and no acceptance is necessary

C There is agreement, but no contract since neither Alf nor Bert knew that their offers had been accepted.

D There is a contract but is lacks consideration since neither Alf nor Bert has paid a price for the other's promise.

An offer was made by letter posted in London and delivered in Birmingham. A reply was made by facsimile machine in Manchester and received by the offeror's machine in Liverpool.

Where is the contract made?

A Where the offer was made – in London.

B Where the acceptance was put into the facsimile machine – in Manchester.

C Where the acceptance was received on the facsimile machine – in Liverpool.

D Where the letter making the offer was received – in Birmingham.

KAPLAN PUBLISHING

4 Consideration

The basic rule

Every simple contract must be supported by consideration from each party. However, contracts made by deed (specialty contracts) do not require consideration unless the terms of the agreement require it.

Definition

'Consideration is an act or forbearance (or the promise of it) on the part of one party to a contract as the price of the promise made to him by the other party to the contract': **Dunlop Pneumatic Tyre Co v Selfridge & Co Ltd (1915)**.

'Some right, interest, profit or benefit accruing to one party, or some forbearance, detriment, loss or responsibility given, suffered or undertaken by the other': **Currie v Misa (1875)**.

Types of consideration

Executory consideration is given where there is an exchange of promises to do something in the future.

Executed consideration means that the consideration is in the form of an act carried out at the time the contract is made.

Sufficient consideration

Consideration must be sufficient but need not be adequate.

Sufficient means that:

*   there must be some monetary value to the consideration
*   it must be capable in law of amounting to consideration.

The words 'need not be adequate' mean that there is no need for each party's consideration to be equal in value.

Chappell v Nestle Co Ltd (1959)

Facts: Records were sold for 1s 6d plus three chocolate wrappers.
Held: The wrappers were part of the consideration even though they had minimal value.

Thomas v Thomas (1842)

Facts: A promise to lease a house to a widow for rent of £1 a year was binding.

Held: The consideration had some value, and so was sufficient at law, even though it was inadequate as a years rent.

White v Bluett (1853)

A son's promise to stop complaining did not amount to consideration as it had no monetary value.

Past consideration

Past consideration is insufficient and therefore is **not valid**.

Consideration is past if the consideration is an act which has been wholly performed before the other party gives his promise.

Re McArdle (1951)

Facts: A mother and her three grown-up children lived together in a house. One of the sons and his wife did some decorating in the house and later the other two children promised to pay towards the decorating costs and signed a document to this effect.

Held: It was held that the promise was unenforceable as all the work had been done before the promise was made and was therefore past consideration.

However, the situation in **Re McArdle (1951)** can be contrasted with that in **Re Casey's Patent (1892)**.

Facts: A and B owned a patent and C was the manager who had worked on it for two years. A and B then promised C a one-third share in the invention for his help in developing it. The patents were transferred to C but A and B then claimed their return.

Held: C could rely on the agreement. Even though C's consideration was in the past, it had been done in a business situation, at the request of A and B and it was understood by both sides that C would be paid and the subsequent promise to pay merely fixed the amount. There was an implied promise to pay as the development of the patent had been requested by A and B.

Performance of an existing duty

As a general rule, performance of an existing statutory duty is not sufficient consideration.

Collins v Godefroy (1831)

Facts: A witness was promised payment if he would attend court and give evidence.

Held: This did not amount to consideration as he was legally required to attend court.

Similarly, performance of an existing contractual duty is not consideration.

Stilk v Myrick (1809)

Facts: A captain promised to share the wages of the deserting seamen with the rest of the crew who had contracted to sail the ship home.

Held: The promise was not binding as there was no extra consideration from the seamen, they were merely doing what they had contracted to do.

However, there are three exceptions:

(1) If the existing contractual or statutory duty is exceeded, there is sufficient consideration.

Glasbrook Bros Ltd v Glamorgan County Council (1925)

Facts: Glasbrook Bros Ltd requested the police to provide protection in excess of the statutory requirement.

Held: The police had provided sufficient consideration to give entitlement to remuneration by providing the extra officers over and above the statutory requirement.

Hartley v Ponsonby (1857)

Facts: A high number of desertions from a merchant ship rendered the vessel unseaworthy since it was now undermanned. Extra pay was offered to the crew if they remained loyal and sailed the ship home.

Held: The promise of extra money was recoverable by the seamen who remained loyal, since they were now working in a dangerous situation not contemplated by their original contractual undertaking (i.e. they were doing more than required by their original contract).

(2) The performance of an existing contractual duty may be sufficient if it confers some benefit of a practical nature on the other party.

Williams v Roffey Bros (1990)

Facts: W agreed to do some carpentry in a block of flats for R at a fixed price of £20,000, by an agreed date. The contract contained a 'time penalty' clause and R agreed to pay an extra £10,000 to ensure that the work was completed on time. If the work had not been completed on time, R would have suffered a penalty in his own contract with the owner of the flats.

Held: The Court of Appeal decided that, even though W was in effect doing nothing over and above the original agreement to complete the work by an agreed time, there was a new contract here for the £10,000. The court decided that both W and R benefited from the new contract. Two reasons were given:

- Even though W merely did what he was already contracted to do, this nevertheless conferred a practical benefit on R in that R not only avoided penalties under the head contract, but also the cost and aggravation of employing substitute contractors.

- R's promise to pay the extra £10,000 had not been extracted by fraud or pressure. (It was R who had approached W and had volunteered the extra money.) It would be inequitable to go back on his promise.

(3) The performance of an existing contractual obligation is sufficient consideration to support a promise from a third party.

Shadwell v Shadwell (1860)

Facts: The claimant was engaged to E (at this time an engagement was an enforceable contract). The claimant's uncle wrote him a letter saying "I will pay you £150 per year during my life until your income as a barrister shall reach 600 guineas pa" if you marry E. When the uncle died the claimant sought to recover outstanding amounts. The deceased's personal representatives argued that the claimant was already under a contractual obligation to marry when the uncle made the offer, and therefore the claimant supplied no consideration.

Held: There was sufficient consideration as the uncle had promised the claimant a reward and in return the uncle had received a promise to which he previously had no right. The contract was between the claimant and E. The uncle was a third party and the claimant promised to marry E in consideration of the payments

Illegal acts

An illegal act is insufficient to amount to consideration.

KAPLAN PUBLISHING

Test your understanding 4

(1) **Which of the following examples of performance amount(s) to good consideration?**

I   The performance of an existing duty under the general law.

II   The performance of an existing contract where it confers some extra benefit of a practical nature on the other party.

III The performance of an act, followed by a promise to pay for that act.

A   (I) only.

B   (II) only.

C   (I) and (II) only.

D   (III) only.

(2) **The law enforces bargains not bare promises. The presence of which of the following indicates the former?**

A   Intention to create legal relations.

B   Consideration.

C   Capacity.

D   Legality.

(3) **Consideration need not be adequate but must be:**

A   Money.

B   Sufficient.

C   Of equivalent value to the goods.

D   Accepted.

The part-payment problem

The problem – if A accepts £400 from B in full and final settlement of a debt of £500, can A sue for the remaining £100?

General rule - the rule in **Pinnel's case (1602)** states that payment of a smaller sum does not discharge a debt of a greater amount. This has been affirmed in **Foakes v Beer (1884)**.

Exceptions

There are four exceptions to the rule in **Pinnel's case**:

- Where the part payment is made by a third party

- composition with creditors (i.e. the creditors all agree to accept a sum which is less than they are owed)
- accord and satisfaction
  - accord means that both the parties agree freely to the part payment.
  - satisfaction (i.e. consideration) might be payment at an earlier date, payment at a different place, payment in a different currency, etc.
- the equitable doctrine of promissory estoppel.

D & C Builders v Rees (1966)

Facts: R owned money to D & C and knew that D & C were in financial difficulties. R offered to pay a smaller sum to be accepted in full and final payment of whole amount. R stated that it was not accepted , the claimant would get nothing. The claimant reluctantly accepted the smaller sum but later sued for the balance.

Held: Claimant was successful because claimant's agreement had not been freely given. Payment by cheque was not a different mode of payment. The doctrine of promissory estoppel did not apply because the defendant had not acted fairly.

Promissory estoppel

The doctrine of promissory estoppel is based on the principles of fairness and justice. It prevents a person going back on his promise to accept a lesser amount.

The principle was established in **Central London Property Trust v High Trees House (1947)**.

Central London Property Trust v High Trees House (1947)

Facts: Claimants let a block of flats to the defendants in 1937 at an annual rent of £2,500 pa. The defendants were then going to sublet the flats. Owing to World War II and London being bombed, some of the flats became empty and it was impossible to re-let them. In addition the existing tenants had their rent reduced. The claimants agreed to accept half the rent for the rest of the war.

Held: The full rent was payable from the end of the war. The doctrine of promissory estoppel would stop the claimants from recovering the full rent foregone during the war years. High Trees House were expected to reduce their rent as a result of the rent reduction by Central London Property Trust, which they did thereby proving their reliance on the waiver.

The principle is subject to the following conditions:

- There must be an existing contract between the parties.
- The claimants must voluntarily waive their rights under the contract.
- There must be an intention that the defendants should rely on the waiver.
- The defendants must alter their legal position because of the waiver.

The doctrine has a number of limitations:

- It is a shield not a sword, i.e. it is a defence not a cause of action.
- It may only have a suspensory effect, as shown in the **High Trees case**. (The claimant's rights were suspended during World War II, but reinstated for the future once the war had finished.)
- The party seeking to use it as an equitable defence must also have acted fairly in their dealings with the claimants.

5 Privity of contract

The general rule

Only the parties to a contract:

- acquire rights and obligations under it
- can sue and be sued on it.

Exceptions

There are a number of exceptions to the general rule regarding privity of contract:

- The Contracts (Rights of Third Parties) Act 1999 allows a person who is not a party to a contract to enforce it so long as the contract was for his benefit and he was expressly identified, by name or description.
- Under the rules of land law, restrictive covenants run with the land to which they relate i.e. that a future owner will be subject to restrictions made in previous contracts.

Tulk v Moxhay (1848)

Facts: The owner of several pieced of land sold a plot to another party, making a covenant to keep a particular area "uncovered with buildings" such that it could remain a pleasure ground. Over the following years the land was sold several times over to new parties, eventually to the defendant. The defendant, who was aware of the covenant at the time of purchase, refused to abide by the covenant as he claimed he was not in privity of contract and so was not bound by it.

Held: An injunction was granted against the defendant to restrain a breach of the covenant.

- Insurance law allows a third party to take the benefit of a contract of insurance for example where the policy is for life insurance which will pay out to a third party in the event of the policy holder's death.

- Trust law allows a beneficiary to enforce a trust.

- Agency law allows an agent to make a contract between his principal and a third party, even though the third party may be unaware that he is acting as an agent. Agency is covered later in **chapter 5**.

- An executor can enforce contracts made by the deceased for whom he is acting.

Beswick v Beswick (1967)

Facts: A coal merchant sold his business to his nephew in return for a pension during his lifetime and the payment of a smaller pension to his widow, on his death. After the uncle died, the nephew stopped paying the widow. She sued the nephew in her own personal capacity and in her capacity as the administrator of her husband's estate.

Held: Although she was not a party to the contract and could not sue in her own personal capacity, she could sue in her capacity as the administrator of her husband's estate.

6 Intention to create legal relations

Introduction

In order to create a contract, both parties must intend to enter into a legal relationship. If it is not clear from the contract that the parties intended legal consequences then the law presumes the intention of the parties based on the type of agreement.

Domestic or social agreements

It is presumed that there is no intention to be legally bound, unless it can be shown otherwise.

Balfour v Balfour (1919)

Facts: The defendant, who was about to go abroad, promised to pay his wife £30 per month in consideration of her agreeing to support herself without calling on him for any further maintenance. The wife contended that the defendant was bound by his promise.

Held: There was no legally binding contract between the parties. As it was a domestic agreement it was presumed the parties did not intend to be legally bound.

The usual presumption that agreements between spouses living happily together are not legally enforceable does not apply when they are about to separate, or have already separated. In such instances the circumstances of the case can be shown to rebut the presumption.

Merritt v Merritt (1970)

Facts: A husband, separated from his wife, wrote and signed a document stating that, in consideration of the wife paying off the outstanding mortgage debt of £180 on their matrimonial home, he would transfer the house standing in their joint names into her sole ownership. The wife paid off the outstanding mortgage debt, but the husband refused to transfer title in the house to her, alleging that his promise was a domestic arrangement and did not give rise to legal relations.

Held: The husband's promise was enforceable, the agreement having been made when the parties were not living together amicably. A legal relationship is contemplated where a husband deserts his wife and an agreement is concluded on ownership of the matrimonial home occupied by the wife and children. The circumstances of their separation was enough to rebut the presumption.

The presumption that there is no intention to be legally bound will also be rebutted where the evidence shows that the parties made formal and/or detailed financial arrangements.

Simpkins v Pays (1955)

Facts: Pays and her granddaughter, together with Simpkins, a paying lodger, submitted an entry each week in a fashion competition appearing in the Sunday Empire News. All three devised a separate solution to the competition, but they were submitted on one coupon only, in Pays' name. The entry fees and postage were shared equally. The granddaughter made a correct forecast and Pays received a prize of £750. Simpkins claimed a one-third share of the prize money.

Held: Although this was an arrangement in a domestic context the presumption was rebutted: it was a legally enforceable joint enterprise and the parties clearly intended to share any prize money. 'There was mutuality in the arrangements between the parties and an intention to create legal relations'. It was decided that on the facts this went beyond a mere friendly agreement and became a joint enterprise.

Jones v Vernon's Pools Ltd (1938)

Facts: Jones contended that he had forwarded a winning entry to the defendant company of football pools promoters, but they denied having received it. In order to deal with this type of eventuality, a clause was printed on the pools coupon which Jones had signed, stating that 'any agreement … entered into … shall not … give rise to any legal relationship … but … is binding in honour only'.

Held: A contract did not exist between the parties, since the wording of the agreement clearly negated any such intention. Jones could not, therefore, sue the pools company for breach of contract.

Commercial agreements

It is presumed that there is an intention to be legally bound, unless it can be shown otherwise.

This is a strong presumption that can only be rebutted by clear evidence to the contrary.

7 Capacity and legality

Capacity

Each party must have the legal power to bind itself contractually. For example persons under the age of eighteen (minors) and persons of unsound mind or under the influence of alcohol have limitations on their power to contract.

KAPLAN PUBLISHING

Legality

The courts will not enforce a contract which is deemed to be illegal.

8 Contractual terms

Terms versus representations

A statement, written or oral, made during the negotiations leading to a contract, may be a term of the contract or merely a representation inducing the contract.

A representation is something that is said by the offeror in order to induce the offeree to enter into the contract. It may or may not become a term of that contract.

The distinction between terms and representations is important because, if a statement is untrue, the remedies available to the innocent party differ:

- if the representation becomes a term of the contract, the innocent party has remedies for breach of the term as well as for misrepresentation

- if, however, the representation does not become a term of the contract, the innocent party will have remedies only for misrepresentation which are based on equitable remedies (see section 11).

Sources of terms

Terms may be express or implied.

Express terms are those specifically inserted into the contract by one or both of the parties. They must be clear for them to be enforceable.

Scammell v Ouston (1941)

Facts: An agreement provided for the balance of the price to be paid ....`on hire purchase terms over a period of two years'....

Held: The words 'hire purchase terms' were considered too imprecise as the seller had a range of such terms.

Implied terms are not expressly included in the contract, but they are nevertheless still part of the contract. They may be implied by statute or by the courts, or rarely by custom.

Express terms will generally override implied terms. However, some statutory terms cannot be overridden by express agreement (for example, terms inserted by the Sale of Goods Act 1979).

The sources of terms are summarised in the following diagram:

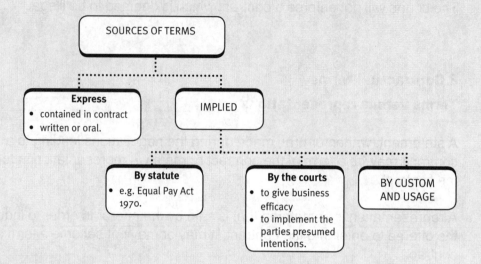

The Moorcock (1889)

There was an agreement by a wharf owner to permit a shipowner to unload his ship at the wharf. The ship was damaged when, at low tide, it was grounded on the bottom of the river on a hard ridge.

The court implied a term into the agreement that the river bottom would be reasonably safe for ships to dry out on.

Types of terms

There are three types of terms:

* conditions

* warranties

* innominate terms.

The distinction between the types of term is important because it determines the remedies that may be available in the event of a breach.

Conditions

A condition is an important term going to the root of the contract.

Breach can result in damages or discharge or both. Discharge entitles the innocent party to repudiate the contract and claim damages.

Poussard v Spiers & Pond (1876)

Facts: An opera singer failed to appear on the opening night.

Held: This was a breach of condition, which entitled the injured party to treat the contract as ended.

Warranties

A warranty is a less important term, which is incidental to the main purpose of the contract.

Breach of warranty results in damages only.

Bettini v Gye (1876)

Facts: An opera singer failed to attend rehearsals.

Held: This was a breach of warranty. The injured party could not treat the contract as ended. They were entitled to damages only.

Innominate terms

An innominate or indeterminate term is neither a condition nor a warranty.

The remedy depends on the effects of the breach:

- if trivial – damages only i.e. term is treated as if it were a warranty.

- if serious – damages, discharge or both i.e. term is treated as if it were a condition.

The Hansa Nord (1976)

Facts: Citrus pulp pellets for use in animal food had been sold for £100,000 under a contract which provided for "shipment to be made in good condition." Part of the goods had not been so shipped and in addition the market value in such goods had fallen at the delivery date. The buyers rejected the goods which were later resold pursuant to a court order and eventually reacquired by the original buyers for just under £34,000. The buyers then used the goods for the originally intended purpose of making cattle food.

Held: The Court of Appeal held that rejection was not justified. The term as to shipment in good condition was neither a condition nor a warranty but an innominate term; and there was no finding that the effect of its breach was sufficiently serious to justify rejection. The buyers seem to have tried to reject, not because the goods were impaired, but because they saw an opportunity of acquiring them at well below the originally agreed price. In these circumstances their only remedy was in damages: they were entitled to the difference in value between damaged and sound goods.

Test your understanding 5

(1) **Which one of the following is incorrect?**

    A   A condition is a term which the parties intended to be of fundamental importance.

    B   A warranty is a term which the parties did not intend to be of fundamental importance.

    C   If a condition is breached, then the contract must be terminated.

    D   If a warranty is breached, then the innocent party cannot terminate the contract.

(2) **Dee Ltd has broken one of the terms of its contract with E Ltd. If that term is a warranty, which of the following is correct?**

    A   E Ltd may repudiate the contract with Dee Ltd.

    B   E Ltd can avoid the contract and recover damages.

    C   E Ltd is entitled to sue for damages only.

    D   E Ltd is entitled to sue for damages or to repudiate the contract.

(3) **'An obligation, which though it must be performed, is not so vital that a failure to perform it goes to the substance of the contract' describes a:**

    A   Warranty.

    B   Condition.

    C   Innominate term.

    D   Representation.

(4) **Which of the following statements is incorrect?**

    A   The remedies of the innocent party for breach of a warranty depend on the seriousness of the breach.

    B   The remedies for breach of a condition are repudiation and damages.

    C   The likely remedy for breach of an innominate term cannot be assessed at the outset of a contractual relationship.

    D   The remedy for breach of a warranty is a legal one and therefore available as of right.

9 Exclusion clauses

Definition

An exclusion clause (or exemption clause) is a term that seeks to exclude a party's liability for breach of contract.

Common law rules

In order to be valid an exclusion clause must satisfy two conditions:

- it must be incorporated into the contract
- its wording must cover the loss.

An exclusion clause can be incorporated into a contract by:

- signature
- notice
- previous dealings.

Signature

The case of **L'Estrange v Graucob (1934)** established that a clause is incorporated by signature even if the signatory did not read or understand the document.

However, the situation in **L'Estrange v Graucob (1934)** can be contrasted with **Curtis v Chemical Cleaning (1951)** in which it was held that a signature does not incorporate the clause if the effect of the term was misrepresented.

Curtis v Chemical Cleaning (1951)

Liability for damage to a wedding dress was not excluded due to misrepresentation of the clause.

Notice

For an exclusion clause to be incorporated by notice, reasonable steps must have been taken to bring it to the attention of the other party at the time the contract was made. What are 'reasonable steps' depend on the circumstances.

Thompson v LMS Railway (1930)

Facts: T bought a railway ticket, which stated that she would travel subject to the company's standard conditions of carriage. These conditions could be inspected at the station; one of them excluded liability for injury to passengers.

T was unable to read, and so was unaware of the clause. She was injured and claimed damages.

Held: The ticket was a document which should be expected to contain terms, being more than a mere receipt for payment. The railway company had taken reasonable steps to bring the exclusion clause to passengers' attention, by incorporating it into the contract document (the ticket). T was bound by the clause (even though she could not read: 'illiteracy is a misfortune, not a privilege') as were all other passengers.

Olley v Marlborough Court (1949)

A clause can be incorporated by notice, provided it was given before making the contract. A notice in a hotel room did not exclude liability as the contract was made at the reception desk.

Previous dealings

For an exclusion clause to be incorporated by previous dealings, there must have been a consistent course of dealings between the parties.

Spurling v Bradshaw (1956)

Facts: The defendant had dealt with the claimant for a number of years. On the contract in question he delivered four full barrels for storage. As usual, he later received a document which acknowledged receipt and contained a clause excluding liability for negligence. When he came to collect the barrels, he found they were empty.

Held: The exclusion clause had been incorporated into the contract, even though it was received after the contract was made. It had been incorporated through the previous course of dealings whereby he had been sent copies of documents containing the clause, even though he had never read them.

However, **Spurling v Bradshaw (1956)** can be contrasted with **Hollier v Rambler Motors (1972)** in which three or four deals between a garage and a private customer over a five-year period were held to be insufficient to constitute a course of dealings.

The wording must cover the loss

Under the contra proferentem rule, the courts interpret the words narrowly against the interests of the person seeking to rely on the clause.

Photo Productions Ltd v Securicor (1980)

Facts: Security guard burned down factory he was guarding. The contract between his employers and the factory owners limited employers' liability for injurious acts and defaults of guards.

Held: The clause was clear and unambiguous and effectively limited their liability even for this fundamental breach.

Statutory rules

Even if a clause passes the common law test, it must also satisfy the statutory rules. These are contained in:

*   UCTA 1977
*   UTCCR 1999.

Unfair Contract Terms Act (UCTA) 1977

UCTA 1977 applies to exemption clauses in contracts made in the course of business.

It states that a clause exempting liability for:

*   death or personal injury due to negligence is void
*   other loss due to negligence is void unless reasonable.

The burden of proving reasonableness is on the party seeking to rely on the clause. In assessing whether a term is unfair or unreasonable, the court has regard to:

*   the strength of the bargaining positions of the parties
*   whether the buyer received an inducement to agree to the term

- whether the buyer knew or ought to have known of the existence and extent of the term
- the ability of the party to insure against the liability.

St Albans City and District Council v International Computers Ltd (1994)

Facts: The defendants had been hired to produce a computer system which would calculate population figures on which the claimants would base their community charges. The contract contained a clause restricting liability to £100,000. The database that the computer system produced was seriously inaccurate and as a result the claimant sustained a loss of £1.3m

Held: The clause was unreasonable. The defendants could not justify the limitation of £100,000 which was small both in relation to the potential risk and the actual loss. In addition, the defendants had insurance of £50m themselves. Therefore, it was reasonable to expect that those who stood to make the profit, and had been well able to insure and had insured, should carry the risk.

Unfair Terms in Consumer Contract Regulations (UTCCR) 1999

UTCCR 1999 applies to contracts where:

- the seller is acting in the course of business
- the other party is a consumer and
- the terms have not been individually negotiated.

The regulations apply to ALL terms of a contract not just exclusion clauses.

A term is unfair if:

- it is not expressed in plain, intelligible language
- contrary to the requirement of good faith, it causes a significant imbalance in the parties' rights and obligations and this is to the detriment of the consumer.

A term is unfair if it allows the seller to alter the terms of the contract unilaterally without a valid reason which is specified in the contract: Sched 3 UTCCR 1999.

If a term is unfair, it is not binding on the consumer, though the rest of the contract can stand.

Summary

> **Does the clause pass the common law rules? i.e.**
> - Is it incorporated into the contract?
> - Does the wording cover the loss?
> - If no, the clause is void.
> - If yes, consider statutory rules.

> If the contract is made in the course of business UCTA 1977 applies.

> If one party is a consumer and the other is in business, UTCCR 1999 applies in addition to UCTA 1977.

> Void if exempts liability for death or personal injury. Other loss – void unless reasonable.

> Unfair (and not binding) if not expressed in plain language or if it causes an imbalance in parties' rights.

Test your understanding 6

(1) **By virtue of the UCTA 1977, an attempt by any person to exclude or restrict liability for damage to property caused by negligence is:**

   A   Void unless reasonable.

   B   Effective only in a non-consumer transaction.

   C   Void.

   D   Valid if the other party to the contract knows of the exclusion clause or has been given reasonable notice of it.

(2) Dave went to drop off his watch for repair. He was handed a note to sign that contained the words, amongst many lines of text, 'the management are not liable for loss or damage to your watch howsoever caused'. He did not read the note but signed it. His watch, worth £350, was lost in transit by the jeweller.

   I   The clause is not incorporated into the contract even though Dave has signed the note.

   II   The clause is automatically void under the UCTA 1977.

Which of the above is correct?

A   (I) only.

B   (II) only.

C   Both (I) and (II).

D   Neither (I) nor (II).

10 Breach of contract

What is meant by breach of contract?

 Breach of contract occurs where one of the parties to the agreement fails to comply, either completely or satisfactorily, with their obligations under it.

 Actual breach is where the breach occurs on the due date for performance.

Anticipatory breach occurs where, before the due date for performance, a party shows an intention not to perform his contractual obligations. It is referred to as renunciation.

Anticipatory breach may be express or implied.

Express anticipatory breach occurs where one of the parties declares, before the due date for performance, that they have no intention of carrying out their contractual obligations.

Hochster v De La Tour (1853)

Facts: In April, De La Tour employed Hochster to act as a travel courier on his European tour, starting on 1 June. On 11 May De La Tour wrote to Hochster stating he would no longer be needing his services. Hochster started proceedings on 22 May. The defendant claimed there would be no cause of action until 1 June.

Held: The claimant was entitled to start the action as soon as the anticipatory breach occurred.

Implied anticipatory breach occurs where one of the parties does something which makes subsequent performance of their contractual undertaking impossible.

KAPLAN PUBLISHING

Omnium D'Enterprises v Sutherland (1919)

Facts: The defendant had agreed to hire a ship to the claimant but before the hire period was to commence, he actually sold the ship to someone else.

Held: The sale of the ship amounted to a clear repudiation of the contract. The claimant could sue for breach from that date.

What are the effects of anticipatory breach?

Anticipatory breach does not automatically bring the contract to an end. The innocent party has two options:

- treat the contract as discharged and bring an action for damages immediately, without waiting for the contractual date of performance as in **Hochster v De La Tour (1853)**

- elect to treat the contract as still valid, complete his side of the bargain and then sue for payment by the other side.

White & Carter (Councils) v McGregor (1961)

Facts: McGregor contracted with the claimants to have advertisements placed on litter bins which were supplied to local authorities. The defendant wrote to the claimants asking them to cancel the contract. The claimants refused to cancel, and produced and displayed the advertisements as required under the contract. They then claimed payment.

Held: The claimants were not obliged to accept the defendant's repudiation, but could perform the contract and claim the agreed price.

The effect of **White & Carter (Councils) v McGregor (1961)** apparently runs contrary to the duty to mitigate losses, as it involves the party in breach paying for more than the mere profit on the contract. There is, however, an element of danger in not accepting the repudiation of the contract when it first becomes apparent. For example, where the innocent party elects to wait for the time of performance, he takes the risk of the contract being discharged for some other reason and thus of losing his right to sue on the basis of the breach of contract.

Test your understanding 7

(1) **Dee Ltd has broken one of the terms of its contract with E Ltd. If that term is a condition, which of the following is correct?**

    A   E Ltd is entitled to damages only.

    B   E Ltd is entitled to sue for damages or to repudiate the contract.

    C   E Ltd is only entitled to repudiate the contract.

    D   E Ltd may repudiate the contract and sue for damages.

(2) **Renunciation occurs when:**

    A   A term going to the root of the contract is broken.

    B   A contracting party states or implies that he does not intend to carry out his future obligations under the contract.

    C   A warranty is breached.

    D   A contract is frustrated.

(3) **A Ltd contracts with B Ltd to supply 1½ tonnes of cement each day for a 100 day period. The thirteenth delivery is defective. Which of the following is correct?**

    A   A fundamental term has been breached and B Ltd can treat the contract as discharged because the contract must be performed exactly.

    B   Damages only will be payable because this is a minor breach in relation to the whole contract.

    C   The contract is frustrated.

    D   An order for specific performance is available to force another delivery.

11 Damages

Introduction

Damages are a common law remedy. They are available as of right for breach of contract.

Damages are intended to be compensatory not punitive.

Liquidated damages and penalty clauses

Where a contract provides for the payment of a fixed sum on breach, it may either be a liquidated damages clause or a penalty clause.

Liquidated damages are a genuine pre-estimate of the expected loss. The amount stated is the amount of damages claimable. The clause is enforceable by the court.

Dunlop Pneumatic Tyre Co v New Garage and Motor Co (1915)

Facts: The claimant supplied the defendant with tyres, under a contract which imposed a minimum retail price. The contract provided that the defendant had to pay the claimant £5 for every tyre they sold in breach of the price agreement. When the defendant sold tyres at less than the agreed minimum price, they resisted the claim for £5 per tyre, on the grounds that it represented a penalty clause.

Held: The provision was genuine attempt to fix damages, and was not a penalty. It was, therefore, enforceable.

A penalty clause threatens large damages for breach. The amount is often very large in relation to the expected loss. It is unenforceable.

A clause is presumed to be a penalty clause if:

- the stipulated sum is extravagant in comparison with the maximum loss that could be incurred

- the same sum is payable in respect of one or more breaches, both trifling and serious

- the sum stipulated is larger than the amount which would actually be payable if the contract were performed.

Assessment of unliquidated damages

Where the contract does not make any provision for damages, the court will determine the damages payable. These are known as unliquidated damages.

There are two factors to consider in determining the amount of unliquidated damages:

- remoteness of loss (i.e. what losses can be claimed for?) and

- measure of damages (i.e. how much are those losses worth?).

Remoteness of loss

Damages cannot not be recovered for all losses suffered. Some losses are too remote.

A loss is not too remote:

- if it arises naturally from the breach (general damages or normal loss)

- it may reasonably be supposed to be within the contemplation of the parties, at the time they made the contract, as a probable result of the breach (special damages or abnormal loss).

Hadley v Baxendale (1854)

Facts: C owned a mill. One of the mill parts had broken and C made a contract with D for the transport of the old part to London as a pattern for making a replacement. D was responsible for a delay in delivering the part and as a result the mill was closed for a longer duration than would have been necessary if there had been no delay. C claimed for loss of profits during the period of delay.

Held: D did not know that the mill was inoperable without the part and whilst he was directly responsible for the delay itself, that stoppage was not a natural consequence of the delay in transportation. C could have had a spare part and did not alert D to the fact that the mill would be inoperable until the new part was made. Accordingly, D was not liable for the loss of profit.

Victoria Laundry v Newman Industries (1949)

Facts: A laundry required a new boiler to enlarge its plant. There was delay in the delivery of the boiler and as a result the laundry lost:

(a) a normal trading profit from the delay in bringing the new plant into use, and

(b) an extra large profit on certain government contracts.

Held: The boiler manufacturer was liable for the loss of normal profits; under the first branch of the rule, he or anyone else would know that an industrial boiler was essential to the operation of the plant and, therefore, to earning normal profits from it. He was not liable for the loss of profit on the government contracts, of which he had no information. (If, of course, he had known of them he would have been liable under the second branch of the rule.)

Jarvis v Swans Tours (1973)

Damages cannot usually be recovered for loss of enjoyment, unless the contract is one designed to give enjoyment. In this case, it was a holiday.

Measure of damages

The measure of damages is the amount which will put the claimant in the position he would have been in had the contract been properly performed.

This is sometimes described as damages for loss of bargain.

It is particularly difficult to measure damages in cases involving **building contracts** as there are two ways in which the damages could, in theory, be measured:

A   the damages could be the difference in value between the building as it has been completed and its value if it had been properly completed, or

B   the cost of rebuilding so that it meets the required specifications.

The usual measure of such damages is the cost of repairing the faulty work. However, this may not be the case where the costs of remedying the defects are disproportionate to the difference in value between what was supplied and what was ordered.

Ruxley Electronics and Construction Ltd v Forsyth (1995)

Facts: The parties had entered into a contract for the construction of a swimming pool. Although the contract stated that the pool was to be 7ft 6in deep at one end, the actual depth of the pool was only 6ft 9in. The total contract price was around £18,000. Fixing the error would have required a full reconstruction and would have cost about £21,000.

Held: The House of Lords considered that, as the costs of reinstatement would have been out of all proportion to the benefit gained, the difference in value only should be awarded. This was £0 as the pool as constructed was just as suitable for swimming and diving as one built to the original specification. However, the House of Lords did uphold the lower court's award of £2,500 for loss of amenity/enjoyment (although they commented that the amount was on the high side).

Reliance damages enable the claimant to recover compensation for expenses incurred in performing his part of the contract before its breach. Where applicable, they are given in place of damages for loss of bargain; the claimant cannot receive both.

Anglia TV Ltd v Reed (1972)

Facts: R was engaged to play the leading role in a TV play. The claimants incurred expenses in preparing for filming. R repudiated the contract. Anglia could not find a suitable replacement and had to abandon the project.

Held: Anglia could recover the whole of their wasted expenditure from R.

Further points:

- If there is no actual loss, the claimant can recover only nominal damages.
- The claimant must take reasonable steps to mitigate (i.e. reduce) their loss.

Brace v Calder (1895)

Facts: Brace was employed by a partnership for a fixed period of two years, but after only five months the partnership was dissolved, thereby prematurely terminating his contract of employment. He was offered identical employment with a reconstituted partnership which was immediately formed to replace the previous one. He refused the offer and sued for wages he would have earned had his job continued for the agreed two year period.

Held: Brace had not mitigated the loss he suffered by his employer's breach of contract, thus he could only recover nominal damages.

- A notional deduction may be made to reflect taxation.

BTC v Gourley (1956)

Facts: A civil engineer was awarded damages by the British Transport Commission in respect of a railway accident. The award included an amount for loss of earnings. The question was whether the amount of damages should be paid to the recipient gross or net of deductions that would have been suffered by the individual had he remained in employment.

Held: It was held that the award should be made net of an amount that would reflect the deductions that would have been made for tax and national insurance in arriving at the settlement figure. The broad general principle which should govern the assessment of damages in cases such as this is that the tribunal should award the injured party such a sum of money as will put him in the same position as he would have been in if he had not sustained the injuries.

- Difficulty in evaluating losses does not prevent their recovery. In **Chaplin v Hicks (1911)**, an amount was awarded representing the loss of opportunity to audition for a theatre role even though there was no guarantee of the claimant being awarded the role.

In the event of a breach of contract, what is the purpose of damages?

I   To punish the contract breaker.

II To compensate the innocent party.

III To put the innocent party in the same position as if the contract had been carried out correctly.

A   (I) only.

B   (II) and (III) only.

C   (III) only.

D   (I), (II) and (III).

12 Equitable remedies

Specific performance	Requires someone to perform their contractual obligations. Not available for personal service contracts. It enforces positive covenants within the contract.
Injunction	Orders someone to do something or not to do something. It enforces negative covenants within the contract.
Rescission	Restores the parties to their exact pre-contractual position.

Equitable remedies are only available at the discretion of the court. They are not granted if:

- damages are an adequate remedy
- the claimant has acted unfairly (i.e. he who comes to equity must come with clean hands)
- the order would cause undue hardship
- the order would require the constant supervision of the court
- there is undue delay in seeking the remedy (i.e. delay defeats the equities).

Warner Brothers Pictures Inc v Nelson (1936)

Facts: The film star, Bette Davis (Miss Nelson) entered into a contract with the claimants, whereby she agreed that she would not undertake other film work or any other occupation without the claimant's written consent. The claimant sought an injunction to restrain her from doing film work for another company in breach of this agreement.

Held: The injunction would be granted. However, no injunction would be granted to prevent her engaging in 'other occupations' as this would force her to work for the claimants.

Page One Records v Britton (Trading as The Troggs) (1967)

Facts: The claimants, as managers of a pop group (The Troggs), sought an injunction to restrain the group from breaching their contract by engaging another manager.

Held: As the group would have been unable to obtain an order of specific performance to compel the claimants to perform their personal services as managers, the claimants could not obtain an injunction against the defendants, as there was no mutuality between the parties.

Test your understanding 9

(1) Which of the following statements is correct?

I   An order for specific performance will not be granted where damages provide an adequate remedy.

II   An order for specific performance will not be granted where the contract is for personal services.

A   (I) only.

B   (II) only.

C   Both (I) and (II).

D   Neither (I) nor (II).

(2) Which one of the following contracts might be specifically enforceable?

A   Alan has contracted to sell his house to Bob but has changed his mind and no longer wishes to sell it.

B   Chris has contracted to buy a new Ford motor car but the garage is now refusing to honour the contract.

C   Diane has contracted to purchase a number of tins of fruit for her business but the seller has now stated that he no longer wishes to proceed with the contract.

D   Eduardo has contracted to sing at a concert organised by Fernando, but Eduardo has withdrawn as he has received a more lucrative offer from Giovanni.

(3) Which one of the following is not an equitable remedy?

A   Damages.

B   Specific performance.

C   Rescission.

D   Injunction.

(4) In breach of contract, C Ltd refused to sell a motor car to D Ltd at the agreed price of £10,000. If the type of motor car is readily available on the market at a price of £9,000, which one of the following is correct?

A   D Ltd is entitled to an order of specific performance, forcing C Ltd to carry out its contract.

B   D Ltd is entitled to damages of £1,000.

C   D Ltd is entitled to nominal damages only.

D   D Ltd is not entitled to damages.

13 Chapter summary

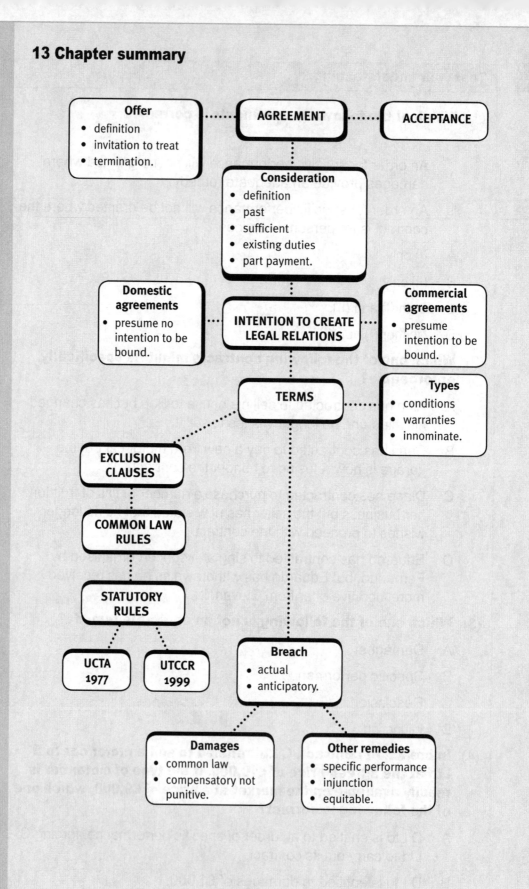

Test your understanding answers

Test your understanding 1

(1) **A**

Statement (i) is correct. An agreement that is binding in honour only is not a contract as there is no intention to create legal relations. However, statement (ii) is incorrect. An enforceable contract does not have to be in writing.

(2) **B**

This is a definition of a 'simple' contract. It does not have to be in any particular form – e.g. it does not have to be in writing – to be binding on the parties.

(3) **C**

The limitation period for a contract made by deed (a specialty contract) is 12 years. All other contracts (simple contracts) have a limitation period of 6 years.

(4) **A**

A contract need not necessarily be in writing. However, a contract is valid only if both parties intend it to be legally binding. Disputes are settled under the civil law.

Test your understanding 2

(1) **D**

An advertisement, such as the statement in the newspaper, is an invitation to treat and is not an offer in itself. An invitation to treat is an invitation to others to make an offer.

(2) **B**

The withdrawal of an offer can be made before acceptance, and if an offer is withdrawn, there cannot be offer and acceptance. In the case of **Dickinson v Dodds (1876)**, it was held that the withdrawal of an offer can be communicated by a reliable third party, and does not have to be made directly by the offeror to the offeree.

Test your understanding 3

(1) **D**

For a contract to exist there must be an offer and an acceptance. The offer was made on 1 September, the acceptance was made on 6 September, within the 10-day period. The contract is valid from 6 September, the date of acceptance.

(2) **B**

An advertisement is an invitation to treat, not an offer. When B Ltd placed an order for 100 television sets, it was making an offer. A Ltd can refuse to accept (but can make a counter-offer to sell the sets at £59).

(3) **C**

For a contract to exist there must be offer and acceptance, so A and B are both incorrect, even though B might seem a logical position. D is clearly incorrect, since payment in advance is not a required condition for consideration in a contract. Since there has not yet been acceptance by either party, Alf is in a position to withdraw his offer, and can also refuse the offer by Bert.

(4) **C**

A fax is treated in the same way as a telephone conversation. The message must be received for the acceptance to be communicated.

Test your understanding 4

(1) **B**

Consideration occurs when one person does something in return for a promise by another party to do something else in return. There must be an exchange of undertakings. This occurs with example (ii). It does not occur when the performance is a legal requirement. It does not apply in (iii), because the performance of the act has not been in return for payment – the offer of payment only came later.

(2) **B**

Based on **Williams v Roffey Bros and Nicholls (Contractors) Ltd (1990)**.

(3) **B**

Consideration need not be adequate, but it must be sufficient.

Test your understanding 5

(1) **C**

Conditions are the most important terms. Failure of a condition is so serious that the other party is not limited to seeking damages; he may also treat the contract as discharged by breach. However, it is incorrect to state that the contract must be terminated. The correct statements in the question provide a useful summary of the difference between conditions and warranties.

(2) **C**

When a warranty is breached, the injured party can only claim damages.

(3) **A**

A warranty is a term which is incidental to the main purpose of the contract. Failure to observe it does not cause the whole contract to collapse.

(4) **A**

The remedy for breach of a warranty is damages. The remedies for breach of a condition are repudiation and damages.

Test your understanding 6

(1) **A**

A clause excluding liability for damage to property through negligence is void unless it can be shown to be reasonable.

(2) **D**

Neither statement is correct. The clause will be included in the contract as Dave signed it. It is not automatically void under UCTA 1977.

KAPLAN PUBLISHING

Test your understanding 7

(1) D

A condition is a major term, going to the root of the contract. When breached, the injured party can repudiate the contract and claim damages. In contrast, when a warranty has been breached the injured party can only claim damages.

(2) B

The term renunciation refers to the situation where one party to the contract states or implies that he does not intend to carry out his future obligations under the contract.

(3) B

This is a minor breach in relation to the whole contract, therefore the remedy is damages.

Test your understanding 8

B

The aim of damages in contract is usually to put the injured party into the position he would have been in if the contract had been properly performed – often referred to as bargain loss. However, in some cases, the courts award 'reliance losses', i.e. losses incurred in trying to perform the contract prior to the breach. Both (ii) and (iii) are therefore purposes of awarding damages. Damages are not intended as a punishment of the person in breach of the contract.

Test your understanding 9

(1) **C**

Although specific performance is given at the discretion of the court, there are certain circumstances where it will not be given. The two statements are examples of those circumstances.

(2) **A**

In English Law, the sale of land and property must be by written contract (the transfer or title is by way of a Deed of Transfer or conveyance). If this contract has been signed, it may be specifically enforceable. (In common parlance, if the parties have 'exchanged contracts' for the purchase of a house, the contract is enforceable even though 'completion' is not until a later date.)

(3) **A**

Damages are a remedy available under common law, not equity.

(4) **C**

Damages are intended to be compensatory and not punitive. In this case, D Ltd has not suffered loss because he can obtain at a lower price the same item that C Ltd has refused to sell. D Ltd is therefore entitled to nominal damages only.

3

The law of torts

Chapter learning objectives

Upon completion of this chapter you will be able to:

- define a tort and show how it is different from a contract
- explain the elements of negligence
- discuss defences to an action in negligence
- relate the basic principles to accountants
- explain the basics of passing off.

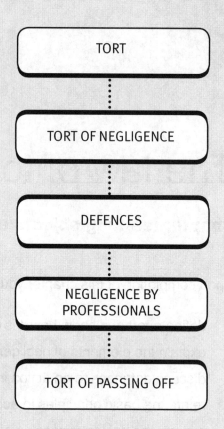

1 Understand the nature of the law of tort

What is a tort?

A tort is a type of civil wrong. It is a breach of a legal duty or an infringement of a legal right which gives rise to a claim for damages.

As a tort is a breach of a legal duty, there is no liability unless the law recognises that the duty exists.

Differences between contracts and torts

A contractual relationship does not have to be established for a claim in tort to be successful. Often the parties have never even met before. For example, in a claim for personal injury as a result of a road accident, the parties will often have had no previous relationship at all.

However, if a contract does exist and a tort has been committed, the claimant may choose the remedy most appropriate.

There are two options:

- Under a valid contract, the amount of damages awarded is intended to put the claimant back in the position he would have been in had the contract been properly performed.

- In tort, the amount of damages awarded is intended to put the claimant in the position he would have been in had the tortious act never taken place.

Limitation periods

- In contract the limitation period is six years from the breach of contract.
- In tort the limitation period is generally six years, but three years for personal injury.

The main elements of a tort

In order to be successful in an action for tort, the following conditions must be satisfied:

- There must be an act or omission by the defendant.
- The act or omission must have directly caused damage or injury to the claimant.
- The courts must be able to establish a legal liability as a result of the damage.

A claim will only be successful if the damage or loss suffered is not 'too remote' i.e. the damage or loss must be as a direct consequence of something the defendant did/or did not do.

2 Negligence

Negligence is the breach of a legal duty to take care, which results in damage to another.

In order for an action in negligence to succeed, the claimant must prove the following:

- That a duty of care was owed to him by the defendant
- The defendant breached that duty
- As a consequence of that breach, damage or loss has been suffered.

Duty of care

There is a duty to take reasonable care not to cause foreseeable harm to others.

The 'neighbour principle'

The case of **Donoghue v Stevenson** (below) was the first to establish that a duty of care may be owed to a person, even where no contractual relationship exists.

Prior to this case, the belief was that to allow an action to be taken where there was no contractual relationship would undermine the principles of contract law. The doctrine of privity states that only parties to a contract can sue or be sued.

Donoghue v Stevenson changed this principle and, as a result, manufacturers of goods owe a duty of care to the ultimate consumer of the product.

Donoghue v Stevenson (1932)

Facts: Mrs Donoghue went to a cafe with a friend. The friend bought her a bottle of ginger beer which Mrs Donoghue drank. She then discovered that there was a decomposed snail in the bottom of the opaque bottle. Mrs Donoghue found this sight so upsetting that she suffered physical illness. She sued the manufacturer, claiming that they were under a duty to see that such outside bodies did not get into the ginger beer.

Held: There was a duty on behalf of the manufacturer to take reasonable care in the manufacture of their products. The manufacturer owes a duty to the consumer to take reasonable care to prevent injury.

Lord Atkin defined those to whom we owe a duty of care in the **'neighbour principle'**:

'You must take reasonable care to avoid acts or omissions which you ought reasonably foresee would be likely to injure your neighbour.'

He defined neighbours as:

'...persons who are so directly affected by my act that I ought reasonably to have them in contemplation'.

The duty of care, which in **Donoghue v Stevenson** just related to physical harm has been extended in subsequent cases.

Bourhill v Young (1943)

In this case the court established that the duty of care could apply to nervous shock provided there was sufficient proximity i.e. that the shock was suffered by someone within the reasonable range of harm.

Facts: A motorcyclist was killed in a road accident for which he has responsible. A pregnant woman who got off a tram near the scene of the accident claimed that when she got to the scene of the accident she saw blood on the road and as a result suffered shock which put her into premature labour which resulted in the loss of her baby. She subsequently brought a claim in relation to nervous shock and the resulting loss.

Held: The House of Lords held that the motorcyclist did not owe a duty of care to the pregnant woman as she was not deemed to be a foreseeable victim. She was not present at the scene of the accident, she arrived after the accident occurred.

White v Chief Constable of South Yorkshire Police (1998)

Facts: The claimants were police constables on duty for maintaining law and order during a football match in April 1989 at Hillsborough Stadium. As a result of overcrowding and the consequent stampede, 95 people died and hundreds of others sustained injuries. The policemen on duty, including the claimants, had to tend to the victims for whom many of them suffered post traumatic stress disorder. Four of them were on duty at the stadium, and the fifth one was responsible for stripping bodies and completing casualty forms at a hospital. Resultantly, they claimed compensation for their psychiatric injury from the police department.

Held: The House of Lords overruled the decision of the Court of Appeal and rejected the claim. It was established that the claimants were a 'secondary victim'. A secondary victim is someone whose personal safety is not threatened, but who suffers psychiatric injury as a result of either fear for the safety of others or the trauma of witnessing a harrowing event. In order to succeed in their claim a secondary victim must satisfy three requirements. First, they must have close ties of love and affection with the person who suffers injury or death in an accident attributable to negligence. Second, they must have been present at the accident or on the scene in its immediate aftermath. And third, the psychiatric injury must have been caused by direct perception of the accident or its immediate aftermath and not upon receiving it second-hand. In this case the claimants did not meet the first criteria.

Economic or financial loss

The case of **Donoghue v Stevenson (1932)** established that an action could be taken if **physical damage was suffered**. However, the law still did not recognise liability in respect of 'pure' economic loss. Pure economic loss is monetary loss which is unconnected to physical injury to a person or damage to other property. Where there is economic loss that is connected to physical injury or damage to property then that is 'consequential' economic loss which is recoverable.

Spartan Steel & Alloys Ltd v Martin & Co (Contractors) Ltd (1973)

Facts: Spartan Steel and Alloys Ltd had a stainless steel factory which obtained its electricity by a direct cable from the power station. Martin & Co Ltd were doing work on the ground with an excavator and negligently damaged that cable. As a consequence, the factory was deprived of electricity for fifteen hours which has caused physical damage to the factory's furnaces and metal, lost profit on the damaged metal and lost profit on the metal that was not melted during the time the electricity was off. Spartan Steel claimed all the three heads of damage.

Held: The Court of Appeal held that Spartan Steel could only recover the damages to their furnaces, the metal they had to discard and the profit lost on the discarded metal. They could not recover the profits lost due to the factory not being operational for fifteen hours. Their main reasoning for this was that while the damage to the metal was "physical damage" and the lost profits on the metal was "directly consequential" upon it, the profits lost due to the blackout constituted "pure economic loss".

In respect of pure economic loss suffered as a result of professional misstatement the case of **Hedley Byrne v Heller** modernised the law in this area. The House of Lords refined the neighbour principle by acknowledging that a claim for financial loss suffered could be made if a 'special relationship' existed between the claimant and defendant (see part 3).

The limits of the duty of care

In the case of **The Nicholas H (Marc Rich & Co v Bishops Rock Marine) (1995)**, four tests were laid down which should be followed in determining whether a duty of care exists.

The issues to be considered are:

• Was the damage reasonably foreseeable by the defendant at the time of the act or omission?

- Is there a neighbourhood principle or sufficient proximity (closeness) between the parties?

- Should the law impose a duty of care between the parties i.e. is it fair and reasonable to do so?

- Is there a matter of public policy which exists or requires that no duty of care should exist?

The **Nicholas H** case focused on financial loss, but these tests should also be applied when determining the duty of care for physical damage cases.

Illustration – Negligence

A was given an ipod for his birthday by his uncle. Due to a design defect, it set fire to his bedroom and caused damage to carpets and furniture. A was made ill by smoke inhalation. A is entitled to claim damages from the ipod manufacturer for:

(1) pain and suffering caused by smoke inhalation

(2) any loss of earnings whilst he recovers

(3) the cost of replacing furnishings and redecoration.

He is not entitled to claim the cost of replacing the defective ipod which would be pure economic loss.

The defect does not give rise to the liability: it is the resultant damage to person or property.

Test your understanding 1

In assessing whether a duty of care exists, which of the following tests will be taken into consideration?

I   Was the damage reasonably foreseeable by the defendant at the time of the act or omission?

II   Was it fair and reasonable for the law to impose a duty of care?

III Has the defendant intentionally caused physical damage or financial loss?

IV   Has the claimant taken reasonable steps to mitigate the loss suffered?

A   (I) and (IV) only

B   (I) and (II) only

C   (III) and (IV) only

D   All of the above

Breach of duty of care

In order for a claim to be successful, a claimant must not only prove that a duty of care existed, but also that the duty was breached by the defendant.

(1) As a question of fact the claimant shows that the defendant was in breach of his duty.

The Breach

Establishing if there has indeed been a breach is a question of fact. Each case must be viewed separately on its own facts.

(2) As a question of law the claimant has to show the defendant has not shown the required standard of care.

The standard of care

The test for establishing breach of duty is an objective one and was set out in **Blyth v Birmingham Waterworks Co (1856)** which stated that a breach of duty occurs if the defendant:

'...fails to do something which a reasonable man, guided upon those considerations which ordinarily regulate the conduct of human affairs, would do; or does something which a prudent and reasonable man would not do.'

The reasonable man is not expected to be skilled in any particular trade or profession.

The following principles have been established by case law:

- Probability of injury/vulnerability of claimant

The degree of care required has to be balanced against the degree of risk involved in the event of the duty being breached. This means that the greater the risk of injury the more that should be done in order to prevent the injury.

KAPLAN PUBLISHING

Glasgow Corporation v Taylor (1992)

Facts: A seven year old child died after eating poisonous berries he had picked from a bush in a park controlled by the defendant.

Held: The provision of a warning notice was not enough. The defendant had breached its duty of care to the child by leaving the berries on the bush.

Children are owed a higher standard of care and a lower standard can be expected from them.

The degree of care to be exercised may be increased if the claimant is more vulnerable i.e. is young, old or less able bodied. This is based on the rule that 'you must take your victim as you find him'.

Haley v London Electricity Board (1965)

Facts: In order to carry out some repairs the defendant made a hole in the pavement. They took sufficient precautions to make the area safe for a sighted person. However, the claimant who was blind fell into the hole, and sustained an injury which made him deaf.

Held: The defendant was in breach of its duty of care to pedestrians as it had failed to ensure that the area was safe for all pedestrians. Although it was reasonably safe for sighted persons clearly it was not for blind persons.

- Particular skill

  As a general rule, the level of skill and care required is that which a reasonable man would possess. However, if the defendant possesses a particular skill, i.e. he is a qualified solicitor or a qualified accountant, the standard of care expected will be that of a reasonable person with that skill.

  Hindsight is irrelevant, the degree of skill is the standard required at the time of the tort.

Roe v Ministry of Health (1954)

Facts: A doctor administered a spinal injection which had become contaminated as a result of minute cracks in the phials. As a result of that the patient was paralysed.

Held: There was no breach of duty since the doctor who had administered the injection had no way of detecting the contamination.

- Lack of skill

Lack of training or the peculiarities of the defendant are not relevant. Therefore, the standard of skill expected from a trainee accountant is the same as that of any reasonable accountant.

Nettleship v Weston (1971)

Facts: During a driving lesson, the defendant who was a learner driver lost control of the car and caused an accident in which the claimant was injured. The defendant argued that the claimant was well aware of her lack of skill and that the court should make allowance for her since she could not be expected to drive like an experienced motorist.

Held: The standard of care for a learner driver would be the usual standard applied to drivers: that of an experienced and skilled driver.

- Cost and practicability

Where there is a forseeable risk this must be balanced against the measures necessary to eliminate the potential risk. If the cost of these measures far outweighs the potential risk it will probably be concluded that there is no breach of duty in not eliminating the risk.

Latimer v AEC Ltd (1952)

Facts: A factory was flooded as a result of a heavy rainstorm and as a result made the floor of the factory very slippery. The defendant who owned the factory arranged for sawdust to be spread on the floor, however there was insufficient sawdust to cover the whole area. The claimant slipped and injured himself.

Held: The defendant was not in breach of its duty as it had taken all the reasonable precautions that would have been expected given the circumstances and had eliminated the risk as so far as was practicable.

- Common practice

Where a particular action is in line with common practice or custom that may be considered to be sufficient to meet the expected standard of care. However, this will not apply if the common practice itself is negligent.

Paris v Stepney BC (1951)

Facts: The defendant employed the claimant as a garage mechanic who had lost the sight of one eye during the war. In order to loosen a stiff bolt he struck it with a hammer; a piece of metal flew off and because he was not wearing goggles struck him in his good eye, causing him to become totally blind.

Held: The court decided that knowing of his disability the defendants should have taken extra care. However, they did make the point that not wearing glasses was common practice and in itself was negligent and therefore could be used as a defence.

Loss caused by the breach

A claimant must demonstrate that he has suffered loss or damage as a direct consequence of the breach. This is sometimes called the 'But For' test - but for the actions of the defendant the claimant would not have suffered the damage.

The claimant must establish a causal link between the defendant's conduct and the damage which occurred:

- If the damage was caused by something or someone else there will be no liability on the defendant's part.

- If the claimant would have suffered the loss regardless of the defendant's conduct then he has not caused the loss.

Barnett v Chelsea and Kensington Hospital Management Commitee (1969)

Facts: The claimant's husband (Mr Barnett) went to hospital complaining of severe stomach pains and vomiting. He was seen by a nurse who telephoned the doctor on duty. The doctor told her to send him home and contact his GP in the morning. Mr Barnett died five hours later from arsenic poisoning.

Held: Even if the doctor had examined Mr Barnett at the time there was nothing the doctor could have done to save him. Therefore, the hospital was not liable as the doctor's failure to examine Mr Barnett did not cause his death.

- If something happened after the defendant's breach that caused or contributed to the damage then the defendant's liability will cease at that point.

- The following losses are normally recoverable:
  - loss as a result of personal injury
  - damage to property
  - financial loss directly connected to personal injury (i.e. loss of wages).

As discussed earlier pure financial loss is very rarely recoverable.

• Even where the claimant is able to show the loss was suffered as a result of the defendant's breach the court will not allow recovery of that loss if it is considered to be too remote (see part 4 below) i.e. must be of a type of loss that is reasonably foreseeable.

Test your understanding 2

Which one of the following is not an essential element of the tort of negligence?

A   A duty of care owed to the claimant

B   A breach of the duty of care

C   An intention to cause loss or injury

D   Loss or injury caused by the defendant's breach

---

3 Professional advice and negligent misstatement

In practice there is no difference between liability arising from negligent misstatement and liability arising from negligent acts. A party can suffer damage by reliance on incorrect advice just as he can be injured by any other negligent conduct.

With respect to a negligent misstatement however, the consequences of this could be far-reaching and affect countless people. Because of this the law had been reluctant to impose a duty of care in the making of statements.

This situation changed in 1964 when the landmark case set out below marked a new approach to the law of negligent misstatement.

Hedley Byrne & Co Ltd v Heller & Partners Ltd (1964)

Facts: The appellants (Hedley Byrne) were advertising agents, who had contracted to place advertisements for their client's (Easipower) products. As this involved giving Easipower credit, they asked the respondents, who were Easipower's bankers, for a reference as to the creditworthiness of Easipower.

Heller gave favourable references (but stipulated that the information was given without responsibility on their part). Relying on this information, the claimants extended credit to Easipower and lost over £17,000 when the latter, soon after, went into liquidation. The claimants sued Easipower's bankers for negligence.

Held: The respondents' disclaimer was adequate to exclude the assumption by them of the legal duty of care. However, in the absence of the disclaimer, the circumstances would have given rise to a duty of care in spite of the absence of a contractual or fiduciary relationship. Thus, but for the disclaimer, the bank was liable on its misleading statement. Note: nowadays the disclaimer might be invalidated under Unfair Contract Terms Act 1977 (UCTA 1977).

The effect of Hedley Byrne

The above case created a new duty situation by recognising liability for negligent misstatement causing economic loss in circumstances where there exists a special relationship between the parties.

Cases involving negligent misstatement are usually concerned with establishing whether or not a duty arises and it is difficult to establish clear principles to apply as the law has evolved on a case-by-case basis.

The meaning of special relationship

A special relationship exists where a professional person advises a known person who relies on the statement for a known purpose.

For an action in negligent misstatement to succeed there must be a special relationship. The considerations outlined in the **Nicholas H** case will still be relevant.

It is clear that liability will only arise where the defendant is in the business of giving professional advice and the statement is given in that context i.e. not on a social or informal occasion.

One important consideration is the relationship of the parties in the context of the damage suffered, for example whether the preparation of accounts is for shareholders or a potential takeover.

Jeb Fasteners Ltd v Marks, Bloom & Co (1982)

Facts: The defendant accountants audited the accounts of X Co. The audit report was negligently prepared. The claimant then took over X Co.

Held: The defendants owed the claimants a duty of care because they knew the claimant company was considering taking over X Co. and thus were likely to rely on the audited accounts. However, the claimant's action for damages failed because they had taken over the company to obtain the services of X Co's two directors and not on the basis of the accounts, so that the breach did not cause the loss suffered and there was no resultant loss.

However the court did express the view that a duty of care was owed by the accountants to the claimant as it was reasonably foreseeable that a potential bidder would rely on the accounts.

If advice is given or financial statements prepared for a specific purpose, then a duty of care is owed to those who are relying on them for that specific purpose.

Morgan Crucible v Hill Samuel Bank (1991)

Facts: MC made a bid for FCE plc which then issued circulars containing profit records and forecasts recommending its shareholders not to accept the bid. Eventually MC increased its bid and, on the FCE board recommending acceptance, MC's bid succeeded. Subsequently MC discovered that the accounts and the profit forecasts grossly overstated FCE's profits and that FCE was worthless. Had MC known the true facts it would never have made the bid, let alone increased it. MC sued FCE's merchant bank, directors and accountants in the tort of negligence in respect of circulars issued after the bid was first made.

Held: Here the claimants knew MC would rely on the circulars for the particular purpose of deciding whether or not to make an increased bid and intended that they should. Thus there might be proximity.

Where there is no special relationship

As a general rule, however, unless the defendant had prior knowledge that a certain bidder would rely on the statement made, no duty of care would exist.

The concept of special relationship has now been redefined in the following leading case:

Caparo Industries Plc v Dickman and Others (1990)

Facts: C, a shareholder in F plc, bought more shares in the company after receiving the audited accounts. He later made a takeover bid.

After the takeover C sued the auditors alleging that the audited accounts had been misleading as they showed a profit when in fact there had been a loss. C said the auditors owed a duty of care to investors and potential investors as they should have been aware that a press release saying that profits would fall significantly had made F vulnerable to a takeover bid and that bidders might rely on the accounts.

Held: The court set out three criteria which had to be fulfilled in order to give rise to a duty of care:

(1) The standard test of foreseeability applied

(2) The concept of proximity limits the duty to circumstances where the statement would be communicated to the claimant either as an individual or a member of an identifiable group in respect of transactions of a particular kind and that the claimant would rely on the statement. It is therefore necessary to look at the purpose for which the statement is made, the statement maker's knowledge of the person relying on the statement and the type of transaction in which it is used.

(3) Whether it is just and equitable that a duty of care should be imposed so that imposing it would not be contrary to public policy. When the court applied these criteria to the Caparo case they found that auditors of a public company owe no duty of care to the public at large who rely on accounts when purchasing shares in a company nor was any duty owed to individual shareholders who purchase additional shares.

This approach is also illustrated in the following case:

James McNaughton Paper Group v Hicks Anderson (1991)

Facts: JMP entered into negotiations with MK Paper for an agreed takeover of MK. The chairman of MK asked its accountants, HA, to prepare draft accounts as quickly as possible for use in the negotiations. The accounts when prepared were shown by MK to JMP. After the takeover was completed, JMP discovered certain discrepancies in the accounts. JMP brought an action against MK's accountants in the tort of negligence.

Held: No duty of care was owed because of lack of proximity between JMP and HA. The prime reasons for lack of proximity included:

- the accounts were produced for MK's use in negotiations not for JMP's use

- draft accounts are not intended to be relied on as if they were final accounts.

Where there is a special relationship

If advice is given or financial statements prepared for a specific purpose, then a duty of care is owed to those who are relying on them for that specific purpose.

Test your understanding 3

Which one of the following is correct?

A Professional advisors cannot be liable in respect of negligent advice in the tort of negligence but may be liable for breach of contract.

B Professional advisors cannot be liable for breach of contract in respect of negligent advice, but may be liable in the tort of negligence.

C Professional advisors may be liable in respect of negligent advice in either contract or tort.

D Professional advisers cannot be liable in respect of negligent advice in either contract or tort.

Test your understanding 4

What forms the basis of the existence of a legal duty of care in negligence for misstatements resulting in economic loss to the claimant?

A Proximity

B Proximity and damage

C Foreseeability

D seeability and proximity

Test your understanding 5

In **Hedley Byrne v Heller & Partners**, the House of Lords held that a banker would owe a duty of care on a reference for a client given voluntarily without consideration to a third party.

What was the basis of this decision?

A That in such a case a duty is owed to persons generally.

B That a duty is owed to those persons who could reasonably be foreseen as relying on the statement.

C That a duty is owed to a person the defendant knew or ought to have known would rely on the statement.

D That a duty is only owed to those with whom the defendant was in a fiduciary or contractual relationship.

4 Remedies and defences in negligence

Remedies in an action in negligence

The principal remedy in any case involving negligence will be an award of damages.

The damage caused to the claimant must be of a type that is 'reasonably foreseeable'.

A loss is reasonably foreseeable if a reasonable man would have foreseen the type of injury, loss or damage.

As a general rule it is for the claimant to prove that the defendant was in breach of the duty of care.

Exceptionally the defendant will have to prove that he was not negligent. This will only occur if:

- the harm would not have normally happened if proper care were taken

- there is no other explanation for what has occurred, known as **res ipsa loquitor**, the thing that speaks for itself

- the defendant was in control of the situation and the victim was not.

Ward v Tesco Stores Ltd (1976)

Facts: The claimant was injured when she slipped on some yoghurt which had been spilt on the floor. At the trial the defendant gave evidence that spillages occurred about ten times a week and that staff had been instructed that if they saw any spillage on the floor they were to stay where the spill had taken place and call somebody to clear it up. Apart from general cleaning, the floor was brushed five or six times every day on which the supermarket was open. There was, however, no evidence before the court as to when the floor had last been cleaned before the claimant's accident.

Held: Even though it could not be said exactly what happened, the yoghurt being spilled spoke for itself as to who was to blame. The claimant did not need to prove how long the spill had been there, because the burden of proof was on Tesco.

Overseas Tankship (UK) v Morts Dock and Engineering Co (The Wagon Mound) (1961)

Facts: Due to the defendants' negligence, oil was spilled and accumulated around the claimant's wharf. The oil ignited and the wharf suffered fire damage.

Held: The defendants were held not liable since, while damage to the wharf by oil pollution was foreseeable, damage by fire was not.

If the type of damage is reasonably foreseeable the defendant is liable. It is irrelevant that the defendant might not have been able to foresee its cause or its severity.

Hughes v Lord Advocate (1963)

Facts: The defendant telephone engineers left an inspection hole covered only by a tent and surrounded by paraffin lamps. A child claimant was badly injured when he fell down the hole carrying a lamp which exploded on impact causing a fireball.

Held: The defendants were liable as they should reasonably have foreseen that a child would be attracted by the lamps and might be burned when playing with them. It was irrelevant that they could not have foreseen the explosion or the severity of the burn damage.

Defences to a claim in negligence

There are three main defences to a charge of negligence:

- contributory negligence
- volenti non fit injuria
- exclusion clauses.

Contributory negligence

If the claimant is partly responsible for his own injuries, the defendant can plead the defence of contributory negligence. The court may then reduce any damages it awards to the claimant depending on the degree to which he is judged responsible for his loss.

The onus is on the defendant to show the claimant was at fault and therefore contributed to their own injury.

It is only a partial defence, the defendant is still liable but the damages are reduced to reflect the extent for which the claimant was responsible for their own injury.

Jones v Livox Quarries (1952)

Facts: The plaintiff was riding down a slope leading to the bottom of a quarry on the back of the defendants' vehicle, contrary to their orders, when another vehicle of the defendants was negligently driven into the back of the first vehicle. As a result, the plaintiff was injured.

Held: The claimant exposed himself not only to the risk of falling off the vehicle but also to the risk of being injured in the particular way in which he was injured. The court therefore found that he was contributorily negligent.

Sayers v Harlow (1958)

Facts: The claimant having paid to use a public toilet found herself trapped inside a cubicle which had no door handle. She attempted to climb out by stepping first on to the toilet and then on to the toilet-roll holder which gave way and as a result she was injured.

Held: The injuries she suffered were a natural and probable consequence of the defendant's negligence, but that the damages would be reduced by 25% since the claimant had been careless in depending for support on the toilet-roll holder.

Volenti non fit injuria

This applies where the claimant has freely consented to the negligent act. It amounts to an agreement by the claimant to exempt the defendant from a duty of care that he would otherwise owe. Consent can be given expressly where the claimant agrees to the risk of injury, or may be implied from the claimant's conduct.

ICI v Shatwell (1964)

Facts: The plaintiff and his brother were certificated and experienced shotfirers employed by ICI Ltd in a quarry owned by the defendant company. Part of the brothers' work included wiring up detonators and checking the electrical circuits. They ignored the defendant's rules relating to safety and tested the detonators without using the shelter provided. One of the brothers was injured and claimed his brother was 50 per cent to blame for the explosion and that the employer was vicariously liable.

Held: Both brothers had impliedly consented to the risks of their actions and therefore the defendant was not liable.

Consent acts as a complete defence and no damages would be awarded if it is shown to apply.

Exclusion clauses

An exclusion clause is a provision within a contract which seeks to exclude or limit liability for negligence. An exclusion clause may fall within the provisions of the Unfair Contract Terms Act 1977 (see Chapter 2).

If an exclusion clause is found be valid, this constitutes a viable defence against any action for negligence.

In addition, liability is excluded if it is possible to say that the act occurred in the course of nature i.e. that it was an 'act of god'; something beyond human foresight which the defendant could not have been expected to provide against.

Test your understanding 6

In the tort of negligence, if a claimant is partly responsible for his own injuries then:

A No compensation can be recovered from the defendant.

B The defendant is fully liable if he was mainly responsible for the injuries.

C If the defendant was negligent he remains fully liable for all the injuries caused.

D The compensation will be reduced to take account of the claimant's share of the responsibility.

Test your understanding 7

If a claimant cannot show precisely how an accident occurred in relation to personal injuries he receives through negligence:

A He cannot claim compensation.

B He can only claim reduced compensation.

C There is no effect on his claim.

D He may assert 'res ipsa loquitor'.

KAPLAN PUBLISHING

5 The tort of passing off

This tort protects the goodwill, reputation and profits of a business.

The tort of passing off arises:

- where one business uses a name which is similar to that of an existing business, and
- it misleads persons into believing that they are the same business, and
- it causes actual damage to that business or will probably do so.

Ewing v Buttercup Margarine Co Ltd (1917)

Facts: Ewing who traded under the name Buttercup Diary Company sued to restrain a newly registered company called Buttercup Margarine Company Ltd from using the name on the grounds that the general public might reasonably believe that there was a link between the two businesses.

Held: The court held that the word 'Buttercup' was so closely associated with Ewing dairy products as to be likely to cause confusion if used by the similar margarine business. An injunction was granted to prevent the defendant company from trading under its name.

If passing off is proved, the court may restrain the business from trading under that name and order that damages be paid to the person whose business has suffered loss.

If a company feels than another company has a name which is too similar to its own, it may object to the Company Names Adjudicator under CA 06. The Adjudicator will consider the case and then make their decision. In most cases the Adjudicator will require a name change, and in some cases the Adjudicator may state the new company name.

6 Chapter summary

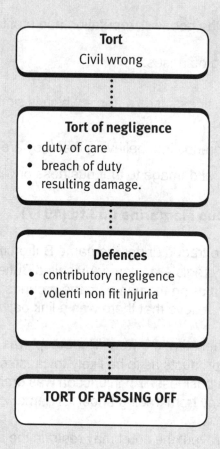

Tort
Civil wrong

Tort of negligence
- duty of care
- breach of duty
- resulting damage.

Defences
- contributory negligence
- volenti non fit injuria

TORT OF PASSING OFF

Test your understanding answers

Test your understanding 1

B

The intention of the defendant is irrelevant to a claim for negligence. The claimant is under no duty to mitigate their loss.

Test your understanding 2

C

The three elements of the tort of negligence are:

- Duty of care: It applies in situations where an individual owes a duty of care to someone else.

- Breach of duty of care: the claimant must show the defendant failed to take the care which a reasonable person would have done in the circumstances.

- Resultant loss: there must be a resultant loss, financial or otherwise, before the tort of negligence can be applied.

Intention to cause harm is not a prerequisite here.

Test your understanding 3

C

Professional advisers may be liable in respect of negligent advice in either contract or tort.

Test your understanding 4

D

The main element is proximity, but some likelihood of damage must have been foreseeable.

Test your understanding 5

C

A duty is owed to a person the defendant knew or ought to have known would rely on the statement. He must also know the purpose to which the information will be put.

Test your understanding 6

D

In the tort of negligence, if the claimant is partly responsible for his own injuries, the compensation awarded by the court will be reduced to take account of the claimant's share of the injuries.

Test your understanding 7

D

If a claimant cannot show how an accident occurred he can assert 'res ipsa loquitor'. This means that 'the thing speaks for itself'. When this doctrine is applied it is not necessary for the claimant to prove that the defendant is negligent: if there was no other way the injury could have happened the negligence of the defendant is presumed.

Employment law

Chapter learning objectives

Upon completion of this chapter you will be able to:

- distinguish between employees and the self-employed
- explain the nature of the contract of employment and give examples of the main duties placed on the parties to such a contract
- distinguish between wrongful and unfair dismissal, including constructive dismissal
- explain what is meant by redundancy
- discuss the remedies available to those who have been subject to unfair dismissal or redundancy.

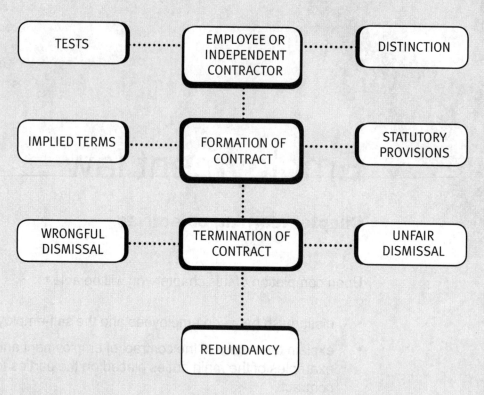

1 Employed versus self-employed
Introduction

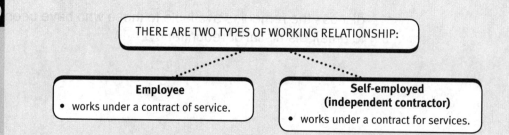

The tests used to determine employment

A number of tests can be used to determine if someone is employed or self-employed:

- **the control test** – employees are subject to control by their employer as to how, where and when they do their work: **Yewens v Noakes (1880).** (Note, however, that this test is inappropriate for skilled workers.)

- **the integration test** – someone is regarded as an employee if their work is an integral part (i.e. part and parcel) of the business and not merely an accessory to it. (Note, however, that this test has become difficult to apply as a sole criterion.)

- **the economic reality test (or multiple test)** – under this test the court takes all the surrounding factors into account.

The test involves asking whether the person who is doing the work, is doing so as a person in business on his own account.

Relevant factors are:

- control
- provision of his own equipment
- whether he hires his own helpers
- degree of financial risk he undertakes
- degree of responsibility he bears for investment and management
- the extent to which he has an opportunity of profiting from sound management in the performance of his task
- whether there is a regular method of payment
- whether the person works regular hours
- whether there is mutuality of obligations.

Ready Mixed Concrete (South East) Ltd v Minister of Pensions & National Insurance & Others (1968)

Facts: The driver of a lorry had a contract with a company under which he drove his lorry only on company business, obeyed instructions of the foreman and wore company colours. He provided his own lorry which he had obtained from the company on hire purchase and which was painted in company colours. He could employ a substitute driver. He was paid on the basis of mileage and quantity of goods delivered. He paid the expenses of repair and maintenance of the lorry and his own national insurance and income tax. The Minister of Pensions claimed that he was an employee and the company had therefore to make the employer's national insurance contributions.

Held: Although the employer exercised some control over his work, the other factors were not consistent with there being a contract of service. In particular, the fact that he owned his own equipment and was operating at his own financial risk to a degree (i.e. was 'a small businessman') meant that he was an independent contractor.

Expandable text

Control test

An example of this test in operation may be seen in **Walker v Crystal Palace Football Club (1910)** in which it was decided that a professional footballer was an employee of his club on the basis that he was subject to control in relation to his training, discipline and method of pay.

However, with developing technology and specialisation, the control test became inappropriate as employers would hire people for particular skills (e.g. a chemical engineer), of which the employer did not have sufficient knowledge or skill to instruct as to the manner in which they carried out their work.

Integration test

An example of the application of the integration test may be seen in **Whittaker v Minister of Pensions & National Insurance (1966)** in which the court found that the degree to which a circus trapeze artist was required to do other general tasks in relation to the operation of the circus in which she appeared, indicated that she was an employee rather than self-employed. As a consequence, she was entitled to claim compensation for injuries sustained in the course of her employment.

The economic reality test

Market Investigations Ltd v Minister of Social Security (1968)

Facts: A market research interviewer worked on and off under a series of contracts whereby she interviewed for a company in accordance with interview instructions issued by the company. She had to complete the work within a specified period, but otherwise had no specified hours of work. There was no provision for holiday or sick pay and she was free to work for others while working for the company.

Held: The company did have some control over the manner in which she did her work and the terms of the contract were consistent with a contract of service. The court emphasised that she did not provide her own tools and took no risk. She was therefore not 'in business on her own account' and was an employee and not an independent contractor. The court also emphasised that there was 'no exhaustive test compiled, nor strict rules laid down' as to the factors which identified a contract of service.

Temporary or casual workers

There are real problems in determining the status of temporary or casual workers.

O'Kelly v Trusthouse Forte Plc (1983)

Facts: A wine waiter was called a 'regular casual' because he was given work when it was required in the banqueting hall. He had no other employment and it was generally accepted that he would be offered work in preference to others when work was available, and that he would accept such work when offered.

Held: He was an independent contractor because there was 'no mutuality of obligation' in that the company was under no duty to offer him work and he was under no duty to accept it. However when at work he wore a company uniform, did not use his own equipment, did not share in the profit and had no investment in the business (aside from his time as a waiter).

Home workers or outworkers

There are also problems with home workers or outworkers. Generally such people will be paid by the number of pieces they produce and will supply their own equipment. Their position is ambiguous and many consider themselves to be self-employed, but the law does not always take this view.

Nethermere (St Neots) Ltd v Taverna and Gardiner (1984)

Facts: Two women, who sewed trousers at home, let the company know when to deliver the material and collect the finished garments. They rarely refused work, but did give warning if they did not want it, e.g. going on holiday. They submitted time sheets and were paid at the same rate as the workers in the factory. The company relied on the work they produced. The company provided the machines.

> **Held:** They were employees because, by the giving and taking of work regularly over a continuous period of time, they had built up a mutuality of obligation (i.e. the company to provide work and the women to accept it).

The importance of the distinction

The type of working relationship has a number of consequences:

- employees receive statutory protection (e.g. unfair dismissal/redundancy)

- there are implied terms in a contract of employment (e.g. duty of obedience)

- an employer is vicariously liable for the acts of employees when they act in the course of the employer's business. The employer is not liable for the acts of independent contractors

- on the insolvency of the employer, an employee is a preferential creditor, whereas someone who is self-employed ranks as an ordinary unsecured creditor

- employees receive their pay net of income tax and national insurance under the PAYE system. Independent contractors are taxed under the trading income provisions

- certain state benefits (e.g. statutory sick pay) are only available to employees.

Test your understanding 1

(1) **Which of the following statements suggest that John is an independent contractor in relation to the work he carries out for Zed Ltd?**

   I   He is required to provide his own tools.

   II   He is required to carry out his work personally and is not free to send a substitute.

   III He is paid in full without any deduction of income tax.

   A   (I) and (II) only.

   B   (II) and (III) only.

   C   (I) and (III) only.

   D   (I), (II) and (III).

(2) H plc carries on its business using both employees and independent contractors. It is important for H plc to be able to distinguish between its employees and independent contractors for a number of reasons.

Which one of the following is incorrect?

A Employees have a right not to be unfairly dismissed, but this does not apply to independent contractors.

B H plc must deduct income tax and national insurance contributions from the wages paid to its employees, but not from the amount paid to independent contractors.

C Both employees and independent contractors can enforce contractual rights against H plc.

D Both employees and independent contractors would rank as preferential creditors in respect of unpaid wages, if H plc went into insolvent liquidation.

(3) **Which of the following is a test to determine a worker's status?**

A The neighbour test.

B The multiple test.

C The reasonableness test.

D The test of remoteness.

(4) **Which of the following statements is correct?**

I An employer is vicariously liable for the torts of employees committed in the course of their employment.

II An employer is vicariously liable for the torts of independent contractors, if they were committed whilst carrying out work for the employer.

A (I) only.

B (II) only.

C Both (I) and (II).

D Neither (I) nor (II).

2 The contract of employment

Contents

A contract of employment will consist of:

- express terms

- terms implied by the courts
- terms implied by statute.

Express terms

Express terms are those agreed by the parties themselves. The agreement may be written or oral.

The Employment Rights Act 1996 (ERA 1996) requires an employer to provide an employee with a written statement of certain particulars of their employment within two months of the commencement of employment.

The statement must include details of:

- pay rates and interval (i.e. weekly, monthly, etc.)
- job title
- hours of work
- place of work
- length of notice
- details of disciplinary or grievance procedures
- date of commencement of employment.

Any change must be notified by written statement within one month.

The statement is not a contract unless both parties agree and it is called a contract. It is strong prima facie evidence of the terms of the contract, but is not conclusive.

Terms implied by the courts

The courts have implied various duties into the employment contract.

Duties of the employee

Duty to obey lawful and reasonable orders

Pepper v Webb (1968)

Facts: A gardener refused to plant the plants where instructed by the employer.

Held: He was in breach of the duty of obedience and this, coupled with the fact that he was rude and surly, justified his summary dismissal.

Duty of mutual co-operation (or the duty to perform the work in a reasonable manner)

The duty of the employer to give, and the employee to obey, lawful instructions is often expressed as the duty of mutual co-operation. The courts have begun to imply a term that the employer must not act in a manner calculated to damage the mutual trust and confidence and this is taken into account in considering the reasonableness of the order. The courts have interpreted the duty to obey lawful and reasonable orders as a duty not to frustrate the commercial objectives of the employer.

Secretary of State for Employment v ASLEF (1972)

Facts: Railway workers 'worked to rule', i.e. obeyed the British Rail rule book to the letter. This resulted in considerable delays in the train service.

Held: There was an implied term that each employee in obeying instructions would not do so in a wholly unreasonable way which had the effect of disrupting the service he was there to provide.

Duty to exercise reasonable care and skill

The employee must act with reasonable care in performing his duties. The standard of care will depend on the circumstances. It is generally accepted that a single act of negligence, unless it is gross negligence, will not justify summary dismissal. There are certain occupations, such as airline pilots, where a single act of negligence in performing essential duties may warrant dismissal.

An extension of this duty of care is a duty to indemnify the employer for any damages which he has had to pay as a result of his vicarious liability for the employee's negligence.

Lister v Romford Ice & Cold Storage Ltd (1972)

Facts: An employee negligently ran over another employee with a fork-lift truck.

Held: He was liable in damages to his employer for breach of contract.

Duty of good faith – a duty to give honest and faithful service

The employee cannot use the employer's property as his own, and must account to his employer for any money or property which he receives in the course of his employment.

Sinclair v Neighbour (1967)

Facts: An employee secretly borrowed from the shop till. He repaid the money the next day.

Held: He was in breach of the duty of good faith and, since this was a serious breach of contract, the employer was justified in summarily dismissing him.

The employee may do other work in his own time. However, the law imposes a duty not to do spare time work which competes with that of his employer and may cause his employer damage.

An employee must not disclose trade secrets to a third party nor misuse confidential information he has acquired in the course of his employment. This implied duty may continue after the employment has ceased. Clearly an employee who uses or sells secret processes, such as chemical formulae, or photocopies list of customers and sells them or uses them for his own purposes will be in breach.

The real problem arises in drawing a line between trade secrets/confidential information and general knowledge and skill acquired by the employee in the course of his employment. An employee may always use skills he has learnt in his employment.

Hivac Ltd v Park Royal Scientific Instruments Ltd (1946)

Facts: Two employees of a company which manufactured sophisticated components for hearing aids worked at the weekends for a rival company.

Held: An injunction was granted as there was potential for misuse of the secret information.

Duty to render personal service

Employees may not delegate the performance of their work to someone else unless they have their employer's express or implied permission to do so.

Duties of the employer

Duty to pay reasonable remuneration

This will be implied in the absence of an express provision regarding pay.

Duty to indemnify the employee

The employer must indemnify his employee where the employee has incurred a legal liability or necessary expenses whilst acting on the employer's behalf.

KAPLAN PUBLISHING

Duty to provide a safe system of work

At common law the employer is under a duty to take reasonable care for the health and safety of his employees. Breach of this duty exposes the employer to liability in negligence to his employees.

In addition, the employer is under various statutory duties, e.g. the Factories Act 1961, the Offices, Shops and Railway Premises Act 1963, and the Health and Safety at Work etc. Act 1974 all regulate work conditions.

The requirement at common law is to take reasonable care to provide a safe system of work and this encompasses such matters as the selection of staff and provision for their supervision; and ensuring that premises, plant and materials are safe.

In assessing the reasonableness of the employer in these matters a number of factors must be considered. For example: what was the risk of injury? What was the cost of prevention? What were the characteristics of the employee?

If the employer has not acted unreasonably, he has not been negligent, and has no common law liability.

Latimer v AEC Ltd (1953)

Facts: Following flood damage, the employer carefully strewed sawdust over a factory floor to prevent employees slipping until the floor could be properly cleared. A small patch remained uncovered and L slipped and was injured.

Held: The employers had not acted unreasonably. They were not liable to L for his injuries.

Duty to give reasonable notice of termination of employment

In practice this implied duty rarely arises since most contracts of employment contain express provision stating the exact length of notice or stating that the contract is to be for a fixed term. Also there are statutory minimum periods of notice.

Duty of mutual co-operation

This duty has already been discussed in respect of employees' duties. The employer has a duty not to behave in a manner calculated to damage the relationship of trust and confidence, e.g. by abusively reprimanding an employee.

Provision of work

There is no general common law duty to provide work. However, such a term may be implied, under the business efficacy test, where failure to provide work would deprive the employee of a benefit contemplated by the contract. For example, if the contract expressly provides for remuneration on a piecework or commission basis it may be possible to imply a duty on the employer to provide sufficient work to enable the employee to earn a reasonable sum.

Similarly, where the employee is skilled and needs practice to maintain those skills, there may be an obligation to provide a reasonable amount of work.

William Hill Organisation Ltd v Tucker (1998)

Facts: T worked as a senior dealer (one of only five authorised to do so) operating in the field of spread betting. He served notice to terminate his contract in order to work for a competitor. WH insisted that he remain on the payroll for the notice period, but stayed at home 'on garden leave'. T sought to start his new job immediately, arguing that WH was in breach of contract in refusing to allow him to work.

Held: WH was in breach by not providing work because T had particular skills which must be exercised to maintain them.

Provision of a reference

There is no duty to provide a reference but, if one is provided, it must be truthful, as shown in:

Spring v Guardian Assurance (1994)

Facts: The claimant had worked as a representative for a company but was dismissed after their sale to Guardian Assurance. He applied to work for the insurance company Scottish Amicable. Guardin Assurance provided Scottish Amicable with a bad reference in respect of the claimant who claimed damages for negligent misstatement. The reference was, the judge said, 'so strikingly bad as to amount to . . . the 'kiss of death' to his career in insurance'.

Held: The defendants did owe the claimant a duty of care in providing a reference, knowing that a bad one might damage his prospects of employment, and that they were in breach of that duty.

Terms implied by statute

ERA 1996	Gives employees certain rights, such as a right not to be unfairly dismissed, a right to a redundancy payment if made redundant and a right to a minimum period of notice to terminate the contract.
Working Time Regulations 1998	Limit the **hours** of work to an average of **48 a week**. It also gives the right to **four weeks' paid leave** a year and **one day off each week**.
Employment Act 2002	Gives **parents of children under seventeen or disabled children under eighteen** the right to request **flexible working** arrangements. The employer must give serious consideration to such a request and can only reject it for clear business reasons. The Act also introduced paternity and adoption leave.
Equal Pay Act 1970	Deals not only with pay, but other terms, e.g. holiday and sick leave. **Implies an equality clause** into all contracts of employment if workers of the opposite sex do the same job or a different job of equal value.
National Minimum Wage Act 1998	Imposes minimum levels of pay.

Test your understanding 2

(1) **Which one of the following is normally implied into a contract of employment?**

    A   A duty to provide a reference.

    B   A duty to provide work.

    C   A duty to pay reasonable remuneration.

    D   An employee's duty to disclose his own misconduct.

(2) **Which one of the following statements is correct?**

    A   An employer is obliged to provide a careful and honest reference.

    B   An employer is obliged to provide a safe system of work.

    C   An employer is obliged to provide employees with smoking facilities during authorised breaks at work.

    D   An employer is obliged to give two days off a week.

(3) **Which of the following are sources of terms of a contract of employment?**

   I   Custom and practice.

   II   A collective agreement between the union and the employer.

   A   (I) only.

   B   (II) only.

   C   Both (I) and (II).

   D   Neither (I) nor (II).

(4) **An employer must provide an employee with a written statement of particulars of the employment:**

   A   Within one month of the employment commencing

   B   As soon after the commencement of employment as possible

   C   Within two months of the employment commencing.

   D   Within a reasonable time of the employment commencing

(5) **Which of the following statements are correct with regard to the terms of the Employment Act 2002?**

   I   Parents of children under six years old have the right to request a flexible working arrangement.

   II   An employer receiving a request from an employee for a flexible working arrangement, in accordance with the Act, is obliged to offer such an arrangement.

   A   (I) only.

   B   Both (I) and (II).

   C   (II) only.

   D   Neither (I) nor (II).

Test your understanding 3

Eric and Freda have worked together as partners for many years. They have decided to take on staff in order to expand the business. They are unsure as to what rights and obligations this will entail.

A   Fill in the gaps.

The choice of status of worker is between that of an .... and an .... These are distinguished mostly by the use of the .... test. Three of the factors in determining that a worker is an .... are:

I

II

III

B   Fill in the gaps.

Under the …………………….....a …………………….....must be given to employees within two months of starting work. That statement must be in writing/can be oral and these are three examples of what it must contain:

I

II

III

C   State the main common law duties owed by an employee to employer

3 Wrongful and unfair dismissal

Minimum notice periods

If a period of notice is not expressly agreed, the ERA 1996 imposes the following minimum notice periods:

Notice by employer

Continuous employment	Period of notice
1 month-2 years	1 week
2-12 years	1 week per complete year
12 years +	12 weeks

Notice by employee

An employee with at least four weeks' continuous employment must give his employer at least one week's notice of his terminating of the contract.

Wrongful dismissal

A claim for wrongful dismissal is a common law action for breach of contract. The claim is available to both employees and independent contractors. The usual rules of breach of contract will apply.

 Wrongful dismissal occurs where the employer terminates the contract:

- without giving proper notice or
- during its fixed term.

 Dismissal without notice is known as summary dismissal.

Summary dismissal is usually wrongful dismissal unless the employee:

- waives their rights or accepts payment in lieu of notice
- repudiates the contract themselves or is in fundamental breach (e.g. wilful refusal to obey orders; failure to show professed skill; serious negligence; breach of duty of good faith).

Remedies

An individual who believes he has been wrongfully dismissed may sue in the County court or High Court for damages. The limitation period for such a claim is six years.

Alternatively, if he is an employee, he can bring a claim to the employment tribunal provided he does so within three months of his dismissal and the claim is for £25,000 or less.

Test your understanding 4

Mario is entitled to one month's notice. Consider both of the following situations and state whether he has been wrongfully dismissed:

A   The employer dismisses Mario on one month's notice, but gives him no reason for the dismissal.

B   The employer dismisses Mario without notice for fighting in the workplace with another employee.

Unfair dismissal

This is a statutory right under the Employment Rights Act 1996. Only employees can bring an action for unfair dismissal.

The employer terminates the contract without justifiable reason.

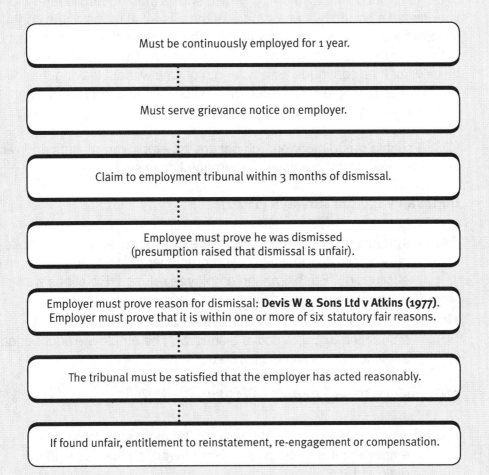

Must be continuously employed for 1 year.

Must serve grievance notice on employer.

Claim to employment tribunal within 3 months of dismissal.

Employee must prove he was dismissed
(presumption raised that dismissal is unfair).

Employer must prove reason for dismissal: **Devis W & Sons Ltd v Atkins (1977)**.
Employer must prove that it is within one or more of six statutory fair reasons.

The tribunal must be satisfied that the employer has acted reasonably.

If found unfair, entitlement to reinstatement, re-engagement or compensation.

Types of dismissal

- Contract terminated by employer with or without notice.
- Fixed-term contract expired and not renewed.
- Constructive dismissal.

Constructive dismissal

Normally employees who resign deprive themselves of the right to make a claim for redundancy or unfair dismissal. However, s95 ERA 1996 covers situations where 'the employee terminates the contract with, or without, notice in circumstances which are such that he or she is entitled to terminate it without notice by reason of the employer's conduct'. This is known as constructive dismissal.

In **Western Excavating (ECC) Ltd v Sharp (1978)** it was held that an employee is entitled to treat himself as constructively dismissed if the employer is guilty of conduct which is a significant breach going to the root of the contract of employment, or which shows that the employer no longer intends to be bound by one or more of the essential terms of the contract. Whether the employee leaves with or without notice, the conduct must be sufficiently serious to entitle him to leave at once. However, he must act quickly, for if he continues for any length of time without leaving, he will be regarded as having elected to affirm the contract and will lose his right to treat himself as discharged.

Where such a repudiatory breach occurs the employee resigns and will have an action against the employer for wrongful dismissal.

Donovan v Invicta Airways (1970)

Facts: The employer put pressure on the employee, an airline pilot, to take abnormal risks on a flight. The employer did this three times in rapid succession. Each time the employee refused. Relations with management deteriorated and he left.

Held: The employer had committed a serious breach of contract amounting to constructive dismissal. The employee succeeded in an action for wrongful dismissal.

Simmonds v Dowty Seals Ltd (1978)

Facts: S had been employed to work on the night shift. When his employer attempted to force him to work on the day shift he resigned.

Held: He could treat himself as constructively dismissed because the employer's conduct had amounted to an attempt to unilaterally change an express term of the employment contract.

Kevin Keegan v Newcastle United Football Club Limited (2010)

Facts: A football club manager resigned from his position and claimed he was constructively dismissed. He contended that when he was appointed manager of the club it was agreed that he would have the final say regarding the transfer of players into the club. The club breached this term by signing a particular player against his express wishes and that he 'had no option but to resign'.

Held: The manager had been constructively dismissed and was awarded in the region of £2m in damages.

In **British Aircraft Corporation v Austin (1978)** a failure to investigate a health and safety complaint was held to be conduct sufficient to entitle the employee to treat the contract as terminated.

If the employee does not resign in the event of the breach, he is deemed to have accepted the breach and waived any rights. However, he need not resign immediately and may legitimately wait until he has found another job: **Cox Toner (International) Ltd v Crook (1981).**

Statutory fair reasons for dismissal

Dismissal for one of the following reasons is **fair unless the employer acted unreasonably** in dismissing for the reason given:

- capabilities/qualifications of employee
- conduct of employee
- redundancy (see below)
- retirement (see below)
- continued employment would contravene statute
- some other substantial reason.

Reasons for dismissal

An employer can only rely on a given reason for dismissal where he knew of it at the date of the dismissal.

Devis W & Sons Ltd v Atkins (1977)

Facts: The employer dismissed the employee and afterwards discovered that the employee had been guilty of dishonesty.

Held: Dishonesty was not the reason for the dismissal and therefore the employer could not rely on it in order to justify the dismissal as fair.

Stevenson v Golden Wonder Ltd (1977)

Facts: A technical manager took part in an unprovoked assault on another employee at a company social function held outside working hours in the company canteen.

Held: This was a fair reason for the dismissal, it was serious misconduct.

An example of 'some other substantial reason' justifying dismissal is the case of **Singh v London Country Bus Services (1976)**, where an employee in a position of trust was convicted of a criminal offence of dishonesty (which he committed off duty).

Reasonableness of employer

Once the employee has shown they were dismissed and the employer has shown that it was for one or more of the six fair reasons it is then for the tribunal to decide whether the dismissal was fair or unfair.

S98(4) ERA 1996 states that the determination of this question 'depends on whether in the circumstances (including the size and administrative resources of the employer's undertaking) the employer acted reasonably or unreasonably in treating it (the reason) as a sufficient reason for dismissing the employee'. The question 'shall be determined in accordance with equity and the substantial merits of the case'.

Case law shows that this 'reasonableness test' involves two questions:

- Whether the reason given was sufficiently serious to justify dismissal.

- Whether the employer adopted reasonable procedures both in coming to the decision to dismiss and in the manner of the dismissal.

The Arbitration, Conciliation and Advisory Service (ACAS) has issued codes of practice for procedures to be followed in coming to the decision to dismiss an employee (e.g. warnings, proper inquiry into alleged misconduct, etc.) which the employment tribunal has regard to. These were illustrated by the House of Lords in **Polkey v Dayton (AE) Services (1987)** where it was stated that:

- in a case of incapability, the employer will normally not act reasonably unless he gives the employee fair warning and an opportunity to mend his ways and show he can do the job

- in a case of misconduct, the employer will normally not act reasonably unless he investigates the complaint fully and fairly and hears whatever the employee wishes to say in his defence or in explanation or mitigation

- in a case of redundancy (this was the situation in **Polkey**) the employer will normally not act reasonably unless he warns and consults any employees affected or their representative, adopts a fair basis upon which to select for redundancy and takes such steps as may be reasonable to avoid or minimise redundancy by redeployment within his own organisation.

Inadmissible reasons for dismissal

Dismissal for one of the following reasons is **automatically unfair**. This means that there is no need to meet the length of employment condition. The tribunal will also make an additional award of compensation.

The inadmissible reasons are:

- victimisation of health and safety complainants or whistleblowers. A whistleblower is a person who raises a concern about wrongdoing occurring in an organisation. The revealed misconduct may be classified in many ways; for example, a violation of a law, rule, regulation and/or a direct threat to public interest, such as fraud, health/safety violations, and corruption

- pregnancy or the exercise of maternity leave rights

- trade union membership/non-membership/activities

- assertion of a statutory right e.g. the exercise of paternity leave rights

- unfair selection for redundancy (see **section 4**).

Retirement

Dismissal on the ground of retirement is fair provided:

- it takes effect on or after the default retirement age of 65 (or on or after the employer's normal retirement age, if there is one); and

- the employer has given the employee written notice of the date of their intended retirement at least six months in advance and told them about their right to request to continue working.

If the employer fails to give six months' notice of the intended retirement date, they may be required to pay compensation for the late notification. If the notification is made within the two weeks prior to the intended retirement date, the dismissal will be automatically unfair.

If the employee wishes to continue working, they must make their request in writing at least three months before the proposed retirement date. Their request must be considered before the employee is retired. Failure to do so will make the dismissal automatically unfair.

Note that although the employer is required to consider any request to work after the normal retirement age, they are entitled to refuse the request. As long as the employer has followed the proper procedure, they may dismiss on the ground of retirement without the dismissal being regarded as unfair or age discriminatory.

Remedies for unfair dismissal

Reinstatement - Employee treated as if not dismissed. Returned to same job with no loss of seniority. **OR** **Re-engagement -** Employee given comparable employment.	Only awarded if the applicant wishes and if it is practicable. The employer's failure to comply with an order for reinstatement or re-engagement results in compensation.

Basic award	Compensatory award	Additional award
18-21 years of age – ½ week's pay for each year of service. 22-40 years of age – 1 week's pay for each year of service. 41 plus – 1½ weeks' pay for each year of service. Maximum – 20 years' service at £380 a week.	Discretionary award of up to £65,300. Based on employee's losses and expenses. Reduced if the complainant contributed to his dismissal.	Given where: • the employer ignores an order for reinstatement or re-engagement • the dismissal is unfair because of race, sex or disability discrimination • the reason cited for dismissal is an inadmissible one.

Test your understanding 5

You have recently been appointed personnel director of a major plc. The board has asked for a review and report on various employment law issues relevant to the employees and working practices within the firm. You investigate the relevant areas of law discussed below.

> **A** **Fill in the gaps.**
>
> The ………………………..sets out a number of reasons why a dismissal will be ………………………
>
> .unfair.
>
> The five major reasons are:
>
> **B** **Explain the remedies for unfair dismissal available to a tribunal.**

4 Redundancy

An employee is redundant if his dismissal is wholly or mainly attributable to the fact that:

* the employer has **ceased**, or intends to cease, **business** for the **purposes** for which the employee has been employed

* the employer has ceased, or intends to cease to carry on the business in the **place** where the employee was employed, or

* the requirements of that business for employees to carry out work of a **particular kind**, or for them to carry out the work in the place where they were so employed, have ceased or diminished.

Note that the work may have ceased altogether or only in the place where the employee was employed.

Redundancy consultation process

If you fail to consult employees - and their representatives if applicable - in a redundancy situation, the redundancy dismissals will almost certainly be unfair.

If you plan to make 20 or more employees redundant in one place of work within a 90-day period, known as a collective redundancy situation, you must:

* Notify the Department for Business, Innovation & Skills; and

* Consult with workplace representatives. These may be either trade union representatives or, where no union is recognised, elected employee representatives instead. If your employees choose not to elect employee representatives, you must give the relevant information directly to each individual.

Consultation must start in good time - when redundancy proposals are in their formative stage - and at least:

- 30 days before the first redundancy where there are 20 to 99 proposed redundancies

- 90 days in advance where there are 100 or more proposed redundancies.

Procedure:

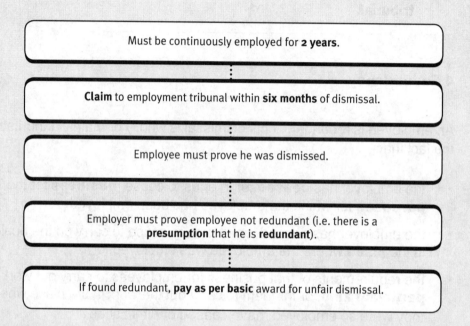

Must be continuously employed for **2 years**.

Claim to employment tribunal within **six months** of dismissal.

Employee must prove he was dismissed.

Employer must prove employee not redundant (i.e. there is a **presumption** that he is **redundant**).

If found redundant, **pay as per basic** award for unfair dismissal.

Expandable text

Is the employee redundant?

European Chefs Catering v Currell (1971)

Facts: A pastry cook was dismissed because the requirement for his speciality (éclairs and meringues) had ceased. He was replaced by a new pastry cook whose speciality was the new requirement (continental pastries).

Held: It was held that the dismissed pastry cook had been dismissed for redundancy as the need for the particular work he contracted to do had ceased.

Vaux and Associated Breweries v Ward (1969)

Facts: A quiet public house was modernised by installing a discotheque. The 57-year-old barmaid, Mrs Ward, was dismissed in order to make way for a younger more glamorous barmaid.

Held: Mrs Ward had not been dismissed for redundancy as there was no change in the nature of the particular work being done.

The place where a person is employed means in this context the place where he is habitually employed and any place where, under his contract, he can be required to work. There will not, therefore, be a redundancy situation where the transfer of location is reasonable or where the contract gives the employer an express or implied right to move (a mobility clause may have been agreed in the contract) the employee in question from one place to another. This is not the case, though, if the employer has no such right: **O'Brien v Associated Fire Alarms (1969).**

Redundancy pay

Redundancy pay is calculated in the same way as the basic award for unfair dismissal.

However, an employee is not entitled to redundancy pay if they unreasonably refuse an offer of fresh employment (made before the old contract expires) to start within four weeks on the same or suitable terms. The employee must be allowed at least a four-week trial period in the new job.

Whether the alternative employment offered is suitable, or the offer was unreasonably refused, are both questions of fact to be determined by reference to such matters as the employee's skill and working conditions, the requirements of his family, change in earnings, age, health, sex, etc. Any dispute arising in this respect is for the tribunal to determine and the onus of proof is on the employer.

Taylor v Kent County Council (1969)

Facts: T was headmaster of a school. The school was amalgamated with another school and a new head appointed to the combined school. T was offered employment in a pool of teachers, standing in for short periods in understaffed schools. He would retain his current salary.

Held: T was entitled to reject this offer and claim a redundancy payment: the new offer was substantially different, particularly in regard to status.

5 Chapter summary

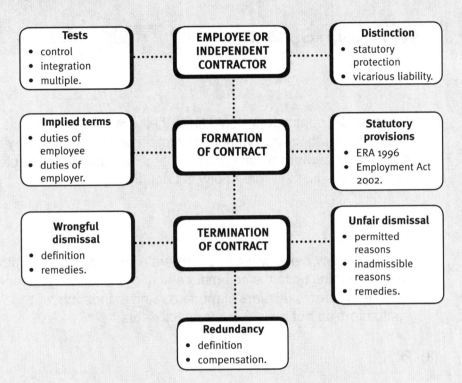

Tests
- control
- integration
- multiple.

EMPLOYEE OR INDEPENDENT CONTRACTOR

Distinction
- statutory protection
- vicarious liability.

Implied terms
- duties of employee
- duties of employer.

FORMATION OF CONTRACT

Statutory provisions
- ERA 1996
- Employment Act 2002.

Wrongful dismissal
- definition
- remedies.

TERMINATION OF CONTRACT

Unfair dismissal
- permitted reasons
- inadmissible reasons
- remedies.

Redundancy
- definition
- compensation.

Test your understanding answers

Test your understanding 1

(1) **C**

Independent contractors would have their own tools, and would be paid in full for their work without deduction of income tax. They may do the work personally; alternatively, they may send a substitute. Items (i) and (iii) therefore apply, but not (ii).

(2) **D**

On a company being wound up, arrears of wages due to employees for four months up to the commencement of the winding up rank as preferential debts. Arrears of money owing to independent contractors do not rank as preferential debts.

(3) **B**

The multiple test is one of the tests used to determine a worker's status. It is sometimes called the economic reality test.

(4) **A**

An employer is vicariously liable for the torts of employees whilst they are at work, but is not liable for the torts of any independent contractor providing services to the employer.

Test your understanding 2

(1) C

A duty to pay reasonable remuneration is normally implied in a contract of employment.

(2) B

An employer does not have to provide a reference for an employee leaving to work somewhere else. Nor does an employer have to provide smoking facilities at work – you might have seen employees standing outside their place of work, smoking in the street, because there is nowhere on the premises to smoke. An employer is obliged to give only one day off a week. However, an employer is under an obligation to provide a safe system of work.

(3) C

The terms of a contract of employment might be subject to a collective agreement between an employer and a trade union, so (ii) is quite clearly correct. In addition, some terms of employment might be derived from custom and practice.

(4) C

A written statement must be provided within two months of commencement.

(5) A

The right of a parent to ask for a flexible working arrangement applies to parents of children under six and disabled children under 18. Statement (i) is correct. An employer is obliged to consider such requests seriously, but may refuse where there is a clear business reason. Statement (ii) is therefore incorrect.

Test your understanding 3

A   employee

independent contractor

multiple/economic reality

employee

Any three of the following:

- control
- provision of his own equipment
- whether he hires his own helpers
- the degree of financial risk he undertakes
- the degree of responsibility he bears for investment and management
- the extent to which he has an opportunity of profiting from sound management in the performance of his task
- whether there is a regular method of payment
- whether the person works regular hours
- whether there is mutuality of obligations.

B   Employment Rights Act 1996

Statement of Particulars

Must be in writing

Any three of the following:

- how pay will be calculated and paid
- job title and nature of the work
- date on which employment began
- intervals of pay
- hours of work
- holidays and holiday pay
- sick pay/leave
- pension scheme details
- place of work
- any collective agreement

KAPLAN PUBLISHING

- length of notice required

- names of employer and employee.

C Duties to obey lawful reasonable orders, of mutual co-operation (care and skill), of good faith and of personal service.

Test your understanding 4

A Mario has not been wrongfully dismissed as he has been given the appropriate amount of notice.

B Mario has not been wrongfully dismissed as his conduct puts him in serious breach of his contract.

Test your understanding 5

A Employment Rights Act 1996

automatically

I complaints/actions by an employee under the Health and Safety at Work etc. Act 1974

II Pregnancy or childbirth

III Trade union related activities

IV Assertion of statutory right

V Unfair selection for redundancy

B A complainant can be compensated, re-instated under the same contract or re-engaged under a different contract in the same organisation.

5

Agency law

Chapter learning objectives

Upon completion of this chapter you will be able to:

- define the role of the agent and give examples of such relationships, paying particular regard to partners and company directors
- explain how the agency relationship is established
- define the authority of the agent
- explain the potential liability of both principal and agent.

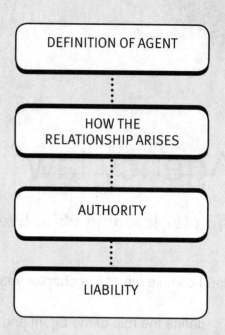

DEFINITION OF AGENT

HOW THE RELATIONSHIP ARISES

AUTHORITY

LIABILITY

1 Definition of an agent

An agent (A) is a person who is authorised to act for another (the principal (P)) in the making of legal relations with third parties.

The resulting contracts are made between the principal and the third party, and not directly with the agent.

An agency relationship exists in lots of situations:

- A director acts as an agent for his company.

- A partner acts as an agent for his partnership.

- An estate agent is appointed by a seller of a house to find a buyer.

- A travel agent is appointed by a holiday company to make bookings with customers.

2 How the agency relationship arises

Introduction

An agency relationship can be established in one of five ways:

- express agreement

- implied agreement

- by necessity

- by ratification

- by estoppel.

Express agreement

This is where P actually appoints A as his agent. The agreement can be made orally or in writing.

Implied agreement

This is where P has not expressly agreed that A should be his agent. However, the agreement can be implied from the parties' conduct or relationship.

By necessity

This requires four conditions to be satisfied:

- P's property is entrusted to A
- an emergency arises making it necessary for A to act
- it is not possible to communicate with P
- A acts in the interest of P.

Great Northern Railway v Swaffield (1874)

Facts: There was a contract between the two parties whereby GNR agreed to transport the defendant's horse to a particular railway station from where it would be collected.

When no one arrived to pick it up, the station master, having tried unsuccessfully to contact the defendant, placed the horse in a stable overnight.

Held: GNR was entitled to recover the costs of stabling because it had become the agent of the defendant by necessity.

By ratification

If a properly appointed agent exceeds his authority, or a person having no authority purports to act as an agent, the principal has no liability on that contract unless the principal 'ratifies' the contract.

The effect of ratification is to backdate A's authority to act as agent. This requires P to:

- have the contractual capacity to make the contract
- have been in existence both when the contract was made and at the date of ratification
- be identified when the contract is made

- be aware of all the material facts
- clearly signify his intention to ratify the whole contract within a reasonable time.

Note that a void or illegal contract cannot be ratified.

Kelner v Baxter (1866)

Facts: The promoters of a company entered into a contract on behalf of a company before it was incorporated, to purchase some property. The other party was not paid.

Held: As the company did not exist at the time the contract was made, the company could not ratify the contract. The promoters were personally liable to the seller.

By estoppel

This arises where P implies that A is his agent even though he is not. He is then prevented or 'stopped' from denying A's authority.

Freeman & Lockyer v Buckhurst Park Properties Ltd (1964)

Facts: The defendant company had four directors, none of whom had been appointed as the managing director. One director effectively ran the business by himself and entered into a number of contracts with the claimants. On previous occasions, the board on behalf of the company had honoured the contracts and paid the claimants. However, on this occasion, the board refused to pay arguing that the director had no express authority to make the contract because he was not the managing director.

Held: Although the director had no express authority to make the contract, the director had acquired authority by estoppel. This was because by honouring similar contracts in the past, the company (as the principal) had given the impression that the director had the authority to make this sort of contract. The claimants had relied on this representation by continuing to deal with the director when purporting to act on behalf of the company.

Test your understanding 1

Peter advertised his car for sale in a local newspaper and then went on holiday leaving his car in the drive. While Peter was away, Tom, having seen the advertisement, went to look at the car and decided to make an offer for it. Peter's neighbour, Alf, pretending to act with Peter's authority, entered into negotiations with Tom and eventually accepted Tom's offer on Peter's behalf.

Alf had no authority to act in this way. When Peter returned from his holiday, he wrote to Tom saying that he was ratifying Alf's act.

Advise Tom as to whether he is bound by the contract.

3 Authority

The authority of an agent is a central issue in the concept of agency. It determines:

- the powers that the agent has on behalf of the principal, and
- for which acts the principal is liable.

If the agent exceeds his powers the principal may still be liable to the third party, but he may have rights against the agent for breach of contract.

There are three ways in which authority may be given:

Express	This is authority that P has explicitly given to A.
Implied	An agent has implied authority to do things which: • are reasonably incidental to the performance of an expressly authorised act • an agent occupying that position would usually have authority to do • have not been expressly prohibited by P.

| Apparent | Such authority arises where A is held out by P as having authority.

The representation by P may arise from:

• the appointment of A to an office or position (in which case A has authority to do those things which are usually done by a person occupying that position)

• previous dealings (allowing A to make contracts in the past is a representation that A has authority to continue to do so in the future).

However, a third party cannot rely on apparent authority when he knows of the lack of actual authority. |

Facts: The new owners of a hotel continued to employ the original owner as the manager. In the agency agreement the new owners ordered the agent not to buy certain items, including cigars. The manager still bought cigars from a third party. The owners then refused to pay for the cigars.

Held: The purchase of the cigars was within the usual authority of a manager of a hotel. The contract was binding on the owners. (If a limitation on the usual authority is going to be effective, it must be communicated to the third party before any contract is made.)

Test your understanding 2

Harry wanted to insure the contents of his house against all loss and damage and appointed Colin to effect a policy, instructing him to 'insure any furniture'. Having obtained quotes from various companies, Colin eventually took out insurance with Hawk Star Limited. Sometime later vandals broke into Harry's house and did substantial damage to his furniture. They did not steal anything. When Harry claimed, Hawk Star refused to pay as the policy covered loss by theft or fire but not damage by vandals.

Advise Harry as to whether he can recover the value of damaged furniture from Colin.

4 Liability

Where the agent acts for a disclosed principal

A principal is disclosed where the existence of the principal has been made known to the third party. It is not necessary for the principal to be identified to the third party.

As a general rule, the contract is between the principal and the third party. The agent is neither liable nor entitled under the contract. However, the agent will be personally liable in the following exceptional circumstances:

- where the agent showed an intention to undertake personal liability, e.g. by signing a written contract in his own name
- trade usage or custom
- where the agent refuses to identify the principal
- where the agent is acting on behalf of a fictitious principal.

Where the agent acts for an undisclosed principal

An undisclosed principal is where the principal's existence has not been made known to the third party. When the third party discovers the existence of P, he can elect to treat P or A as bound by the transaction.

Agent's fiduciary duty

An agent has a fiduciary relationship with his principal. This is a position similar to that of a trustee. It has the following consequences:

- A must not allow his personal interests to conflict with those of P.
- A must always act in the best interests of P.
- A must not make a secret profit.
- A has a duty to account to P for all money and property received.

Where an agent is in breach of his fiduciary duty, the following remedies are available:

- P can repudiate the contract with the third party.
- A can be dismissed without notice.
- P can refuse to pay any money owed to A or recover any money already paid.
- P can recover any secret profit made or any bribe.

Principal's liability to the agent

The agent has the right:

- To claim remuneration or commission for services performed.

Usually the amount of remuneration or commission to be paid is stated in the agency agreement. Where it is not specified and it is a commercial agreement, the court will imply a term into the agreement requiring a reasonable amount to be paid.

- To claim an indemnity against P for all expenses reasonably incurred in carrying out his obligations.

- To exercise a lien over P's property. The lien allows the agent to retain possession of P's property that is lawfully in A's possession until any debts due to A, e.g. arrears of remuneration, have been paid by P.

5 Chapter summary

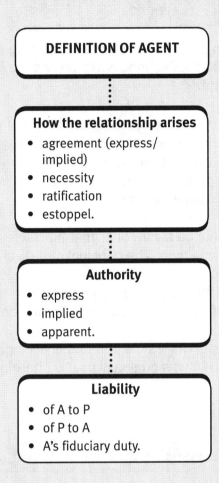

DEFINITION OF AGENT

How the relationship arises
- agreement (express/ implied)
- necessity
- ratification
- estoppel.

Authority
- express
- implied
- apparent.

Liability
- of A to P
- of P to A
- A's fiduciary duty.

Test your understanding answers

Test your understanding 1

Where a person purports to act as another's agent, even though he has no authority to do so, the principal is only bound by the contract if he decides to ratify it.

The principal can only ratify the contract if certain requirements are satisfied. The principal must have the contractual capacity to make the contract both at the time the contract is made and at the time of ratification. The principal must have been identified to the third party at the time the contract was made.

The principal must be aware of all material facts and ratify the contract within a reasonable time. The principal must ratify the whole contract.

It would appear that all these requirements can be satisfied in this situation. Therefore Peter is able to ratify the contract.

When the principal ratifies the contract, it is binding on the parties from the date on which it was originally made. Therefore Tom is bound by the contract.

Test your understanding 2

When an agent is appointed, he is given express authority to act on behalf of the principal. However, where the terms of authority are ambiguous or where the agent is given discretion to act the law implies authority to enable an agent to carry out his express duties. The agent must always act in the best interests of the principal.

Colin's authority is very ambiguous. He can decide which policy to take out 'to insure the principal's furniture'.

If Colin can show that when he made the decision to take this policy as opposed to any other, that he was acting in Harry's best interests, Colin will be acting within his authority. Harry will not be able to recover the value of the damaged furniture from Colin.

6

Types of Business Organisation

Chapter learning objectives

Upon completion of this chapter you will be able to:

- distinguish between different types of business organisation
- explain the meaning of the different types of partnership
- in relation to general or ordinary partnerships:
  - discuss how they are established
  - explain the authority of the partners in relation to partnership activity
  - outline the liability of the partners for partnership debts
  - explain the ways in which they can be brought to an end.

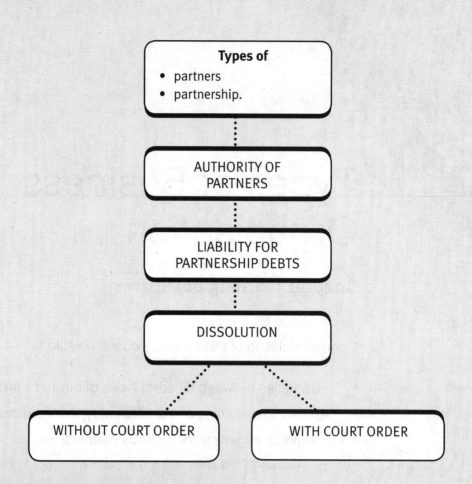

1 Types of Business Organisation

Different forms of business organisation

Sole trader/sole practitionership	• The owner 'is' the business - owns the assets and is liable for all the debts. • No legal formalities are required to set up a sole trader business/practitionership • This form of business is inappropriate for large businesses or those involving a degree of risk.
General partnership	Defined by Partnership Act 1890 (PA 1890) as the relationship which subsists between persons carrying on a business in common with a view to profit. (See below.)
Limited partnership	Formed under the Limited Partnerships Act 1907. (See below.)
Limited liability partnership	An artificial legal entity where the liability of the members is limited to the amount of capital they have agreed to contribute. (See below.)
Company	A corporation is an artifical legal person. (See Chapter 7.)

The rest of this chapter will focus on partnerships.

2 Types of partnership

Definition

A partnership is a relationship which subsists between two or more persons carrying on a business in common with a view to profit: s1 Partnership Act 1890 (PA 1890).

A partnership can be a small operation or as with some large firms of solicitors and accountants partnerships with several hundred partners.

Types of partners

General partner	Actively involved in the day-to-day business.
Sleeping partner	Takes no active part in the running of the business. However, is jointly and severally liable for the debts and contracts of the business.
Limited partner in a limited partnership	Contributes a specific amount of capital. Liability limited to that amount. Cannot take part in the management of the firm.
Salaried partner	Will received a fixed amount in income. Not a real partner unless he also receives a share of the profits.

Types of partnership

General or ordinary partnership	Governed by Partnership Act 1890 - this is the default position if a partnership is not formed under either of the two Acts below.
Limited partnership	Governed by Limited Partnership Act 1907.
Limited liability partnership (LLP)	Governed by Limited Liability Partnerships Act 2000.Legally separate from its members.

Characteristics of a partnership

In order for a partnership to exist, a business must be carried on with a view to profit. This means that the persons involved in the partnership intend the business to yield a profit and they are all entitled to share in that profit.

The following do not necessarily create a partnership:

*   joint ownership of property
*   the sharing of gross returns
*   the sharing of expenses.

Cox v Coulson (1916)

Facts: C agreed with M that M would put on a play at C's theatre. C was to have 60% and M 40% of the gross box office receipts. C paid the expenses of running the theatre and M paid the expenses of putting on the play. During a performance the claimant, who was in the audience, was accidentally shot by one of the actors. The claimant sued C alleging that C was M's partner and was jointly liable with M.

Held: C was not M's partner because they merely shared gross box office receipts.

A partnership begins as soon as the partners start their business activity. The actual agreement may be made earlier or later than that date.

No formalities are required to form general partnerships, no documentation and no registration. The reason for this is that The Partnership Act 1890 applies to every partnership whether written or oral. Many of the Act's provisions apply, unless they are excluded by a **partnership agreement**. The PA 1890 provides that partners shall share profits equally, but in cases where partners contribute different amounts of capital this may not be appropriate and partners will need to agree specific profit sharing arrangements within their partnership agreement.

The partnership agreement is a contract. Like any contract it may be:

- express (e.g. oral, in writing or by deed), or
- implied.

The partners are contractually bound by the terms they have agreed, even if they conflict with PA 1890.

Limited partnerships

 A limited partnership is a partnership in which the liability of one or more partners is limited to their capital contribution.

A limited partnership must fulfil the following conditions:

- There must be at least one partner with unlimited liability.
- The partnership must be registered with the registrar of companies as a limited partnership.
- Limited partners may not participate in the management of the business. If they do, they forfeit their limited liability.

- A limited partner has no power to bind the firm to contracts, i.e. unlike the unlimited partners, he is not an agent of the firm.

3 Authority of partners

Agency relationship

When entering into a contract to carry out the business, each partner is acting as the agent of all the partners:

- The actual authority of a partner is set out in the partnership agreement.
- The apparent authority is set out in s5 PA 1890.

S5 PA 1890 states that every partner is the agent of the firm and of the other partners. This means that each partner has the power to bind all partners to business transactions entered into within their actual or apparent authority.

Apparent authority

Under s5 every partner is presumed to have the implied or apparent authority to:

- sell the firm's goods
- buy goods necessary for, or usually employed in, the business
- receive payments of debts due to the firm
- engage employees
- employ a solicitor to act for the firm in defence of a claim or in the pursuance of a debt.

Trading partnerships

The above implied powers apply to both trading and non-trading partnerships. Partners in trading partnerships have additional powers, such as to borrow money.

In order to be acting within his implied authority, the individual partner must be acting within the usual scope of a partner's powers in the particular business concerned.

Mercantile Credit Co v Garrod(1962)

Facts: P and G entered into a partnership to let lock-up garages and repair cars. P ran the business and G was a sleeping partner. The partnership agreement expressly stated that the firm would not buy and sell cars. P sold a car to a finance company, M. M sued G to recover the £700 which it had paid to P for the car. G denied liability claiming that P when selling the car had been acting outside the agreed limits of the firm's business and therefore P had no actual or apparent authority to make the contract. Evidence was given that other garage businesses of the type carried on by P and G did deal in cars.

Held: The test of what is the firm's business is not what the partners agreed it should be but 'what it appears to the outside world' to be. Under that test P appeared to M to be carrying on business of a kind carried on by such a firm. This contract was within the apparent authority of P and therefore the contract was binding on G.

Test your understanding 1

Jekyll and Hyde are in partnership providing support services to police services. The partnership agreement states that all scientific equipment is to be supplied by James and that neither partner may incur liability of more than £2,000 without consulting the other. Jekyll, although he contributed all the firm's initial capital, does not have any active involvement and visits its premises rarely. Hyde receives a salary, as well as a share of the profits, and works full-time for the firm.

Jekyll now seeks your advice as he has found out that Hyde has ordered £5,000 worth of equipment from Edgar. Advise him.

4 Liability for partnership debts
Is there liability in contract?

The firm is liable for contracts made by a partner if he was acting within his actual or apparent authority.

The firm is not bound by the apparent authority of a partner if:

- the third party knows the partner has no actual authority, or

- the partner has no actual authority and the third party does not know or believe him to be a partner.

Holding out

Every person who by his words or conduct represents himself (or knowingly allows himself to be represented) as a partner is liable as if he is a partner to anyone who thereby gives credit to the firm: s14 PA 1890.

Martyn v Gray (1863)

Facts: G went to Cornwall to discuss the possibility of investing in a tin mine belonging to X. Nothing came of the discussions, but while G was in Cornwall he was introduced by X to M as 'a gentleman down from London, a man of capital'. M later gave X credit believing he was in partnership with G.

Held: The introduction amounted to a representation that G was in partnership with X, and so G was liable for the debt incurred subsequent to the introduction. He should have made the true position clear by correcting the impression made.

Liability in tort

Where a tort is committed during the ordinary course of the partnership's business, or by a partner acting with the authority of the other partners, the partners are jointly and severally liable to the person who has suffered loss.

Misapplication of money or property

The partnership is liable to make good the loss where a third party's money or property is misapplied:

- after being received by a partner within his actual or apparent authority, or
- while it is in the custody of the firm, such as in the partnership bank account.

Which partners are liable?

General rule	Every partner is jointly and severally liable for the debts and contracts of the business. Outsiders can sue one partner alone or the firm.
New partners	A new partner is not personally liable for debts incurred before they became a partner.
Retiring partners	A retiring partner remains liable for any debts incurred while he was a partner. If no notice of the retirement is given, the firm continues to be bound by his actions as he is still being held out as a partner.
Change in partners	Where a third party deals with a partnership after a change in partners, all of the partners of the old firm are still treated as partners, until the third party receives notice of the change: • Previous customers require actual notice. • Third parties who were not existing customers can be notified by a notice in the London Gazette: s36 PA 1890. This is known as constructive notice. Notification must take place prior to retirement if the retiring partner is to avoid liability for contracts entered into after his retirement.
Novation	A creditor agrees with the outgoing, continuing and/or incoming partners that liability for an existing debt will be that of the continuing and incoming partners. (Thus the liability of the outgoing partner is removed and the incoming partner becomes liable for the debt even though it was incurred before he became a partner.)
Indemnity	The continuing and incoming partners may agree to indemnify the outgoing partner against debts incurred pre- and/or post-retirement.

Test your understanding 2

Following their earlier dispute, Jekyll and Hyde do not believe that they can continue in partnership. It is proposed that Jekyll will retire and Edgar will be admitted as a partner.

What will be the liability for the firm's debts of (i) Jekyll and (ii) Edgar once these changes have been made?

5 Dissolution

Without court order

The partnership will automatically end in the following situations:

- The expiry of a fixed term or the completion of a specific enterprise.

- One of the partners gives notice (unless the partnership agreement excludes this right).

- Death or bankruptcy of a partner (the partnership agreement will usually make provision for the partnership to continue if a partner should die).

- Where continuation of the partnership would be illegal.

Hudgell, Yeates and Co v Watson (1978)

Facts: Practising solicitors are required by law to have a practising certificate. One of the partners in a firm of solicitors forgot to renew his certificate which meant that it was illegal for him to practice.

Held: The failure to renew the practising certificate brought the partnership to an end, although a new partnership continued between the other two members.

By court order

Under s35 PA 1890, the court can bring a partnership to an end in any of the following situations:

- Partner has mental disorder or permanent incapacity.
- Partner engages in activity prejudicial to the business.
- Partner wilfully or persistently breaches the partnership agreement.
- Partner conducts himself in a way that it is no longer reasonably practicable for the others to carry on in business with him.
- Business can only be carried on at a loss.
- It is just and equitable to do so.

6 LLPs

A limited liability partnership (LLP) is a corporate body which combines the features of a traditional partnership with a company.

LLP's are covered in the next chapter once we have covered the characteristics of a company.

7 Chapter summary

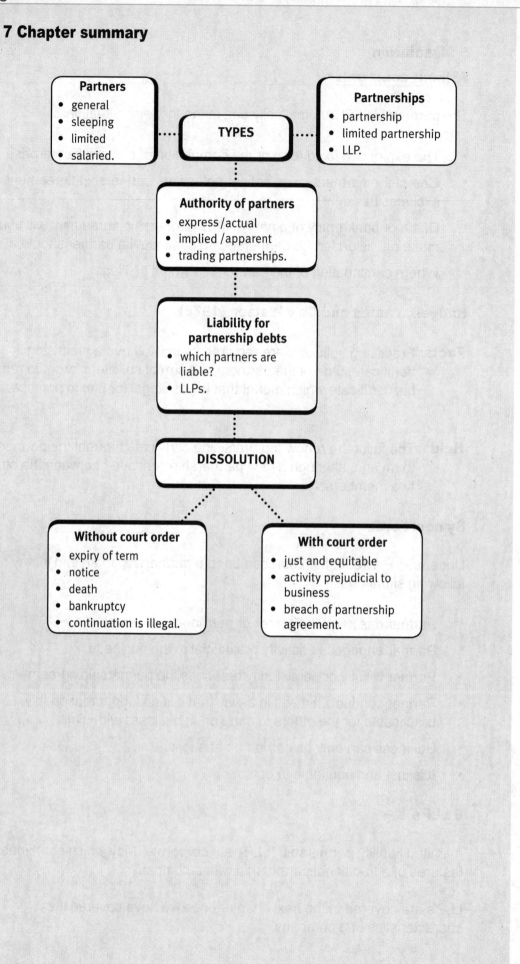

Partners
- general
- sleeping
- limited
- salaried.

TYPES

Partnerships
- partnership
- limited partnership
- LLP.

Authority of partners
- express /actual
- implied /apparent
- trading partnerships.

Liability for partnership debts
- which partners are liable?
- LLPs.

DISSOLUTION

Without court order
- expiry of term
- notice
- death
- bankruptcy
- continuation is illegal.

With court order
- just and equitable
- activity prejudicial to business
- breach of partnership agreement.

Test your understanding answers

Test your understanding 1

PA 1890 states that a partnership is a relationship which subsists between two or more persons carrying on a business with a view to profit. Each partner is liable for the debts of the firm.

Jekyll is a sleeping partner who takes no part in the running of the business, but he is treated as any other partner with respect to his liabilities.

Hyde is a salaried partner which means that he can run the business. Any act done within the ordinary course of the firm's business is binding on all partners and they are jointly and severally liable for the debts of the business.

When Hyde enters into the contract with Edgar, he is exceeding the actual authority given to him in the partnership agreement. However, the partnership agreement is not a public document and Edgar could not be expected to know of any limitation imposed upon Hyde's authority. In addition to actual authority, every partner has the apparent authority under s5, to enter into contracts on behalf of the business. As long as the equipment could be used in the ordinary course of the business, the contract will be binding on both parties.

When Hyde enters into the contract with Edgar, he is acting in breach of the partnership agreement. Jekyll can sue for breach of agreement and recover damages for any loss he suffers.

Test your understanding 2

A partner who has retired from the firm is not liable for any debts that arise after his or her retirement. He or she must notify the partnership's usual suppliers of his retirement and make sure that his name is taken off the list of partners including from the firm's stationery. This is actual notice.

A notice should also be placed in the London Gazette to give notice to the persons who have not previously dealt with the firm that he is no longer a partner. This will be constructive notice.

Jekyll will continue to be liable for the debts that arose while he was still a partner. However, it is possible to avoid this by agreement with Hyde, Edgar and the creditors.

An incoming partner is only liable for the debts arising after he became a partner. However, if there is an arrangement with the creditors by which the new partners assume the obligations of the old, Edgar will be liable for the old debts as well. This agreement can be express or it can be implied from the conduct of the partnership.

Corporations and legal personality

Chapter learning objectives

Upon completion of this chapter you will be able to:

- explain the meaning and effect of limited liability
- explain meaning of LLPs and compare companies and partnerships
- analyse the different types of companies, especially public and private companies
- illustrate the effect of separate personality
- recognise instances where separate personality will be ignored
- explain the role and duties of company promoters
- describe the procedure for registering companies, both public and private
- describe the contents of model articles of association
- analyse the effect of a company's articles
- explain how articles of association can be changed
- describe the statutory books, records and returns that companies must keep or make.

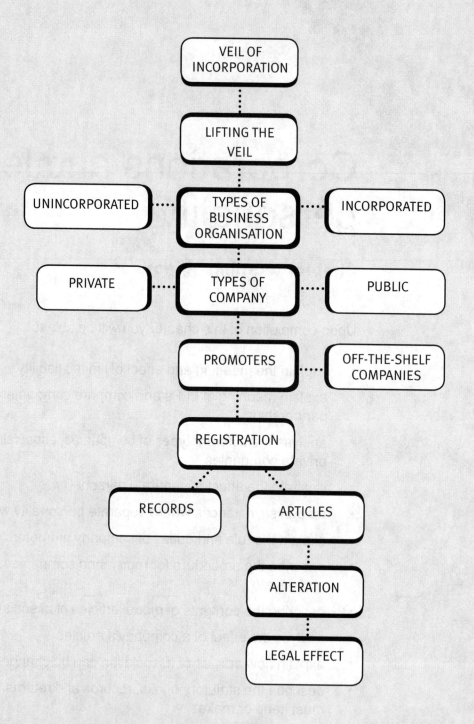

1 The doctrine and veil of incorporation

Meaning

The company is separate legal entity (i.e. separate from its shareholders, the part owners and its directors, the managers).

Salomon v Salomon & Co Ltd (1897)

Facts: S transferred his business to a limited company. He was the director and majority shareholder and a secured creditor. The company went into liquidation and the other creditors tried to obtain repayment from S personally.

Held: S as shareholder and director had no personal liability to creditors, and he could be repaid in priority as a secured creditor. This enshrined the concepts of separate legal personality and limited liability in the law.

Lee v Lee's Air Farming Ltd (1960)

Facts: This case concerned an aerial crop-spraying business. Mr Lee owned the majority of the shares (all but one) and was the sole working director of the company. He was killed while piloting the aircraft.

Held: Although Lee was the majority shareholder and sole working director of the company, he and the company were separate legal persons. Therefore he could also be an employee of the company for the purposes of the relevant statute with rights against it when killed in an accident in the course of his employment.

Macaura v Northern Life Assurance (1925)

Facts: M owned a forest. He formed a company in which he beneficially owned all the shares and sold his forest to it. He, however, continued to maintain an insurance policy on the forest in his own name. The forest was destroyed by fire.

Held: He could not claim on the policy since the property damaged belonged to the company, not him, and as shareholder he had no insurable interest in the forest.

Consequences of incorporation

There are a number of consequences of being a separate legal entity:

- Limited liability. A company is fully liable for its own debts. If a company fails, the liability of the shareholders is limited to any amount still unpaid on their share capital (or any amount they have agreed to contribute if the company is limited by guarantee).

- A company enters into contracts in its own name and can sue and be sued in its own name.

- A company owns its own property.

- A company has perpetual succession, irrespective of the fate of shareholders.

- The management of a company is separated from its ownership.

- A company is subject to the requirements of the Companies Act 2006 (CA06).

- Where a company suffers an injury, it is the company itself that must take the appropriate remedial action. This is known as the rule in **Foss v Harbottle**.

Foss v Harbottle (1843)

Facts: Two minority shareholders initiated legal proceedings against, among others, the directors of the company. They claimed that the directors had missapplied the company's assets.

Held: The court dismissed the claim and held that when a company is wronged by its directors it is only the company that has standing to sue.

2 Lifting the veil of incorporation

Meaning

The phrase 'lifting the veil of incorporation' means that in certain circumstances the courts can look through the company to the identity of the shareholders.

The usual result of lifting the veil is that the members or directors become personally liable for the company's debts.

Statutory examples

There are a number of occasions on which statute will intervene to lift the veil:

- S399 of CA06 requires accounts to be prepared by a group of related companies, therefore recognising the common link between them.

- Under the Insolvency Act 1986 (IA 1986), members and/or directors liable for wrongful or fraudulent trading may be personally liable for losses arising as a result. (See chapter 13).

- If a public company starts to trade without first obtaining a trading certificate, the directors can be made personally liable for any loss or damage suffered by a third party: S767 CA06.

- Under the Company Directors Disqualification Act 1986, if a director who is disqualified participates in the management of a company, that director will be jointly or severally liable for the company's debts.

Case law examples

Sham companies

The veil will be lifted only where **'special circumstances** exist indicating that it is a mere facade concealing the true facts': **Woolfson v Strathclyde Regional Council (1978)**

Gilford Motor Co Ltd v Horne (1933)

Facts: An employee had a covenant in his contract of employment which stated that he would not solicit his former employer's customers. After he left their employment he formed a company to solicit those customers and claimed it was the company approaching the customers and not him.

Held: The court held that the company could be restrained from competition, as the previous employee had set it up to evade his own legal obligations. An injunction was granted against him and the company.

Jones v Lipman (1962)

Facts: Mr. Lipman contracted to sell his land and thereafter changed his mind. In order to avoid an order of specific performance he transferred his property to a company.

Held: The veil was lifted in order to prevent the seller of a house evading specific performance. An order of specific performance was granted against him and the company to transfer the property to the buyer.

Nationality

In times of war it is illegal to trade with the enemy. It may be possible to lift the veil of incorporation so as to impute to a company the same nationality as its members.

Daimler v Continental Tyre & Rubber Co (1916)

Facts: C sued D for debts owing. C was a UK company, however all shareholders but one were German. D argued that they should not pay the debt to German individuals to prevent money going towards Germany's war effort.

Held: As C was German, D need not discharge their debt to C since effective control of the latter was in enemy hands and hence to do so would be to trade with the enemy.

Groups

Although each company within a group is a separate legal entity, there have been a number of cases where the courts have lifted the veil between a holding company and its various subsidiaries. This has generally been done in order to:

- benefit the group by obtaining a higher compensation payment on the compulsory purchase of premises.

- benefit creditors of an insolvent company by making other companies within the group liable for its debts.

DHN Food Distributors v London Borough of Tower Hamlets (1976)

Facts: DHN carried on business from premises owned by a subsidiary. The subsidiary itself had no business activities. Both companies had the same directors. The local authority acquired the premises compulsorily but refused to pay compensation for disturbance of the business since the subsidiary, which owned the premises, did not also carry on the business.

Held: The companies were, in economic terms, mutually interdependent on each other and therefore they should be regarded as a single economic entity. Thus there was a valid claim for disturbance since ownership of the premises and business activity were in the hands of a single group.

The above case can, however, be contrasted with the more recent case of **Adams v Cape Industries (1990)** which represents the current position:

Adams v Cape Industries (1990)

Facts: Cape was an English registered company. One of its subsidiaries, CPC, a company incorporated and carrying on business in the United States, had a court judgement against it.

Held: It was unsuccessfully argued that the veil should be lifted between the companies so as to enable the judgement to be enforced against Cape. The Court of Appeal said there were no special circumstances indicating that CPC was a mere facade for Cape such as was the situation in **Jones v Lipman**.

There was no agency as CPC was an independent corporation under the control of its chief executive

The DHN doctrine of economic reality would not be extended beyond its own facts to facts such as these where the effect would be to make a holding company liable for its subsidiary's debts.

Test your understanding 1

In the context of company law explain:

A   what is meant by, and what are the consequences of, the 'veil of incorporation' (5 marks)

B   under what circumstances the 'veil' will be lifted. (5 marks)

(ACCA June 2003)

3 LLPs

Ordinary (or general) partnerships lack the characteristics of a company in the sense that they do not have limited liability or separate legal personality. Over time the government was pressurised to recognise the needs of some partnerships (especially professional partnerships such as solicitors, accountants and auditors) to limit their liability and have separate legal personality without having to form a company. This resulted in the Limited Liability Partnerships Act 2000 (LLPs).

LLPs have similar features to private limited companies, for example, their members (i.e. not called partners) are not directly responsible for the debts of the partnership.

Incorporation	• Incorporation document must be delivered to registrar stating name of LLP, location and address of registered office, names and addresses of members (minimum two). • Must send a declaration of compliance that LLP satisfies requirements of the Limited Liability Partnerships Act 2000. • Registrar issues a certificate of incorporation.
Membership	• First members sign incorporation document. Later members join by agreement with the existing members. • Membership ceases on death, dissolution or in accordance with agreement with other members • Rights and duties are set out in membership agreement. If no agreement, governed by Limited Liability Partnership Regulations 2001 • Each member acts as an agent of the LLP.

Designated members	• Perform the administrative and filing duties of the LLP.
	• Incorporation document specifies who they are.
	• Must be at least two designated members. If there are none, all members will be designated members.
Name	• Must end with Limited Liability Partnership, llp or LLP.
	• Rules on choice are the same as for companies.
Taxation	• Members are treated as if they are partners carrying on business in a partnership, i.e. they pay income tax, not corporation tax.
Liability for debts	• The liability of a member of an LLP to contribute to its debts is limited to his capital contribution. However, there is no requirement for a capital contribution, and any contribution made can be withdrawn at any time.

	• If an LLP goes into liquidation, the court can order the members to repay any drawings made in the previous two years if it can be shown that the member knew or had reasonable grounds to believe that the LLP:
	   – was unable to pay its debts at the date of withdrawal, or
	   – would become unable to pay its debts because of the withdrawal: s214A Insolvency Act 1986 (IA 1986).
	
	 The fraudulent and wrongful trading provisions of IA 1986 apply to members of LLPs in the same way as they apply to directors of companies **(see chapter 13).**

Differences between LLP and partnership	• The liability of the members of an LLP is limited to the amount of capital they have agreed to contribute.
	• The LLP must file annual accounts and an annual report with Companies House.
	• LLP is an artificial legal entity with perpetual succession. It can hold property in its own right, enter into contracts in its own name, create floating charges, sue and be sued.

Company versus partnership

Company	General Partnership
Created by registration – with a written constitution.	No special formality required for creation.
Separate legal person, i.e. can own property, sue or be sued, and contract in own name.	Not a separate legal person – the partners own any property, are jointly liable on contracts and are liable if sued.
Shares are transferable. However, the articles of private companies usually restrict transfer.	Limits on transfer of shares (may require dissolution of partnership or consent of other partners to enable partners to realise their share).
Can create both fixed and floating charges as security for borrowing.	Can only create fixed charges as security for borrowing. More usual to have personal guarantees.
Managed by directors, who may or may not also be shareholders.	Managed by partners, who are also the owners of the business.
The company cannot usually return capital to its members (except on dissolution).	Partners may withdraw their capital.
The company is liable for its debts. (No personal liability for shareholders beyond any unpaid portion of the price of their shares or the amount they have agreed to contribute.)	The partners are personally liable for the debts of the firm. Their liability is joint and several.
Must make information about financial affairs and ownership publicly available.	Private business. No disclosure of results.
The business is run by the directors. Members have no right to participate.	Every partner has the right to take part in the management of the business.
Must comply with Companies Act requirements concerning meetings, special resolutions, filing accounts and annual return.	No administrative requirements regarding meetings.
Formal dissolution procedure (known as liquidation). Death/bankruptcy of any member/director does not dissolve the company.	May dissolve by agreement. Automatically dissolved on the death/bankruptcy of any partner.
Companies pay corporation tax.	Partners pay income tax.

Test your understanding 2

(1) **X Ltd, Y Ltd and Z Ltd have formed the XYZ partnership. If the partnership should become insolvent, which of the following statements is correct?**

    A   The shareholders of each company are fully liable for the firm's debts.

    B   X Ltd, Y Ltd and Z Ltd are fully liable for the firm's debts.

    C   The directors of each company are fully liable for the firm's debts.

    D   The liability of X Ltd, Y Ltd and Z Ltd for the firm's debts is limited to the amount of their capital contributions.

(2) **In relation to E Ltd, a company limited by shares, which one of the following statements is correct?**

    A   The liability of the company and its shareholders is limited, but the directors are fully liable for the company's debts.

    B   The liability of the company and its directors is limited, but the shareholders are fully liable for the company's debts.

    C   The liability of the company, its directors and shareholders is limited.

    D   The liability of the directors and shareholders is limited, but the company is fully liable for its own debts.

(3) Mr X owns shares in Y Ltd. This means that Mr X:

    I   is a part-owner of Y Ltd

    II   is a part-owner of Y Ltd's property.

Which of the above is/are correct?

    A   (I) only.

    B   (II) only.

    C   Both (I) and (II).

    D   Neither (I) nor (II).

4 Types of company

Introduction

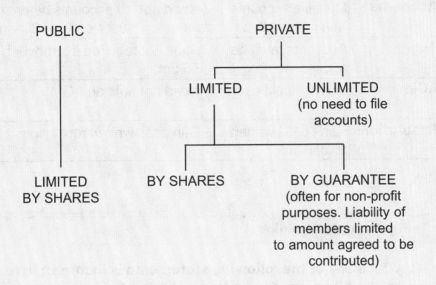

Private company versus public company

The following table summarises the basic differences between public companies and private companies.

	Public companies	Private (limited) companies
Definition	Registered as a public company.	Any company that is not a public company.
Name	Ends with plc or public limited company.	Ends with Ltd or limited.
Capital	In order to trade, must have allotted shares of at least £50,000.	No minimum (or maximum) requirements.
Raising capital	May raise capital by advertising its securities (shares and debentures) as available for public subscription.	Prohibited from offering its securities to the public.
Start of trading	Must obtain trading certificate from registrar before commencing trading.	Can begin from date of incorporation.
Directors	Minimum two.	Minimum one.
Secretary	Must have one. Must be qualified.	Need not have one.

Accounts	Must file accounts within 6 months.	Need not lay accounts before general meeting. Must file within 9 months.
Audit	Accounts must be audited.	Audit not required if turnover below £6.5m.
AGM	Must be held each year.	Need not hold an AGM.
Resolutions	Can't pass written resolutions.	Can pass written resolutions.

Test your understanding 3

(1) **Which one of the following statements is incorrect in relation to a public company limited by shares?**

    A   The company must have at least one director.

    B   The company must have at least two shareholders.

    C   The company must have an allotted share capital of at least £50,000.

    D   The company must be registered as a public limited company.

(2) **What is the main requirement of the Companies Act 2006 relating to a private company?**

    A   The allotted capital must not exceed £50,000.

    B   It must not have more than 50 members.

    C   The liability of its members must be limited.

    D   It must not invite the public to subscribe for its shares.

(3) **Which of the following is a requirement for any public company?**

    A   No restrictions may be placed on the transfer of its shares.

    B   Its shares must be publicly for sale.

    C   It must have a minimum paid up capital of £50,000.

    D   The final words of the company's name must be 'public limited company' (or plc).

Test your understanding 4

Spencer and his brother Trevor have decided to leave their employment as software engineers and set up a consultancy. Spencer has come to you for advice; he is unsure about the type of business organisation he should commence trading as.

A **Fill in the gap, delete as appropriate and complete the sentence.**

The term 'partnership' is defined in ……………………….. People can form such organisations informally or formally and they need/do not need written agreements.

The definition of a partnership is …

(Your answer must not exceed 20 words.)

B **Fill in the gaps, delete as appropriate and complete the sentence.**

The major advantage of incorporating a business is that the ………………………..of the ………………………..is ……………………….. On company insolvency, the amount the shareholders/directors can be obliged to contribute to the company's assets is ….

(Your answer must not exceed 10 words.)

C **Delete as appropriate.**

The formalities required to form a company are less/more onerous than for other types of business organisation. In addition there is less/more regulation in relation to the officers of a company compared to partners. Partnerships are also less/more private in that they do/do not have to publish annual accounts.

D **Spencer and Trevor may one day wish to become a public company. What are the main characteristics of this business entity?**

(Your answer must not exceed 20 words.)

5 Promoters

Definition

There is no statutory definition of a promoter.

According to case law, a promoter is a person who 'undertakes to form a company and who takes the necessary steps to accomplish that purpose': **Twycross v Grant (1878)**.

The definition excludes people just acting in a professional capacity, such as accountant or solicitor.

Duties

A promoter is under a fiduciary duty to:

- disclose any interest in transactions to the company and not to make a 'secret profit'
- disclose any benefit acquired to an independent board and/or to the shareholders.

If a promoter does make a secret profit, the company may:

- Rescind the contract – but this is not always possible, e.g. if a third party has acquired rights under the contract.
- Obtain damages – but this requires the company to prove loss.
- Recover the profit – the company must prove that the promoter has failed to disclose his profit from a transaction.

Pre-incorporation contracts

A pre-incorporation contract is where a person enters into a contract before a company has been registered.

The position at common law is that a company, prior to its incorporation, does not have contractual capacity and after its formation it cannot ratify or formally adopt a pre-incorporation contract. The promoter is therefore personally liable under any such contract. (This is because a company does not legally exist until it is incorporated.)

Kelner v Baxter (1866)

Facts: A, B and C entered into a contract with the claimant to purchase goods on behalf of the proposed Gravesend Royal Alexandra Hotel Co. The goods were supplied and used in the business. Shortly after incorporation the company collapsed.

Held: As the Gravesend Royal Alexandra Hotel Co was not in existence when the contract was made it was not bound by the contract and could not be sued for the price of the goods. Neither could it ratify the contract after incorporation.

S51 CA06 reinforces the common law position by providing that, subject to any agreement to the contrary, the person making the contract is personally liable. Clear and express words are needed in order to negate liability: **Phonogram Ltd v Lane (1981)**.

The promoter can protect his position by:

- including a term in the contract giving the company the right to sue under the Contracts (Rights of Third Parties) Act 1999 (see Privity of Contract: **Chapter 2**)

- postponing finalising contracts until the company is formed

- entering into an agreement of novation (this involves discharging the original contract and replacing it with a new one) or assigning (transferring) the contract. All parties must agree

- agreeing with the company that there is no personal liability for the promoter

- buying an 'off-the-shelf' company, so it is ready to contract without waiting for incorporation.

Off-the-shelf companies

An 'off-the-shelf' company is one that has already been formed. Buying off the shelf has a number of advantages as follows:

- cheap and simple

- can trade immediately

- no problem of pre-incorporation contracts.

Test your understanding 5

(1) **Which of the following statements is true in respect of a promoter in breach of their duty not to make a secret profit?**

    A   The company can always sue the promoter for damages.

    B   The company can only rescind the contract with the promoter when the promoter owned the property before the promotion began.

    C   The company can always rescind the contract with the promoter.

    D   The company can only rescind the contract with the promoter when the promoter acquired the property after the promotion began.

(2) **Which of the following are correct?**

    I   Purchasing an 'off-the-shelf' company enables a business to commence more quickly.

    II   It is generally cheaper to purchase an 'off-the-shelf' company than to arrange for a solicitor or accountant to register a new company.

    III   Incorporating a company by registration enables the company's documents to be drafted to the particular needs of the incorporators.

    A   (I) and (II) only.

    B   (II) and (III) only.

    C   (I) and (III) only.

    D   (I), (II) and (III).

(3) **A company's contractual capacity before incorporation is limited in that it may:**

    A   only make contracts necessary to form the company.

    B   only ratify, once formed, contracts necessary to form the company.

    C   only make or ratify, once formed, contracts necessary to form the company.

    D   not make or ratify, once formed, any contract even if necessary to form the company.

(4) Tom ordered goods from Seller Ltd on behalf of H Ltd before H Ltd had obtained its certificate of incorporation. Tom signed the order 'Tom, for and on behalf of H Ltd.' Upon receipt of a certificate of incorporation, the board of H Ltd agreed that the company should adopt the contract with Seller Ltd.

If the contract with Seller Ltd is broken, who is liable for the breach?

A   Tom.

B   H Ltd.

C   The board of H Ltd.

D   The shareholders of H Ltd.

Test your understanding 6

Alfred and Betty have carried on a business as a partnership for some years. They have now decided to incorporate their business.

A   **Explain the difference in liability for business debts between partners and shareholders.**

(Your answer must not exceed 25 words.)

B   **Fill in the gaps, delete as appropriate and complete the sentence.**

Alfred bought some stationery on credit before the date of incorporation. Alfred is/is not personally liable for the debt because

....

(Your answer must not exceed 10 words.)

The company can/cannot unilaterally adopt the contract.

A range of better solutions might have included

....

(Your answer must not exceed 25 words.)

6 Registration

Documents to Registrar

The following must be submitted to the Registrar in order to form a company.

Memorandum of association	• Used to be a more important document under previous company legislation.
	• Signed by all subscribers and stating that they wish to form a company and agree to become members of the company.
	• In relation to a company limited by shares, the memorandum provides evidence of the members' agreement to take at least one share each in the company.
	• Is not possible to amend or update the memorandum of a company formed under CA06.
Application for registration	S9 CA06 sets out the information that must be delivered to the Registrar when an application for registration is made. In all cases, the application form must include:
	• the proposed name of the company
	• whether the members will have limited liability (by shares or guarantee)
	• whether the company is to be private or public
	• details of the registered office.

Documents to be sent with application:	
Statement of capital and initial shareholdings	Essentially is a 'snapshot' of a company's share capital at the point of registration This must state: • the number of shares • their aggregate nominal value • how much has been paid up.
OR	
Statement of guarantee	This states the maximum amount each member guarantees to contribute in a winding up.
Statement of proposed officers	This gives details of the first directors (and company secretary, if applicable) and their consent to act.
Statement of compliance	This provides confirmation that CA06 has been complied with. It may be made in paper or electronic form.
Registration fee	Currently £20 approximately.

Note: As the model articles will apply if no articles are supplied, it is not a requirement that articles must be sent, although all companies will have articles.

Registrar's duties

On receipt of the above documents the registrar must:

- **Inspect the documents** and ensure that Companies Act requirements are fulfilled.
- **Issue certificate of incorporation** which is conclusive evidence that Companies Act requirements have been fulfilled: s15 CA06. The company exists from the date on the certificate of incorporation.

Trading certificate – public companies only

A plc cannot commence trading until the registrar has issued a trading certificate.

In order to obtain a trading certificate, an application must be made to the registrar which states:

- The nominal value of allotted share capital ≥ £50,000.

- That at least a quarter of the nominal value and all of any premium have been paid up (i.e. at least £12,500 of nominal capital).

- The amount of preliminary expenses and who has paid or is to pay them.

- Any benefits given or to be given to promoters.

If it trades before the certificate is issued:

- The company and any officers in default are liable to a fine.

- It is a criminal offence to carry on business, but any contracts are still binding on the company.

- The directors are personally liable if the company defaults within 21 days of due date.

- It is a ground for winding up if not obtained within one year: s122 IA 1986.

Test your understanding 7

(1) Bob and Mike decided to form a company. On 1 March 20X6, they sent the necessary documents to the registrar. On 10 May 20X6, they received the certificate of incorporation dated 1 May 20X6. Subsequently they discovered that the company was registered on 1 June 20X6.

What was the date of incorporation?

A 1 March 20X6.

B 1 May 20X6

C 10 May 20X6.

D 1 June 20X6

(2) **Which of the following documents need not be submitted to register a company limited by shares?**

A A memorandum of association.

B Articles of association.

C A statement of the first directors and secretary.

D A statutory declaration of compliance with the requirements of the Companies Acts.

Test your understanding 8

Adam and Ben have carried on business together in partnership for a number of years. They have now decided to operate their business through the medium of a private company limited by shares called AB Ltd.

A **Complete this sentence.**

As partners, the liability of Adam and Ben for the firm's debts was

....

(Your answer must not exceed 3 words.)

B **In order to register a private company limited by shares the partners will need to submit the following documents to the registrar of companies.**

I

II

III

IV

V

VI

C **Complete this sentence:**

If the Registrar of Companies is satisfied with the documents submitted to him for registration, he will issue a .... which enables the company to commence trading immediately.

D **Explain the liability of Adam and Ben in the event of AB Ltd becoming insolvent.**

(Your answer must not exceed 20 words.)

Name of company

The name of the company must comply with the following rules:

- It must have limited (Ltd) or public limited company (plc) at the end as applicable.

- It cannot be the same as another in the index of names.

- it cannot use certain words which are illegal or offensive.

- It must have the Secretary of State's consent to use certain words (e.g. England, Chartered, Royal, National, University, Insurance, etc.) or any name suggesting a connection with the government or any local authority.

- It must avoid the tort of passing off (see chapter 3).

The Secretary of State can force a company to change its name in the following circumstances:

Reason	Period
The name is the same as, or too like, an existing registered name.	12 months
The name gives so misleading an indication of the nature of the company's activities as to be likely to cause harm to the public.	No time limit
Misleading information or undertakings were given when applying for a name that required approval.	5 years

S77 CA06 allows a company to change its name by special resolution.

As discussed at the end of chapter 3 if a company feels that another company has a name which is too similar to its own, it may object to the Company Names Adjudicator.

KAPLAN PUBLISHING

Test your understanding 9

(1) **Which of the following names could not without further consent be a permissible name under the Companies Act for a company, the main object of which is to contract refuse collection services for Westminster City Council?**

    A   Westminster City Refuse Services Ltd.

    B   Council (Refuse Collection) Services Ltd.

    C   Refuse Collection (Westminster) Ltd.

    D   City Waste Disposal Ltd.

(2) **Which of the following statements is correct?**

    I   It is not possible to register a company limited by shares with the same name as a company already on the register.

    II   Once on the register, a company limited by shares cannot change its registered office.

    A   (I) only.

    B   (II) only.

    C   Both (I) and (II).

    D   Neither (I) nor (II).

(3) **A business has been registered under the name 'The Mark Jones Partnership Co Ltd'. What type of business organisation must this be?**

    A   A partnership.

    B   A private limited company.

    C   A public limited company.

    D   Any of the above as this is a business name.

7 Articles of association

Introduction

The articles of association form the company's internal constitution. They:

- set out the manner in which the company is to be governed and

- regulate the relationship between the company, its shareholders and its directors.

There are no mandatory contents.

Model articles

For companies incorporated under Companies Act 2006, model articles have been prescribed by the Secretary of State.

There are three model articles which cover the following companies:

- private companies limited by shares; or
- private companies limited by guarantee; or
- public companies.

These model articles will apply where a company is formed without registering articles or where the articles registered do not exclude or modify the model articles.

A company:

- may adopt the model articles in full or in part;
- is deemed to have adopted the model articles if there is no express or implied provision to exclude them; or
- may draft its own unique articles.

8 Alteration of articles

General rule

- The articles can usually be altered by a special resolution (75% majority).
- Copies of the amended articles must be sent to the Registrar within 15 days.

Exceptions

1. Entrenchment

It is possible to entrench some of the articles. This means that a specified procedure (e.g. unanimous consent) may be required to change them.

2. Members increase liability

S25 CA06 prevents a member being bound by any alteration made after he becomes a member that requires him to increase his liability or contribute further to the company.

3. Common law restriction

Any change to the articles must be 'bona fide in interests of the company as a whole': **Allen v Gold Reefs of Africa (1900)**.

- It is for the members to decide whether the change is bona fide in the interests of the company as a whole.

- The court will not interfere unless no reasonable person would consider the change to be bona fide.

- If the change is bona fide, it is immaterial that it happens to inflict hardship or has retrospective operation.

- The change will be void if actual fraud or oppression takes place.

- An alteration is not invalid merely because it causes a breach of contract - but that does not excuse breach.

Greenhalgh v Arderne Cinemas Ltd (1950)

Facts: The issue was the removal from the articles of the members' right of first refusal of any shares which a member might wish to transfer; the majority wished to make the change in order to admit an outsider to membership in the interests of the company.

Held: The benefit to the company as a whole was held to be a benefit which any individual hypothetical member of the company could enjoy directly or through the company and not merely a benefit to the majority of members only. The test of good faith did not require proof of actual benefit but merely the honest belief on reasonable grounds that benefit could follow from the alteration.

In several cases the court has held that actual and foreseen detriment to a minority affected by the alteration was not in itself a sufficient ground of objection if the benefit to the company test was satisfied.

Brown v British Abrasive Wheel Co (1919)

Facts: The articles were altered to enable the majority to purchase at 'a fair value the shares of the minority'. The intention was to invoke the clause against some minority members who were refusing to inject further capital into the company. They objected to the alteration.

Held: This was not a bona fide alteration as it would benefit the majority shareholders, rather than the company as a whole.

Sidebottom v Kershaw, Leese & Co (1920)

Facts: The company altered its articles to empower the directors to require any member who carried on a business competing with that of the company, to sell his shares at a fair price to persons nominated by the directors. The minority against whom the new article was aimed did carry on a competing business and they challenged the validity of the alteration on the ground that it was an abuse of majority power to 'expel' a member.

Held: The Court of Appeal held that the evidence showed that the claimant might cause the defendant company loss by information which he received as a member, and as the power was restricted to expulsion for competing, the alteration was for the benefit of the company as a whole and was valid.

Allen v Gold Reefs of West Africa Ltd (1900)

Facts: Z held fully paid up and partly paid up shares in the company. The company's articles provided for a lien for all debts and liabilities of any member upon all partly paid shares held by the member. The company by special resolution altered its articles so that the lien was available on fully paid up shares as well.

Held: The company had power to alter its articles by extending the lien to fully paid shares.

Southern Foundries (1926) Ltd and Federated Foundries Ltd v Shirlaw (1940)

Facts: Following a merger the members of the new group of companies agreed to make alterations in the articles regarding directors. The amended articles gave the group the power to remove any director of the company and also stipulated that a managing director should cease to hold office if he ceased to be a director. Shirlaw was removed from office as a director which meant that he could no longer be a managing director, however, his contract still had some time to run.

Held: The House of Lords held that the company could not be prevented from altering its articles but that the only remedy for an alteration which has caused a breach of contract was damages.

9 Legal effect of company's constitutional documents

S33 CA06 states that the provisions of a company's constitution bind the company and its members to the same extent as if there were covenants on the part of the company and of each member to observe those provisions. This means that the articles form a statutory contract between the company and its members, and the members between themselves, even if they do not sign them.

(1) The articles are enforceable by the members against the company.

Hickman v Kent or Romney Marsh Sheepbreeders' Association (1920)

Facts: The company's articles included a clause to the effect that all disputes between the company and its members were to be referred to arbitration. A member brought court proceedings against the company.

Held: The proceedings were stopped. The company could enforce the arbitration clause against a member.

(2) The articles are enforceable by the members against the company.

Pender v Lushington (1877)

Facts: The articles provided for one vote per ten shares, with no member to have more than 100 votes. A member with more than 1,000 shares transferred the surplus to a nominee and directed him how to vote. The chairman refused to accept the nominee's votes.

Held: The right to vote was enforceable against the company and should have been recognised by the company as a breach of the articles.

(3) The articles also operate as a contract between individual members in their capacity as members.

Rayfield v Hands (1958)

Facts: The articles required the directors to be members, i.e. to hold qualification shares and to purchase shares from any member who wished to sell.

Held: This was enforceable against the directors in their capacity as members.

However, the articles do not bind the company to non-members nor do they bind the members in any other capacity.

Eley v Positive Government Security Life Assurance Co (1876)

Facts: The articles provided that Eley should be solicitor to the company for life.

Held: This was not a right given to him as a member and he could not rely on the articles as a contract for professional services. The right to be a director of a company has also been held to be an outsider right (i.e. a non-membership) right.

Beattie v EF Beattie (1938)

Facts: The company's articles contained an arbitration clause. B, a member and director of the company, was in dispute with the company concerning his rights as director. He brought court proceedings against the company.

Held: He was not bound by the arbitration clause since he was acting in his capacity as director, not a member.

However, even where the articles are not a relevant contract for this purpose, the terms may be evidence of another contract made independently.

New British Iron Co, ex parte Beckwith (1898)

Facts: The articles stated that directors were entitled to be paid £1,000 on taking office.

Held: The contract was implied from the directors' action in taking office. The provision in the articles was merely evidence of that separate contract.

It is important in an examination question to check the capacity in which the person is claiming. Is it as a member, or in some other capacity, such as a director or an accountant? Obviously the articles have no effect as a contract between the company and a person who is not a member even if they are named in them and given apparent rights against the company. In **Eley's** case above, Eley's membership was irrelevant to his claim; as solicitor he had no claim – he was attempting to enforce an employment right <u>not</u> a members right.

Test your understanding 10

(1) **Which of the following statements is/are correct?**

I   The articles of association of a company limited by shares contain the internal regulations of the company.

II   The articles of association form a contract between the shareholders and the company.

A   (I) only.

B   (II) only.

C   Both (I) and (II).

D   Neither (I) nor (II).

(2) **The articles of association of a company limited by shares form a contract between:**

A   the shareholders and the company in respect of all provisions in the articles.

B   the shareholders and the directors in respect of all provisions in the articles.

C   the company and the directors in respect of directors' rights only.

D   the company and the shareholders in respect of shareholder rights only.

Test your understanding 11

Explain the meaning and effect of a company's articles of association, paying particular attention to the following issues:

A   the operation of the model articles of association

B   the effect of the articles on both members and non-members

C   the procedure for altering the articles of association.

(Adapted from ACCA June 2004 examination)

10 Statutory books, returns and records

Registers

Register	Contents
Members	Names, addresses, date became/ceased, number of shares, class of share, amount paid up. Any member of the company can inspect the register without charge. A member of the public has the right of inspection but must pay.
Directors and company secretary	Names (present and former), address, date of birth, occupation, residency, nationality, other directorships within the last five years. The register does not include shadow directors (see chapter 9). The register must be open to inspection by a member without charge or by any other person for a fee.
Charges	This register contains details of fixed or floating charges created over the company's property (see chapter 8). The register will have details of the name of chargee, type of charge, brief description of property charged, amount and date created. The company must also keep copies of every instrument creating a charge at its registered office or some other place of which the Registrar has been notified. Any member or creditor may inspect the register free of charge, any other member of the public can inspect for a fee.
Other documents	Minutes of general meetings.
Resolutions and meetings	Records must be kept for a minimum period of 10 years.

The registers must normally be kept at the company's registered office (although the register of members and register of directors' interests can be kept where they are made up) and must be available for public inspection by a member free of charge or by any other person for a fee.

Requests for inspection must provide details about the person seeking the information, the purpose of the request and whether the information will be disclosed to others. The company may apply to the court for an order that it need not comply with the request.

The register of directors' addresses should now contain service addresses rather than details of the directors' residential addresses. The service address can be simply 'the company's registered office'.

The company must also keep a separate register of the directors' residential addresses. Both the service and the residential addresses will need to be supplied to the Registrar of Companies.

The residential addresses will be withheld from the public register. However, they will generally remain available to the Registrar and certain specified public bodies and credit reference agencies.

Annual return

The annual return must be filed with the Registrar annually within 28 days of the return date (which is the anniversary of incorporation). The return must be signed by a director or a secretary. It must include:

- the address of the company's registered office

- the type of company

- the company's principal business activities

- details of directors and company secretary where applicable (see chapter 10)

- a statement of capital which states the total number of shares of the company, the aggregate nominal value of the shares and the amount paid up and unpaid on each share.

- for each class of shares, the right of those shares, the total number of shares in that class and their total nominal value.

- details of the members of the company as at the return date

- details of members who have cease to be members since the last return was made

- details of the number of shares of each class held by members at the return date.

Accounting records

The company must keep accounting records containing sufficient information to show and explain the company's transactions and its financial position.

At any time it should be possible:

- to disclose with reasonable accuracy the company's financial position at intervals of not more than six months

- for the directors to ensure that any accounts that needs to be prepared comply with Companies Act 2006 and International Accounting Standards.

In particular the records **must** show:

- daily entries of all money received and spent

- a record of assets and liabilities

- statement of stocks at end of the financial year

- statements of stocktaking to back up the above

- statements of all goods sold and purchased, showing the goods and the buyers and sellers (except in the retail trade).

Accounting records must be kept for three years in the case of a private company and six years in that of a public one. They should be kept at the company's registered office or at some other place thought fit by the directors.

Failure to keep sufficient accounting records is an offence by the officers in default.

Annual financial statements

Companies are required to produce annual financial statements for each accounting reference period. This includes a:

- balance sheet/statement of financial position and profit and loss account/statement of comprehensive income showing true and fair view

- directors' report stating the amount of any dividend and likely future developments.

The annual financial statements must be approved and signed on behalf of the board of directors and a copy filed with Registrar.

11 Chapter summary

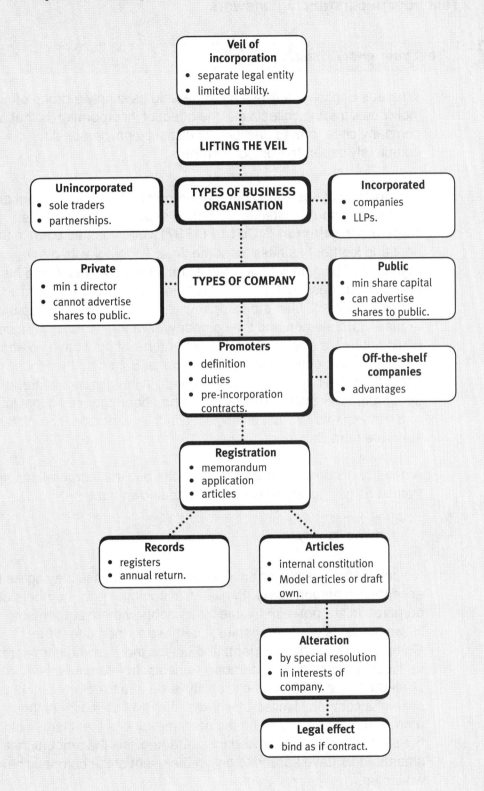

Veil of incorporation
- separate legal entity
- limited liability.

LIFTING THE VEIL

Unincorporated
- sole traders
- partnerships.

TYPES OF BUSINESS ORGANISATION

Incorporated
- companies
- LLPs.

Private
- min 1 director
- cannot advertise shares to public.

TYPES OF COMPANY

Public
- min share capital
- can advertise shares to public.

Promoters
- definition
- duties
- pre-incorporation contracts.

Off-the-shelf companies
- advantages

Registration
- memorandum
- application
- articles

Records
- registers
- annual return.

Articles
- internal constitution
- Model articles or draft own.

Alteration
- by special resolution
- in interests of company.

Legal effect
- bind as if contract.

Test your understanding answers

Test your understanding 1

A   Whereas English law treats a partnership as simply a group of individuals trading collectively, the effect of incorporation is that a company once formed has its own distinct legal personality, completely separate from its members.

The doctrine of separate or corporate personality is an ancient one, but the case usually cited in relation to separate personality is: **Salomon v Salomon & Co Ltd (1897)**. Salomon had been in the boot and leather business for some time. Together with other members of his family he formed a limited company and sold his previous business to it. Payment was in the form of cash, shares and debentures. When the company was eventually wound up it was argued that Salomon and the company were the same, and since he could not be his own creditor, his debentures should have no effect. Although lower courts had decided against Salomon, the House of Lords held that under the circumstances, in the absence of fraud, his debentures were valid. The company had been properly constituted and consequently it was, in law, a distinct legal person, completely separate from Salomon.

A number of consequences flow from the fact that corporations are treated as having legal personality in their own right.

I   Limited liability

No one is responsible for anyone else's debts unless they agree to accept such responsibility. Similarly, at common law, members of a corporation are not responsible for its debts without agreement. However, registered companies, i.e. those formed under the Companies Acts, are not permitted unless the shareholders agree to accept liability for their company's debts. In return for this agreement, the extent of their liability is set at a fixed amount. In the case of a company limited by shares, the level of liability is the amount remaining unpaid on the nominal value of the shares held. In the case of a company limited by guarantee, it is the amount that shareholders have agreed to pay in the event of the company being wound up.

II   Perpetual existence

As the corporation exists in its own right, changes in its membership have no effect on its status or existence. Members may die, be declared bankrupt or insane, or transfer their shares, all without any effect on the company. As an abstract legal person the company cannot die, although its existence can be brought to an end through the winding-up procedure.

III   Business property is owned by the company

Any business assets are owned by the company itself and not the shareholders. This is normally a major advantage in that the company's assets are not subject to claims based on the ownership rights of its individual members. It can, however, cause unforeseen problems as may be seen in **Macaura v Northern Assurance Co (1925)**. The plaintiff had owned a timber estate and later formed a one-man company and transferred the estate to this company. However, he continued to insure the estate in his own name. When the timber was lost in a fire it was held that Macaura could not claim on the insurance as he had no personal interest in the timber, which belonged to the company.

IV   Legal capacity

The company has contractual capacity in its own right and can sue and be sued in its own name. The extent of the company's liability, as opposed to the members, is unlimited and all its assets may be used to pay off debts. The company may also be liable in tort for any injuries sustained as a consequence of the negligence of its agents or employees.

V   The rule in **Foss v Harbottle (1843)**

This states that where a company suffers an injury, it is for the company, acting through the majority of the members, to take the appropriate remedial action. Perhaps of more importance is the corollary of the rule, which is that an individual cannot raise a legal action in response to a wrong suffered by the company.

B   **Lifting the veil of incorporation**

There are a number of occasions, both statutory and at common law, when the doctrine of separate personality will not be followed. On these occasions it is said that the veil of incorporation, which separates the company from its members, is 'pierced', 'lifted' or 'drawn aside'. Such situations arise as follows:

I   Under statute

If a public company starts to trade without first obtaining a trading certificate, the directors can be made personally liable for any loss or damage suffered by a third party: S767 CA06.

Under the Company Directors Disqualification Act 1986, if a director who is disqualified participates in the management of a company, that director will be jointly or severally liable for the company's debts.

Under the Insolvency Act 1986, members and/or directors held liable for wrongful or fraudulent trading may be made personally liable for losses arising as a result.

II   At common law

As in most areas of law that are based on the application of policy decisions, it is difficult to predict when the courts will ignore separate personality. What is certain is that the courts will not permit the corporate form to be used for a clearly fraudulent purpose or to evade a legal duty. Thus in **Gilford Motor Co Ltd v Horne (1933)** an employee had covenanted not to solicit his former employer's customers. After he left their employment he formed a company to solicit those customers and it was held that the company was a sham and the court would not permit it to be used to avoid the contract.

The courts are prepared to ignore separate personality in times of war in order to defeat the activity of shareholders who might be enemy aliens. See **Daimler Co Ltd v Continental Tyre and Rubber Co (GB) Ltd (1916)**.

Where groups of companies have been set up for particular business purposes, the courts will not usually ignore the separate existence of the various companies, unless they are being used for fraud. Although there is authority for treating separate companies as a single group (as in **DHN Food Distributors Ltd v London Borough of Tower Hamlets (1976)**) later authorities have cast extreme doubt on this decision (see **Woolfson v Strathclyde Regional Council (1978)**). More recent cases would appear to suggest that the courts are now more reluctant to ignore separate personality where the company has been properly established (**Adams v Cape Industries plc (1990)**).

Test your understanding 2

(1) **B**

The partners of a partnership are fully liable for all of the firm's debts. The fact that the partners in this case are limited companies is irrelevant.

(2) **D**

Answer D gives a definition of liability for a limited liability company limited by shares.

(3) **A**

A shareholder is a part-owner of the company, but is not a part-owner of the property owned by the company. In law, this property belongs to the company itself, which is a legal person.

Test your understanding 3

(1) **A**

A public company must have at least two directors. Statements B, C and D are correct.

(2) **D**

A private company cannot invite the public to subscribe for its shares. This is the key difference between a public and a private company.

(3) **D**

A public limited company must have a name ending with the words 'public limited company' (or the letters 'plc'). It may have its shares traded publicly, but this is not a requirement of plc status. It must have allotted share capital of £50,000, but this need not be fully paid up.

Test your understanding 4

A   the Partnership Act 1890

do not need

…the relationship which subsists between persons carrying on a business in common with a view to profit.

B   liability

members

limited

shareholders

…any unpaid portion of the price of their shares.

C   more

more

more

do not

D   A public limited company must have a minimum allotted share capital of £50,000 and a trading certificate.

KAPLAN PUBLISHING

Test your understanding 5

(1) **A**

The company can always sue the promoter for damages. However, the right to rescission may be lost where, for example, there has been unreasonable delay.

(2) **D**

Buying a company off the shelf means that the company has already been incorporated. It saves the time of going through the procedures for incorporation. Other non-urgent changes can then be made, such as changing the company name. A company can be bought off-the-shelf for about £100, which is much cheaper than using a solicitor or accountant to register a new company. However, the registered details (such as the name and directors) may need to be changed. All three statements are therefore correct.

(3) **D**

The position at common law is that a company cannot be bound by a contract that was made before it was formed, and after its formation it cannot ratify or formally adopt a pre-incorporation contract. S51 CA06 provides that a person acting for the company should have personal liability on a pre-incorporation contract that he enters into.

(4) **A**

S51 CA06 deems the person purporting to act on behalf of a company personally liable on a pre-incorporation contract, unless otherwise agreed. Merely signing as agent (e.g. using the words 'for and on behalf of') is not sufficient to avoid personal liability. The company cannot unilaterally adopt (or 'ratify') a pre-incorporation contract.

Test your understanding 6

A   Partners are liable for business debts to the extent of their personal wealth, whereas shareholders' liability is limited to the unpaid portion of their shares.

B   is

the company cannot make contracts before it comes into existence.

cannot

assigning the contract, making an agreement of novation or acquiring an 'off-the-shelf' company before making the contract.

Test your understanding 7

(1) **B**

Regardless of the actual date of registration, the only date that matters is the date on the certificate of incorporation.

(2) **A**

Provisional contracts are valid although if not paid within 21 days, the directors become jointly and severally liable with the company.

(3) **B**

It is not necessary to submit articles of association and if a company limited by shares (or guarantee) does not do so, the model articles will apply.

Test your understanding 8

A   joint and several

B

    I   An application

    II   Articles of Association (unless the model articles are to apply).

    III Memorandum of Association

    IV A statement of capital and initial shareholdings

    V   A statement of proposed officers containing the names of the first directors and company secretary (if applicable).

    VI A statement of compliance.

C   Certificate of incorporation

D   Adam and Ben are only liable for any unpaid portion of the price of their shares.

Test your understanding 9

(1) **B**

S54 CA06 prohibits a company, unless given approval by the Secretary of State for the Department for Business, Innocation and Skills from having a name that would be likely to give the impression that the business is carried on in connection with the government or a local council. Here, the use of the word 'Council' in the business name would not be permitted.

(2) **A**

A company cannot take the same name as a company that has been registered already with the same name. Once registered, a company can change its registered office, and must notify the registrar of any such change.

(3) **B**

The fact that the name ends with the letters 'Ltd' indicates that it is a private limited company.

Test your understanding 10

(1) **C**

The articles of association form a contract between the shareholders and the company, in respect of the rights of the ordinary shareholders. The articles set out the internal regulations or constitution of the company, e.g. the articles set out the rights of shareholders and the powers of the directors.

(2) **D**

The articles of association form a contract between the ordinary shareholders and the company, but only in respect of individual articles that affect the rights of the shareholders.

Test your understanding 11

A   Model articles are prescribed by the Secretary of State. They apply where a company is formed without registering articles or where the articles registered do not exclude or modify the model articles.

A company:

–   may adopt the model articles in full or in part;

–   is deemed to have adopted the model articles if there is no express or implied provision to exclude them; or

–   may draft its own unique articles.

B   S33 CA06 states that the provisions of a company's constitution bind the company and its members to the same extent as if there were covenants on the part of the company and of each member to observe those provisions. This section has three effects.

I   The documents establish a contract which binds each member to the company. Thus in **Hickman v Kent or Romney Marsh Sheepbreeders' Association (1920)**, the company was able to enforce an article against a member that provided that disputes involving the member and the company should go to arbitration.

II   The company is contractually bound to each of its members. On this basis in **Pender v Lushington (1877)** a member was able to sue in respect of the wrongful denial of his right to vote at a company meeting.

III   The articles constitute a contract between the members. In **Rayfield v Hands (1958)**, the articles of the company provided that, where shareholders wished to transfer their shares, they should inform the directors of the company, who were obliged to take the shares equally between them at fair value. When the directors refused to purchase the plaintiff's shares, the court held that the directors were bound as members by the articles and therefore had to comply with the procedure set out there.

Articles only operate as a contract in respect of membership rights and obligations. Consequently it has been held that, although members can enforce them, non-members, or members suing in some other capacity than that of a member, will not be able to enforce promises established in the company's articles. In **Eley v Positive Government Security Life Assurance Co (1876)**, the articles of a company stated that the plaintiff was to be appointed as the company's solicitor. It was held that Eley could not use the articles to establish a contract between himself and the company as those articles only created a contract between the company and its members. Although Eley was in fact a member, he was not suing in that capacity but in the capacity of solicitor, which was not a membership right.

C   A company can normally alter its articles by passing a special resolution. However, if certain provisions are entrenched, they can only be altered by following the specified procedure; this may require unanimous consent.

Any alteration must be made 'bona fide in the interest of the company as a whole', although the exact meaning of this phrase is not altogether clear. It is evident that it involves a subjective element in that those deciding the alteration must actually believe they are acting in the interests of the company. There is additionally, however, an objective element. In **Greenhalgh v Arderne Cinemas Ltd (1950)** it was stated that any alteration had to be in the interests of the 'individual hypothetical member'.

In **Brown v British Abrasive Wheel Co (1919)** an alteration to the articles of the company was proposed to give the majority shareholders the right to buy the shares of the minority. It was held that the alteration was invalid as it would benefit the majority shareholders rather than the company as a whole. However, in **Sidebottom v Kershaw, Leese & Co (1920)**, an alteration to the articles gave the directors the power to require any shareholder, who entered into competition with the company, to transfer their shares to nominees of the directors at a fair price. It was held that under those circumstances the alteration was valid as it would benefit the company as a whole.

8

Capital and financing

Chapter learning objectives

Upon completion of this chapter you will be able to:

- examine the different meanings of capital

- illustrate the difference between various classes of shares

- explain the procedure for the variation of class rights

- define companies' borrowing powers

- explain the meaning of debenture

- distinguish loan capital from share capital

- explain the concept of a company charge and distinguish between fixed and floating charges

- describe the need and the procedure for registering company charges

- explain the doctrine of capital maintenance and capital reduction

- examine the effect of issuing shares at either a discount or a premium

- explain the rules governing the distribution of dividends in both private and public companies.

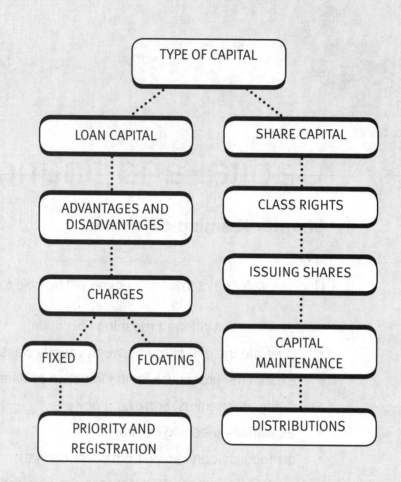

1 Share capital

Definition of a share

A share is 'the interest of a shareholder in the company measured by a sum of money, for the purpose of a liability in the first place, and of interest in the second, but also consisting of a series of mutual covenants entered into by all the shareholders': **Borland's Trustee v Steel Bros & Co Ltd (1901)**.

A shareholder is a member of the company and therefore has voting rights, depending on the class of shares held. They are also entitled to dividends depending on the availability of profits.

In the event of liquidation, depending on the type of share, a shareholder receives payment after all other creditors, but can participate in surplus assets.

2 Types of shares

	Preference shares	Ordinary shares
Voting rights	None, or restricted by the articles of association.	Full
Dividend rights	Fixed dividend paid in priority to other dividends, usually cumulative	Paid after preference dividend. Not fixed.
Surplus on winding up	Prior return of capital, but cannot participate in surplus	Entitled to share surplus assets after repayment of preference shares.

Test your understanding 1

Freeco is a public limited company. Geoffrey owns 11,000 6% £1 preference shares in the company and his sister, Gertrude, owns 10,000 £1 ordinary shares.

A   **Delete as appropriate and complete the sentence.**

Both Geoffrey and Gertrude are/are not members of the company. Geoffrey can/cannot attend general meetings. He can/cannot usually vote in the same way as Gertrude. Gertrude and Geoffrey can/cannot receive a dividend.

On liquidation, the position of both in relation to creditors is ….

(Your answer must not exceed 20 words.)

> **B** **Explain why Geoffrey's investment may be seen as less risky than Gertrude's.**
>
> (Your answer must not exceed 30 words.)

3 Class rights

What are they?

Class rights are the special rights attached to each class of shares, such as dividend rights, distribution of capital on a winding up and voting. (See above concerning the different rights that normally attach to ordinary shares and preference shares.)

How can they be varied?

The procedure for varying class rights depends on whether any procedure is specified in the articles:

Is procedure to vary specified?	Method of variation
Yes	Procedure set out in articles must be followed.
No	Variation needs special resolution or written consent of 75% in nominal value of the class: S630 CA06.

Minority protection

Under S633 CA06, the holders of 15% of the nominal value of that class, who did not consent to the variation, may ask the court to cancel the variation within 21 days of the passing of the resolution.

The court may confirm or cancel the variation. However, it will only cancel the variation if the petitioner proves it is unfairly prejudicial.

The court draws a distinction between:

- a variation that affects the value, enjoyment or power derived from the rights and
- a variation that changes the rights themselves.

The court will only intervene in the latter case.

Cumbrian Newspapers Group Ltd v Cumberland & Westmorland Herald (1986)

Facts: The claimant and the defendant were both publishers of newspapers. They negotiated a transaction whereby D would acquire one of C's papers and C would acquire 10 per cent of D's share capital. D issued the 10 per cent share holding and as part of the agreement under which the shares were issued amended its articles to give C certain rights including pre-emption rights over other ordinary shares. The purpose of such rights was to enable C as a shareholder to prevent a takeover. Subsequently, a few years later D called a meeting to pass a special resolution to cancel the articles which gave special rights to C. C sought a declaration that the rights were class rights which could not be cancelled without his consent.

Held: The declaration was granted. The special rights granted were rights which could not be varied or cancelled without C's consent.

White v Bristol Aeroplane Co (1953)

Facts: The company made a bonus issue of new ordinary and preference shares to the existing ordinary shareholders who alone were entitled to participate in bonus issues under the articles. The existing preference shareholders objected on the basis that this reduced their proportion of the class of preference shares and was a variation of class rights to which they had not consented.

Held: Bonus issue is not a variation of class rights since the existing preference shareholders had the same number of shares as before.

Greenhalgh v Arderne Cinemas Ltd (1950)

Facts: The company had two classes of ordinary shares, 50p and 10p shares, with every share carrying one vote. A resolution was passed to subdivide each 50p share into five 10p shares, thereby multiplying the votes of that class by five.

Held: The subdivision of shares is not a variation of class rights. The rights of the original 10p shares had not been varied since they still had one vote per share as before.

4 Terminology

Issued share capital	Issued share capital comprises share capital that has actually been issued, released or sold by the company
Paid up share capital	The amount which shareholders have actually paid on the shares issued.
Called up share capital	The amount of unpaid share capital which has been called for from shareholders but not yet paid.
Uncalled share capital	The amount of unpaid share capital that has not yet been called for from shareholders and therefore also remains unpaid.
Bonus issues	Carried out by using some of the company's non-distributable reserves to issue fully paid shares to existing shareholders in proportion to their shareholdings. Do not raise any new funds.
Rights issues/Statutory pre-emption rights	New shares offered to existing shareholders in proportion to their shareholdings. Statutory pre-emption rights only apply where ordinary shares are issued for cash. Raise new funds. Shares usually offered at discount to current market value (but not at discount to nominal value).

Test your understanding 2

A public company with a stock market listing has just sold a new issue of ten million £1 ordinary shares. All the shares were bought by existing shareholders in the company.

Which one of the following conclusions can be inferred from this statement?

A   The company has undertaken a rights issue.

B   The company has raised exactly £10 million to finance the expansion of the business.

C   As a new issue, the shares could be sold only to personal shareholders and not to institutional shareholders.

D   Since there were no new shareholders, the company's share capital was not extended.

5 Issuing shares

Allotment of shares

This is where the shares are allocated to a person under a contract of allotment. Once the shares are allotted and the holder is entered in the register of members, they become a member of the company.

Authority

The directors need authority in order to allot shares. This may be given:

- by the articles, or
- by passing an ordinary resolution.

The authority must state:

- the maximum number of shares to be allotted
- the expiry date for the authority (maximum five years).

The directors of a private company with only one class of shares may allot shares of that class unless it is prohibited by the articles: S550 CA06.

Issue at discount

Every share has a **nominal value** which is fixed at the time of incorporation of the company in the statement of capital and initial shareholding. The nominal value of the share represents the extent of a shareholders potential liability.

The common law rule is that a company cannot issue its shares for a consideration which is at a discount on their nominal value.

Ooregum Gold Mining Co of India v Roper (1892)

Facts: Shares in a company which had a nominal value of £1 were trading at a market price of 12.5p. In an honest attempt to refinance the company, new £1 preference shares were issued and credited with 75p as paid up. The company subsequently went into liquidation.

Held: The holders of the shares were required to pay a further 75p per share.

The common law rule is given statutory effect in S580 CA06. In addition S582 CA06 states that shares are only treated as paid up to the extent that the company has received money or money's worth.

If this rule is breached the issue is still valid, but the allottee must pay up the discount plus interest. This applies to any subsequent holder of such a share who was aware of the original underpayment: S588 CA06.

Issue at premium

Where a share is allotted at a value greater than its nominal value, the excess over the nominal value is share premium. This is where the market value of the share is greater than the fixed nominal value.

S610 CA06 requires any premium to be credited to a share premium account, which may only be used for:

- writing off the expenses of the issue of new shares
- writing off any commission paid on the issue of new shares
- issuing bonus shares.

Paying for shares – private companies

Private companies may issue shares for non-cash consideration. The court will interfere with the valuation only if there is fraud or the consideration is 'illusory, past or patently inadequate'.

Paying for shares - public companies

There are a number of additional rules relating to the issue of shares in public companies contained in CA06:

S584	Subscribers to the memorandum must pay cash for their subscription shares.
S585	Payment for shares must not be in the form of work or services.
S586	Shares cannot be allotted until at least one-quarter of their nominal value and the whole of any premium have been paid.
S587	Non-cash consideration must be received within five years.
S593	Non-cash consideration must be independently valued and reported on by a person qualified to be the company's auditor.

Test your understanding 3

What can the share premium account be used for?

6 Capital maintenance

Purpose

The share capital of a limited company is regarded as a buffer fund for creditors. (Note that the creditors' buffer is an accounting fund, not real money. The actual cash or assets subscribed can be used by the company.)

The rules on maintenance of capital exist in order to prevent a company reducing its capital by returning it to its members, whether directly or indirectly. This means that, **as a general rule**, a limited company cannot reduce its share capital. There is, however, an exception to this general rule which is discussed below.

Exception

Reduction of capital

Under S641 CA06, a company can reduce its capital at any time, for any reason.

Reduce or cancel liabilities on partly-paid shares, i.e. the company gives up any claim for money owing.

Return capital in excess of the company's needs, i.e. the company reduces its assets by repaying cash to its shareholders.

Cancel the paid-up capital that is no longer represented by the assets, i.e. if the company has a debit balance on reserves it can write this off by reducing capital and thereby does not need to make good past losses.

Procedure for public companies:

> Pass a special resolution

> Apply to the court to confirm the special resolution.

> If reduction involves one of the first two methods above, court must require company to settle a list of creditors entitled to object.

> The court must not confirm the reduction until it is satisfied that all creditors have either consented to the reduction or had their debts discharged or secured.

> The company must file documents with the Registrar. If the share capital of a public company falls below £50,000, it must re-register as a private company.

Simplified procedure for private companies:

> Pass a special resolution supported by a solvency statement.

> The solvency statement is a statement by each of the directors that the company will be able to meet its debts within the following year.

> A solvency statement made without reasonable grounds is an offence punishable by fine and/or imprisonment.

> Copies of the resolution, solvency statement and a statement of capital must be filed with the Registrar within 15 days.

KAPLAN PUBLISHING

Test your understanding 4

(1) **A public company limited by shares may reduce capital by:**

    A   passing an ordinary resolution and obtaining the court's permission

    B   passing a special resolution and obtaining the court's permission

    C   passing an ordinary resolution with special notice

    D   passing a special resolution with special notice.

(2) Under S641 Companies Act 2006 a private limited company can reduce its issued share capital if certain conditions are fulfilled.

    Which one of the following is not a necessary condition?

    A   The articles must not prohibit the reduction.

    B   The directors must make a solvency statement.

    C   A special resolution must be passed.

    D   The sanction of the court must be obtained.

7 Distributions

Introduction

A company can only make a distribution (e.g. pay a dividend) out of profits available for that purpose, i.e. distributable profits.

Distributable profits

Distributable profits are the accumulated realised profits (so far as not previously utilised by distribution or capitalisation) less the accumulated realised losses (so far as not previously written off in a reduction of capital): S830 CA06.

- Profit/loss – trading or capital.

- Accumulated – overall profit/loss, not just one year in isolation.

- Realised – not revaluation reserve. However, provisions (e.g. depreciation) are deemed realised.

Additional rules for a public company

A public limited company can only declare a dividend if both before and after distribution its net assets are not less than the aggregate of its called up share capital and undistributable reserves.

Undistributable reserves are:

- share premium account
- capital redemption reserve
- unrealised profits (i.e. revaluation reserve)
- reserves that the company is forbidden to distribute.

The latest audited accounts are used to make the calculations.

Model articles

Under the model articles, the directors recommend the payment of a dividend and the company declares it by passing an ordinary resolution. The amount paid cannot exceed the amount recommended by the directors.

However, a shareholder is not entitled to a dividend as of right.

Test your understanding 5

A company had a balance on its profit and loss account reserve at the beginning of its accounting year of losses of £3,000. During the year the company made trading profits of £7,000 and revalued its fixed assets by £5,000.

What are the profits available for distribution?

Consequences of an unlawful dividend

If a dividend is not paid in accordance with the rules on distributions then the company can recover the distribution from:

- shareholders who knew or had reasonable grounds to know the dividend was unlawful
- any director unless he can show he exercised reasonable care in relying on properly prepared accounts
- the auditors if the dividend was paid in reliance on erroneous accounts.

However, if a director has to make good to the company an unlawful dividend he may claim indemnity from the shareholders who when they received the dividend knew it was an unlawful dividend.

8 Loan capital

All companies have the implied power to borrow for the purpose of business.

Loan capital comprises all the longer term borrowing of a company such as:

*   permanent overdrafts at the bank

*   unsecured loans either from a bank or other party

*   loans secured on assets either from a bank or other party.

Companies often issue long-term loans in the form of **debentures**.

Debentures

A debenture is a document issued by a company containing an acknowledgment of its indebtedness whether charged on the company's assets or not.

There are three main types of debentures:

*   a single debenture e.g. a company obtains a secured loan or overdraft facility.

*   debentures issued as a series and usually registered

*   debenture stock subscribed to by a large number of lenders.

Advantages of debentures

*   The board does not (usually) need the authority of a general meeting to issue debentures.

*   As debentures carry no votes they do not dilute or affect the control of the company.

*   Interest is chargeable against the profit before tax.

*   Debentures may be cheaper to service than shares.

*   There are no restrictions on issuing debentures at a discount or on redemption.

Disadvantages of debentures

*   Interest must be paid out of pre-tax profits, irrespective of the profits of the company. If necessary must be paid out of capital.

- Default may precipitate liquidation and/or administration if the debentures are secured.

- High gearing will affect the share price.

Test your understanding 6

Edward and Frederick wish to invest in Fizz, a listed plc. They have the choice of investing by buying shares or by subscribing to an issue of debentures.

A   **Fill in the gaps and complete the sentence.**

Most people understand a debenture to mean a
…………………………...

Strictly speaking it is a ….

(Your answer must not exceed 10 words.)

B   **Fill in the gaps and delete as appropriate.**

Edward and Frederick will have the choice of being
…………………… shareholders or
…………………….....shareholders. The …………………….....
have the real voting rights while the …………………….... will have
a less risky investment.

C   **List three differences between debentures and shares.**

9 Fixed versus floating charges

Fixed charge

A fixed charge is a legal or equitable mortgage on a specific asset (e.g. land), which prevents the company dealing with the asset without the consent of the mortgagee.

A fixed charge has three main characteristics:

- It is on an identified asset.

- The asset is intended to be retained permanently in the business.

- The company has no general freedom to deal with (e.g. sell) the asset.

Floating charge

The judge in **Re Yorkshire Woolcombers' Association (1903)** stated that a floating charge has three main characteristics:

- It is on a class of assets, present and future.
- The assets within the class will change from time to time.
- The company has freedom to deal with the charged assets in the ordinary course of its business.

A floating charge cannot be created by a partnership.

Crystallisation

A floating charge does not attach to any particular asset until crystallisation.

Crystallisation means the company can no longer deal freely with the assets. It occurs in the following cases:

- liquidation
- the company ceases to carry on business
- any event specified (e.g. the company is unable to pay its debts; the company fails to look after its property; the company fails to keep stock levels sufficiently high).

Advantages of a floating charge

A floating charge has the following advantages for the company:

- The company can deal freely with the assets.
- A wider class of assets can be charged.

Disadvantages of a floating charge

A floating charge has a number of disadvantages for the chargee:

- The value of the security is uncertain until it crystallises.
- It has a lower priority in order of repayment than a fixed charge.
- It may be challenged by a liquidator if it was created within 12 months preceding a winding up. This is to prevent a company from giving preference to one of its unsecured creditors by giving a floating charge over its assets.

Test your understanding 7

(1) JIH Ltd has borrowed money from K Bank plc and has provided security by executing a fixed charge debenture in favour of the bank.

A fixed charge is:

A   a charge over specific company property that prevents the company from dealing freely with the property in the ordinary course of business

B   a charge over a class of company assets that enables the company to deal freely with the assets in the ordinary course of business

C   a charge over specific company property that enables the company to deal freely with the assets in the ordinary course of business

D   a charge over company land enabling the company to deal freely with the land in the ordinary course of business.

(2) HIJ Ltd has borrowed money from K Bank plc and has provided security by executing a floating charge debenture in favour of the bank.

A floating charge is:

A   a charge over specific company property that prevents the company from dealing freely with the property in the ordinary course of business

B   a charge over a class of company assets that enables the company to deal freely with the assets in the ordinary course of business

C   a charge over specific company property that enables the company to deal freely with the assets in the ordinary course of business

D   a charge over company land enabling the company to deal freely with the land in the ordinary course of business.

10 Priority and registration of charges

Priority

The priority of a charge depends on the type of charge and whether or not it has been registered:

- Equal charges – first created has priority.

- Fixed charge – has priority over a floating charge.
- An unregistered registerable charge has no priority over a registered charge.
- A chargeholder can prohibit the creation of a later charge with priority, but the prohibition is only effective if a subsequent chargee has notice of the prohibition as well as the charge.

Registration

The company must also notify the registrar within 21 days of the creation of the charge.

Registration can be undertaken by:

- the company
- the chargeholder.

Failure to register:

- renders the charge void against the liquidator
- results in a fine on the company and every officer in default
- renders the money secured immediately repayable.

If the charge relates to land it must also be registered with HM Revenue and Customs.

The company must also include all charges in its own register of charges. However, failure to include the charge in the company's own register does not invalidate the charge.

Test your understanding 8

(1) **Which of the following is the correct period within which company charges must be registered with the registrar of companies?**

   A   7 days following the creation of the charge

   B   14 days following the creation of the charge

   C   21 days following the creation of the charge

   D   28 days following the creation of the charge. Which one of the following statements is correct?

11 Loan capital versus share capital

Loan capital versus share capital

	Loan capital	Share capital
Definition	A debenture is a document issued by a company containing an acknowledgment of its indebtedness.	A share is the interest of a shareholder in a company measured by a sum of money. It is a bundle of rights and obligations.
Voting rights	A debenture is a creditor of the company and therefore has no voting rights.	A shareholder is a member (owner) of the company and therefore has voting rights, depending on the class of shares held.
Income	A debenture has a contractual right to interest, irrespective of the availability of profits.	Dividends depend on the availability of profits.
Liquidation	A debenture has priority with respect to repayment.	Depending on the type of share, shareholders receive repayment after creditors, but can participate in surplus assets.
Maintenance of capital	Does not need to be maintained.	Must be maintained.

12 Chapter summary

TYPE OF CAPITAL

Loan capital
- creditor
- interest
- preferential right to repayment.

Share capital
- preference or ordinary
- member
- dividend
- voting rights.

Advantages
- interest is tax deductible
- no dilution of voting control

Disadvantages
- interest payable irrespective of profits.

Class rights
- definition
- variation
- minority protection.

CHARGES

Issuing shares
- at discount
- at premium
- for non-cash consideration.

Fixed
- specific
- can not deal freely.

Floating
- class of assets crystallisation.

Capital maintenance
- reduction of capital.

Priority and registration
- fixed have priority over floating
- notify registrar within 21 days.

DISTRIBUTIONS

Test your understanding answers

Test your understanding 1

A   are

     can

     cannot

     can

     …that they cannot receive any payment until all amounts due to creditors have been paid.

B   The dividend is fixed. Preference shares have priority when dividends are declared and on winding up. Dividends are cumulative and arrears of dividend will be paid when profits are available.

Test your understanding 2

A   A sale of a new issue of shares to the existing shareholders is a rights issue.

Test your understanding 3

The share premium account may only be used for:

- writing off the expenses of the issue of those shares
- writing off any commission paid on the issue of those shares
- issuing bonus shares.

KAPLAN PUBLISHING

Test your understanding 4

(1) **B**

Once the special resolution to reduce the share capital has been passed, it must be approved by the court. The procedure involving a special resolution supported by a solvency statement is only available to private companies.

(2) **D**

The Articles must not prohibit the reduction of capital. A special resolution must be passed, supported by a solvency statement. However, it is not necessary for the reduction of capital by a private company to be sanctioned by the court.

Test your understanding 5

The company can distribute up to £4,000. This represents the £7,000 profit for the year, less the accumulated losses of £3,000. The unrealised profit on the revaluation of fixed assets is excluded.

Test your understanding 6

A   loan

...written acknowledgment by a company of an amount owed.

B   ordinary

preference

ordinary shareholders

preference shareholders

C

I   Shareholders are members, debenture holders are creditors.

II   Shareholders receive a dividend, debenture holders receive interest.

III   Shares cannot be issued at a discount, debentures can.

Test your understanding 7

(1) **A**

A fixed charge is a charge over a specific asset which attaches to the asset immediately upon its creation. This means that the company cannot deal freely with the asset in the ordinary course of business.

(2) **B**

Answer B provides a good basic definition of a floating charge.

Test your understanding 8

(1) **C**

Charges must be notified to the registrar of companies within 21 days.

KAPLAN PUBLISHING

9

Directors

Chapter learning objectives

Upon completion of this chapter you will be able to:

- explain the role of directors in the operation of the company

- discuss the ways in which the directors are appointed, can lose their office or be subject to a disqualification order

- distinguish between the powers of the board of directors, the managing director and individual directors to bind the company

- explain the duties that directors owe to their companies

- demonstrate an understanding of the way in which statute law has attempted to control directors.

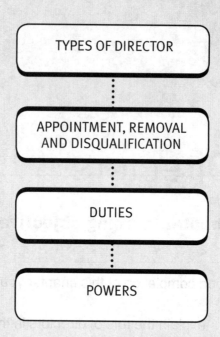

1 Directors

Definition of director

The term 'director' includes 'any person occupying the position of director, by whatever name called': s250 CA06.

The decision as to whether someone is a director is therefore based on their function, not their title.

There must be at least one director who is a 'natural person'. In addition, a director must normally be aged at least 16.

KAPLAN PUBLISHING

Types of director

Managing director (MD)	• The model articles allow the board to delegate to the MD any powers they see fit. • The MD has a dual role – member of board and also executive officer. • **Freeman & Lockyer (A Firm) v Buckhurst Park Properties (Mangal) Ltd (1964)** – the MD has the apparent authority to enter into all contracts of a commercial nature.
Shadow director	• 'A person in accordance with whose directions or instructions the directors of a company are accustomed to act': s251 CA06. • Not a shadow director if advice is given only in a professional capacity.
Executive director	• Likely to be a full-time employee involved in management.
Non-executive director (NED)	• Part-time. • Brings outside expertise to board. • Not an employee. • Exerts control over executive directors.
Chairman of board	• Chairs meetings of board. • Acts as spokesman for the company. • Has a casting vote.

2 Appointment, disqualification and removal

Appointment

First Directors	• Appointed in Statement of Proposed Officers. • Public companies need a minimum of two; private companies need one. • There is no statutory maximum, but the articles may specify a maximum number.
Appointment procedure	• Usually appointed by the existing directors or by ordinary resolution. • Directors of public companies should generally be voted on individually: s160 CA06. • A director's actions are valid notwithstanding that his appointment was defective: s161 CA06.

Model articles for public companies	• At the first annual general meeting (AGM) all the directors retire and offer themselves for re-election by ordinary resolution.
	• At each AGM one-half retire (those most senior). They can be re-elected.
	• Casual vacancies are filled by the board until the next AGM when the new directors must stand for election.
Publicity	• The company must notify Companies House within 14 days of new appointments and any changes in particulars. It must also enter details in the register of directors.
Service contracts	• Cannot exceed two years unless they have been approved by the shareholders by ordinary resolution: s188 CA06.
	• If s188 CA06 is breached the service contract is deemed to state that the company can terminate the contract at any time by giving reasonable notice.
	• The service contract must be kept open for inspection at the company's registered office.
	• The directors of a quoted company must prepare a directors' remuneration report for each financial year of the company. The report will contain for each person who was a director during the year: a) date of the contract, the unexpired term and the details of any notice periods; b) any provision for compensation payable upon early termination of the contract; and c) such details of other provisions in the contract as are necessary to enable members of the company to estimate the liability of the company in the event of early termination of the contract.
Compensation for loss of office	• Gratuitous payments must be disclosed to all members and approved by ordinary resolution. If not approved, director holds payment on trust for the company.

Disqualification

Model articles – Directors must vacate their office if they become bankrupt or insane.

Company Directors (Disqualification) Act 1986 (CDDA 1986)

The CDDA 1986 was introduced to prevent the misuse of the limited liability status of companies by directors who would set up a new company to carry on essentially the same business as an old company which had ceased trading with unpaid debts.

A disqualified director cannot be concerned in the management of a company directly or indirectly or act as a liquidator, receiver or promoter.

The CDDA 1986 identifies three distinct categories of conduct:

(1) General misconduct in connection with companies. This includes:

- Conviction of a serious offence in connection with the management of a company (maximum fifteen years disqualification).

- Persistent breaches of CA06, e.g. failure to file returns (maximum five years disqualification).

(2) Disqualification for unfitness. This includes:

- Where an investigation by the Department for Business, Innovation and Skills finds the director unfit to be concerned in the management of the company.

- Where a liquidator's report finds the director unfit to be concerned in the management of a company (minimum two years, and maximum fifteen years, disqualification).

(3) Other cases for disqualification. This includes:

- participation in fraudulent or wrongful trading (maximum 15 years disqualification).

- where an undischarged bankrupt has been acting as a director

Breach of a disqualification order:

- This is a criminal offence, which could result in a fine and imprisonment.

- The disqualified director (or any person who acts on his instructions) is personally liable for the debts of the company while so acting.

Removal

Under s168 CA06, a company may by ordinary resolution remove a director before expiration of his period of office notwithstanding anything in:

- its articles, or

- any agreement between him and it.

Thus a director can be removed despite any provision to the contrary in his service contract, although he can sue for damages if the removal is in breach of his contract. The company must follow this procedure to remove a director:

> Special notice (28 days) is required of the resolution by persons wishing to remove a director.
> The company must forward a copy of the resolution to the director concerned.

> Notice of the meeting goes to the director and all members entitled to attend and vote.

> The director in question can require the company to circulate written representations to members.

> At the meeting, the director can read out representations if there was no time for prior circulation.
> The director must be allowed to attend the meeting and to speak.
> An ordinary resolution is needed to remove the director.

The power of the members to remove a director may be limited:

Bushell v Faith (1970)

Facts: A provision in the articles tripled the number of votes of shares held by directors on a resolution to remove them. Statute only required an ordinary resolution and made no provision as to how it could be obtained or defeated.

Held: The weighted voting rights provided in the articles were valid.

Test your understanding 1

Which of the following states the requirements for removal of a director?

A   Special resolution with ordinary notice

B   Ordinary resolution with special notice

C   Ordinary resolution with ordinary notice

D   Special resolution with special notice

---

3 Duties

The low level of care shown in **Re City Equitable Fire Insurance Co (1925)** was raised in:

Dorchester Finance Co Ltd v Stebbing (1989)

Facts: The company was a money-lending company and had three directors, Parsons, Hamilton and Stebbing. All three had considerable accountancy and business experience (Parsons and Hamilton were chartered accountants). No board meetings were ever held and Parsons and Hamilton left all the affairs of the company to Stebbing. Parsons and Hamilton did, however, turn up from time to time and signed blank cheques on the company's account which they left Stebbing to deal with. Stebbing loaned the company's money without complying with statutory regulations applying to money lending, such that the loans were unenforceable.

Held: All three were liable in negligence. If a director has a special skill (e.g. as an accountant) he is expected to use it for the benefit of the company.

Duty to avoid conflicts of interest: s175

A director must avoid any situation which places him in direct conflict with the interests of the company or the performance of any other duty.

IDC v Cooley (1972)

Facts: Cooley, the managing director of IDC, had been negotiating a contract on behalf of the company, but the third party wished to award the contract to him personally and not to the company. Without disclosing his reason to the company (or its board) he resigned in order to take the contract personally.

Held: He was in breach of fiduciary duty as he had profited personally by use of an opportunity which came to him through his directorship: it made no difference that the company itself would not have obtained the contract. He was therefore accountable to the company for the benefits gained from the contract.

The IDC case also illustrates that an individual may still be subject to the duties even after he ceases to be a director.

The accountability arises from the mere fact of having made a profit, it is not a question of loss to the company.

Regal (Hastings) Ltd v Gulliver (1942)

Facts: The claimant company owned one cinema and wished to buy two others with the object of selling all three together. They formed a subsidiary to buy the cinemas but could not provide all the capital needed to finance the purchase. The directors bought some of the shares in the subsidiary to enable the purchases to be made and later sold their shares at a profit.

Held: The directors must account to the claimant company for the profit on the grounds that it was only through the knowledge and opportunity they gained as directors of that company that they were able to obtain the shares and consequently to make the profit.

Duty not to accept benefits from third parties: s176

A director must not accept any benefit from a third party which arises by reason of him being a director or performing/not performing an act as a director, unless acceptance cannot reasonably be regarded as likely to give rise to a conflict of interest.

Boston Deep Sea Fishing & Ice Co v Ansell (1888)

Facts: Ansell was managing director of the claimant company. He accepted a 'commission' (bribe) from a supplier to order goods from that supplier, on behalf of the company. When the company found out, he was dismissed.

Held: The defendant was in breach of his fiduciary duty as the agent of the company. Therefore the company could recover the commissions paid to him.

Duty to declare interest in proposed transaction or arrangement: s177

A director is required to declare the nature and extent of any interest, either direct or indirect through a connected person, that they have in relation to a proposed transaction or arrangement with the company. Even if the director is not a party to a transaction, the duty may apply if they are aware or ought reasonably to have been aware, of the interest.

This declaration can be made in writing, at a board meeting or by a general notice that he has an interest in a third party.

Aberdeen Railway v Blakie (1854)

Facts: A company bought some chairs from a firm. At the time of the contract one of the company's directors, unknown to the company was a partner in the firm.

Held: The company could avoid the contract because of this undisclosed interest in the transaction.

The low level of care shown in **Re City Equitable Fire Insurance Co (1925)** was raised in:

Dorchester Finance Co Ltd v Stebbing (1989)

Facts: The company was a money-lending company and had three directors, Parsons, Hamilton and Stebbing. All three had considerable accountancy and business experience (Parsons and Hamilton were chartered accountants). No board meetings were ever held and Parsons and Hamilton left all the affairs of the company to Stebbing. Parsons and Hamilton did, however, turn up from time to time and signed blank cheques on the company's account which they left Stebbing to deal with. Stebbing loaned the company's money without complying with statutory regulations applying to money lending, such that the loans were unenforceable.

Held: All three were liable in negligence. If a director has a special skill (e.g. as an accountant) he is expected to use it for the benefit of the company.

Duty to avoid conflicts of interest: s175

A director must avoid any situation which places him in direct conflict with the interests of the company or the performance of any other duty.

IDC v Cooley (1972)

Facts: Cooley, the managing director of IDC, had been negotiating a contract on behalf of the company, but the third party wished to award the contract to him personally and not to the company. Without disclosing his reason to the company (or its board) he resigned in order to take the contract personally.

Held: He was in breach of fiduciary duty as he had profited personally by use of an opportunity which came to him through his directorship: it made no difference that the company itself would not have obtained the contract. He was therefore accountable to the company for the benefits gained from the contract.

The IDC case also illustrates that an individual may still be subject to the duties even after he ceases to be a director.

The accountability arises from the mere fact of having made a profit, it is not a question of loss to the company.

Regal (Hastings) Ltd v Gulliver (1942)

Facts: The claimant company owned one cinema and wished to buy two others with the object of selling all three together. They formed a subsidiary to buy the cinemas but could not provide all the capital needed to finance the purchase. The directors bought some of the shares in the subsidiary to enable the purchases to be made and later sold their shares at a profit.

Held: The directors must account to the claimant company for the profit on the grounds that it was only through the knowledge and opportunity they gained as directors of that company that they were able to obtain the shares and consequently to make the profit.

Duty not to accept benefits from third parties: s176

A director must not accept any benefit from a third party which arises by reason of him being a director or performing/not performing an act as a director, unless acceptance cannot reasonably be regarded as likely to give rise to a conflict of interest.

Boston Deep Sea Fishing & Ice Co v Ansell (1888)

Facts: Ansell was managing director of the claimant company. He accepted a 'commission' (bribe) from a supplier to order goods from that supplier, on behalf of the company. When the company found out, he was dismissed.

Held: The defendant was in breach of his fiduciary duty as the agent of the company. Therefore the company could recover the commissions paid to him.

Duty to declare interest in proposed transaction or arrangement: s177

A director is required to declare the nature and extent of any interest, either direct or indirect through a connected person, that they have in relation to a proposed transaction or arrangement with the company. Even if the director is not a party to a transaction, the duty may apply if they are aware or ought reasonably to have been aware, of the interest.

This declaration can be made in writing, at a board meeting or by a general notice that he has an interest in a third party.

Aberdeen Railway v Blakie (1854)

Facts: A company bought some chairs from a firm. At the time of the contract one of the company's directors, unknown to the company was a partner in the firm.

Held: The company could avoid the contract because of this undisclosed interest in the transaction.

Breach of directors' duties

Directors owe their duties to the company as a whole, not to individual members.

Percival v Wright (1902)

Facts: A director of a company bought shares from a member at a price less than that for which the director knew that a third party had expressed interest in buying all the shares in the company. The third party interest came to nothing, but the selling member sued the director for breach of duty to the member in not disclosing the interest expressed by the third party.

Held: The purchasing director was under no obligation to disclose to the selling member the third party interest. A director's duties are owed to the company and not to individual members.

Breach of duty may carry the following consequences:

- The director may be required to make good any loss suffered by the company.

- Contracts entered into between the company and the director may be rendered voidable.

- Any property taken by the director from the company can be recovered from him if still in his possession.

- Property may be recovered directly from a third party, unless that third party acquired it for value and in good faith.

- An injunction may be an appropriate remedy where the breach has not yet occurred.

S232 CA06 provides that any provision to exempt a director from or indemnify him against any liability for breach of duty or negligence is void.

S239 CA06 states that the company can ratify a breach of duty by passing an ordinary resolution.

Jack has acted in breach of his duty to disclose his interest in a contract as a director of JK Ltd.

Which one of the following is correct?

A   The breach cannot be ratified by the shareholders.

B   The breach may be ratified by a written or ordinary resolution.

C   The breach may be ratified by a provision in the company's articles.

D   The breach may be ratified by a resolution of the board of directors.

4 Powers

The division of power within a company

The division of power within a company is between the board of directors who manage the business on a day-to-day basis and the members who make major decisions about the running of the company's business in a general meeting.

Directors are required to exercise their powers in accordance with the company's constitution i.e. the articles, which usually authorise the directors 'to manage the company's business' and to 'exercise all the powers of the company for any purpose connected with the company's business'.

Note that the power to manage the business of the company is given to the board as a whole, not to the individual directors. Where a company's articles delegate the management of the company's business to the board, the members have no right to interfere in decisions made by the board. Directors are not agents of the members and are not subject to their instruction as to how to act.

Shaw v John Shaw (1935)

Facts: The company's board of directors resolved that the company commence litigation against two errant directors. At a subsequent member's meeting an ordinary resolution was passed that the litigation be discontinued.

Held: It was for the board to decide whether or not the company should commence litigation and therefore the ordinary resolution had no legal effect.

There are some restrictions which mean that power is placed in the hands of the members rather than the directors:

- some actions require a resolution

- a director can be removed at any time by an ordinary resolution of the members and they may see fit to exercise this right should their views be ignored

- the members can alter the articles by passing a special resolution. This power could therefore be used to restrict the directors' powers.

The control of directors

Although the directors manage the company on a day-to-day basis, a company is ultimately controlled by its members. Most decisions require a majority of over 50% (although some require 75%) therefore shareholders who are in the minority may find that their wishes are ignored.

Members can exercise their votes in their own interests. They are not required to act for the benefit of the company.

Certain matters require the approval of the members in a general meeting in order to be valid. For example, substantial property transactions: s190 CA06.

A substantial property transaction occurs where a director acquires from the company (or vice versa) a substantial non-cash asset.

 An asset is 'substantial' if its value either exceeds £100,000 or exceeds 10% of the company's asset value and is more than £5,000.

Failure to obtain the members' approval results in the following consequences:

- the transaction is voidable by the company, unless the members give approval within a reasonable period

- the director is liable to account to the company for any gain or indemnify it against any loss.

Authority of directors

At common law

Individual directors cannot bind the company without being given authority to do so. There are three ways in which this authority may be given:

Express	• Where authority is expressly given, all decisions taken are binding.
Implied	• Authority flows from a person's position.
	• The person appointed as the managing director has the implied authority to bind the company in the same way as the board.
	• The managing director is assumed to have all powers usually exercised by a managing director.
Apparent/ Ostensible	• Such authority arises where a director is held out by the other board members as having the authority to bind the company.
	• If a third party acts on such a representation, the company is estopped from denying its truth: **Freeman & Lockyer v Buckhurst Park Properties (1964)** (see Chapter 5: Agency Law).

Transaction beyond the board's powers

S40 CA06 states that the power of the directors to bind the company, or to authorise another to bind the company, will not be limited by anything in the company's constitution, **provided** the other party is acting in good faith.

S40 goes on to state that even where there is **actual knowledge** of the lack of authority this is not enough to count as lack of good faith so, on the face of it, any contract entered into by the board of a company will be binding.

Where, however, the third party to the transaction is also a director of the company or a person associated with a director, the transaction becomes **voidable** at the company's instance: s41 CA06. Moreover, the third party director or associate, and any director who authorised the transaction is then liable to **compensate** the company for any profit made or to indemnify the company for any loss or damage arising, whether the company chooses to avoid the contract or not.

5 Chapter summary

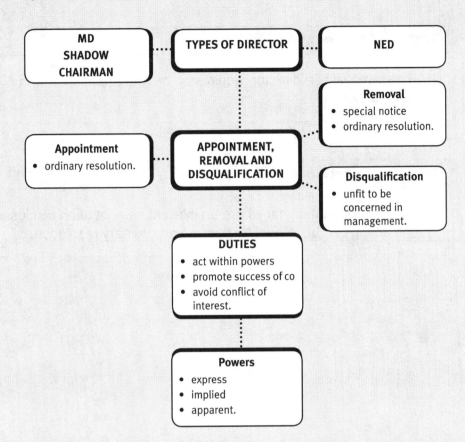

MD
SHADOW
CHAIRMAN

TYPES OF DIRECTOR

NED

Removal
- special notice
- ordinary resolution.

Appointment
- ordinary resolution.

APPOINTMENT, REMOVAL AND DISQUALIFICATION

Disqualification
- unfit to be concerned in management.

DUTIES
- act within powers
- promote success of co
- avoid conflict of interest.

Powers
- express
- implied
- apparent.

Test your understanding answers

Test your understanding 1

B   The removal of a director requires an ordinary resolution with special notice.

Test your understanding 2

B   S239 CA06 states that where an interest has not been disclosed, the action can be ratified by passing an ordinary resolution.

Corporate administration

Chapter learning objectives

Upon completion of this chapter you will be able to:

- discuss the appointment, duties and powers of, a company secretary

- discuss the appointment, duties and powers of, the company auditors

- distinguish between types of meetings: general meetings and annual general meetings

- explain the procedure for calling such meetings

- detail the procedure for conducting company meetings

- distinguish between types of resolutions: ordinary, special, and written.

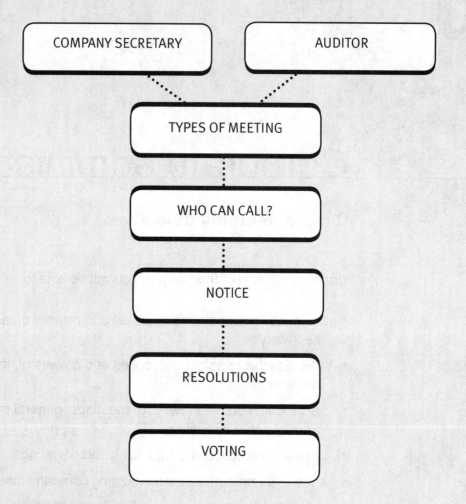

1 Company secretary

Introduction

Every public company must have a qualified company secretary. Private companies may choose to appoint a secretary, but are not obliged to do so.

The secretary is usually appointed and removed by the directors.

Qualifications

The secretary of a **public** company must be **qualified** under one of the following conditions:

- They must have held the office of company secretary in a public limited company (plc) for at least three out of the preceding five years.

- They must be a solicitor, barrister or member of ICAEW, ACCA, CIMA, ICSA, CIPFA.

- They must appear to be capable of discharging the functions by virtue of another position or qualification.

Duties

There are no statutory duties, therefore the duties will be whatever the board decides. The company secretary will typically undertake the following:

- check that documentation is in order
- make returns to the registrar
- keep registers
- give notice and keep minutes of meetings
- countersign documents to which the company seal is affixed.

Powers

The company secretary has the authority to bind the company in contract. There are two types of authority:

- actual authority – this is the authority delegated by the board
- apparent authority regarding contracts of an administrative nature.

Panorama Developments (Guildford) v Fidelis Furnishing Fabrics (1971)

The company secretary ordered services for his own, not the company's, use. It was held that the contract was binding on the company as the contract was of the sort that a company secretary should be able to carry out.

'He is no longer a mere clerk…He is entitled to sign contracts connected with the administrative side of a company's affairs, such as employing staff, and ordering cars, and so forth.'

However, two other cases indicate that there is a limit to the company secretary's authority:

- It does not extend to making commercial as opposed to administrative contracts: **Re Maidstone Building Provisions (1971)**.
- It does not usually carry the authority to borrow money: **Re Cleadon Trust Ltd (1938)**.

Test your understanding 1

In relation to the company secretary, which one of the following statements is correct?

A   Both a public and a private company must have a company secretary.

B   The company secretary is appointed by the members.

C   In a public company the company secretary must be qualified.

D   Company secretaries can bind companies in a contract if acting outside their actual or apparent authority.

2 The auditor

Qualifications

The auditor must be either:

- a member of recognised supervisory body (ICAEW, ICAS or ACCA) and eligible under their rules, or

- qualified by a similar overseas body and authorised by the Department for Business, Innovation and Skills.

The auditor must not be:

- an officer or employee of the company

- the partner of an officer or employee of the company.

Appointment

The auditors should generally be appointed by the shareholders by ordinary resolution. However, the directors can appoint the company's first auditor and fill casual vacancies.

A company must inform the Secretary of State if it has failed to appoint an auditor within 28 days of circulating its accounts. The Secretary of State has power to appoint an auditor in those circumstances.

Audit exemption for small companies

For financial years starting on or after 6 April 2008, to qualify for total audit exemption a company must:

- have a turnover of not more than £6.5m; and
- have gross assets not more than £3.26m.

However, these exemptions do not apply to public companies, banking or insurance companies or those subject to a statute-based regulatory regime.

Resignation

An auditor can resign at any time by giving written notice to the company: s516 CA06.

The resignation is effective from the date it is delivered to the company's registered office, or from a specified later date. To be effective it must be accompanied by the statement required by s519 (see below).

A company whose auditor resigns is required to inform the registrar: s517 CA06. Failure to do so is an offence.

Under s518 CA06, an auditor who resigns can require the directors to convene a general meeting to consider his explanation of the circumstances that led to his resignation. The directors have 21 days to send out a notice convening a meeting and it must be held within 28 days of the notice.

Removal

An auditor can be removed by ordinary resolution: s510 CA06. The resolution must be passed at a general meeting; a written resolution cannot be used to remove an auditor.

Special notice of the resolution is needed (i.e. 28 days). The company must send a copy of the resolution to the auditor and he has the right to make a statement of his case. The company then has to circulate his statement to the shareholders. However, if time does not allow for circulation, the statement can be read out at the meeting.

Notice of the resolution removing the auditor must be sent to the Registrar within 14 days.

Statement by departing auditor

Under s519 CA06, a departing auditor is required to make a statement and to deposit it with the company:

- For quoted companies, this statement must explain the circumstances surrounding his departure.

- For other public companies and all private companies, it should explain the circumstances surrounding his departure, unless the auditor thinks that there is no need for them to be brought to the attention of the shareholders or creditors. In that case, the statement should state that there are no such circumstances.

Unless there are no circumstances to be brought to the attention of shareholders and creditors, the company is obliged to circulate the statement to everyone to whom it needs to send the annual accounts. It must do this within 14 days of receiving it.

If the company does not want to circulate the statement, it can apply to the court for an order that it need not circulate the statement.

Duties

The auditor has a statutory duty to report to the members on whether the accounts:

- give a true and fair view and

- have been properly prepared in accordance with the Companies Act and the relevant financial reporting framework.

The auditor must investigate and form an opinion as to whether:

- proper books of accounting records have been kept

- proper returns adequate for their audit have been received from branches not visited by them

- the accounts are in agreement with the books of account and returns

- the information given in the directors' report is consistent with the accounts.

If the auditor is dissatisfied with the findings of his investigation he must qualify the audit report.

The report (whether qualified or unqualified) must state the name of the audit firm, or if an individual has been appointed as auditor, his name. Where the auditor is a firm, the senior statutory auditor must sign the report in his own name on behalf of the firm.

Under s507 CA06 it is a criminal offence to knowingly or recklessly cause an audit report to include anything that is misleading, false or deceptive, or to omit a required statement of a problem with the accounts or audit. The offence carries an unlimited fine.

There could also be liability under the tort of negligence for including misleading accounts (see **Chapter 3**).

Companies Act liability for auditor's report and audited accounts

s507 of the Companies Act 2006 (s507 CA06) makes it an offence for an auditor to recklessly cause an auditor's report to contain any matter that is misleading or false to a material extent. The offence is punishable by a fine.

s532 CA06 makes any provision exempting auditors from or indemnifying them against liability for negligence void in relation to providing audited accounts.

s534 CA06 provides that a company may enter into a liability limitation agreement with an auditor, limiting his liability for negligence (among other things) in the course of auditing accounts.

Powers

The auditor has the right to:

- receive notice of, attend and speak at general meetings.

- access the books at all times

- require such information and explanations from the company's officers and employees as the auditor thinks fit for the performance of his duties (it is a criminal offence to fail to provide the information requested, unless it was not reasonably practicable to do so).

Test your understanding 2

If a company's auditor is to be removed before his term of office expires, what type of resolution is required and what period of notice must be given?

3 Meetings

Annual general meeting (AGM)

Timing	Public companies must hold an AGM within the six months following their financial year end: s336.
Failure to hold	The company and every officer in default can be fined if an AGM is not held. Any member can apply to the Department for Business, Innovation and Skills to convene the meeting.
Private companies	Private companies are not required to hold an AGM.
Notice	**21 days' notice** is required unless every member entitled to attend and vote agrees to a shorter period. The notice must state that the meeting is an AGM.
Business	Usual business includes: • consider accounts • appoint auditors • elect directors • declare dividends.
Resolutions	• Members holding at least 5% of the voting rights (or at least 100 members holding on average £100 paid-up capital) have the right to propose a resolution for the AGM agenda and to require the company to circulate details of the resolution to all members. • If the members' request is received before the financial year end, the members are not required to cover the costs of circulation. Otherwise, the members requesting the resolution must deposit a sum to cover the company's costs.

General meetings (GM)

Timing	Held **whenever required**. Must be held by a plc if a serious loss of capital has occurred, i.e. net assets have fallen to less than half of the called up share capital.
Notice	At least **14 days**.
Business	The person who requisitions the meeting sets the agenda.

Class meetings

Purpose	Meeting of a class of shareholders, usually to consider a variation of their class rights.
Procedure	Notice, etc. as for general meetings.
Quorum	Two persons holding or representing by proxy at least one-third in nominal value of the issued shares of the class in question.

4 Calling a meeting

Who can call a meeting?

Directors	The articles usually delegate the power to the directors
Members	Members may require the directors to call a GM if they hold at least 5% of the paid up voting capital. The directors must call a meeting within 21 days of receiving a requisition. The meeting must take place within 28 days of the notice convening the meeting. If the directors do not call a meeting, the members who requested the meeting (or any members holding over 50% of the total voting rights) may themselves call a meeting to take place within three months of the initial request and recover their expenses from the company.
Resigning auditor	A resigning auditor may require the directors to convene a meeting so he can explain the reasons for his resignation.
Court	A court can call a meeting on the application of a director or member where it would otherwise be impracticable e.g. to break a deadlock.

Notice

Who must receive notice?	Every member and every director: s310.
Failure to give notice	Accidental failure to give notice to one or more persons does not invalidate the meeting: s313.
Contents of notice	Date, time and place of the meeting. The general nature of the business to be transacted. The text of any special resolutions.
Length of notice period	**AGM – 21 days** Less if every member entitled to attend and vote agrees. **GM – 14 days** Less if members holding at least 95% of shares agree. (Where company is private, can be reduced to 90%).
Special notice	Requires 28 days' notice. Required for the removal of a director or auditor

5 Resolutions

Resolutions are the way in which companies take decisions. They are voted on by the members in person or by proxy. There are three types of resolution:

Type	% required to pass	To Registrar?	Purpose of resolution
Special	≥75%	Yes – within 15 days	• Alter name. • Wind up company. • Alter articles. • Reduce share capital.
Ordinary	>50%	Only if required by statute	Used whenever the law or the articles do not require a special resolution.

Written (private companies only)	Same majority as required in GM	Yes if a 75% majority is required	The purpose can be anything apart from resolutions requiring special notice. Members cannot revoke their agreement.
			The date of the resolution is the date when the necessary majority has been reached.
			The resolution must generally be passed within 28 days from its circulation.

Test your understanding 3

Fill in the gaps:

(1) An annual general meeting requires ……..days' notice.

(2) Members may require the directors to call a GM if they hold at least ….% of the paid up voting capital

(3) Special notice requires …. days' notice.

(4) A special resolution must be filed with the Registrar within …. days.

6 Procedure at meetings

A **quorum** is the minimum number of members that needs to be present at a meeting in order to validate business. It is generally two persons who can be members or proxies: s318 CA06.

Voting is by a **show of hands** initially, unless a poll is demanded. A show of hands means one member one vote, irrespective of the number of shares held.

A **poll** may be demanded by members holding at least 10% of the total voting rights (or by not fewer than 5 members having the right to vote on the resolution). A poll means one vote per share. The result of a poll replaces the result of the previous show of hands. Quoted companies must publish the results of polls on their website: s341 CA06.

Members have a statutory right under s 324 CA06 to appoint one or more persons as their ' **proxy** '. A proxy can attend meetings, vote and speak on behalf of the member for whom he is acting.

7 Chapter summary

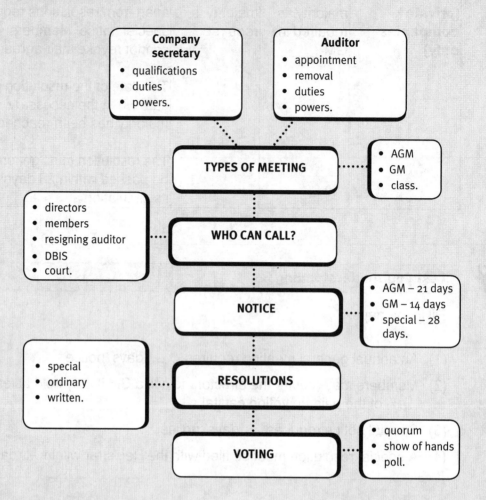

Company secretary
- qualifications
- duties
- powers.

Auditor
- appointment
- removal
- duties
- powers.

TYPES OF MEETING
- AGM
- GM
- class.

- directors
- members
- resigning auditor
- DBIS
- court.

WHO CAN CALL?

NOTICE
- AGM – 21 days
- GM – 14 days
- special – 28 days.

- special
- ordinary
- written.

RESOLUTIONS

VOTING
- quorum
- show of hands
- poll.

Test your understanding answers

Test your understanding 1

C Only a public company is required to have a company secretary. The secretary is appointed by the directors and must be qualified. To bind a company, the secretary must be acting within his actual and/or apparent authority.

Test your understanding 2

Removal of an auditor before his term of office expires requires an ordinary resolution of which 28 days' special notice has been given.

Test your understanding 3

(1) An annual general meeting requires **21** days' notice.

(2) Members may require the directors to call a GM if they hold at least **5%** of the paid up voting capital

(3) Special notice requires **28** days' notice.

(4) A special resolution must be filed with the Registrar within **15** days.

Insolvency

Chapter learning objectives

Upon completion of this chapter you will be able to:

- explain the meaning of and the procedure involved in voluntary liquidation

- explain the meaning of and the procedure involved in compulsory liquidation

- explain administration as an alternative to liquidation.

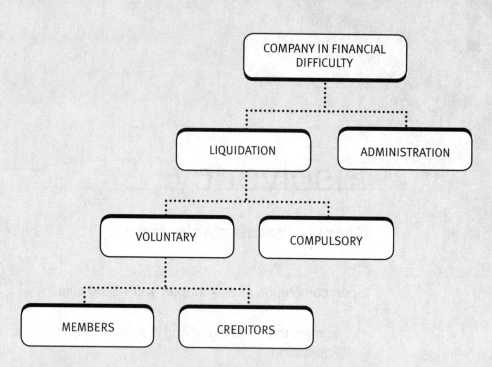

1 Voluntary liquidation: s84 Insolvency Act (IA 1986)

Introduction

If a company finds itself in financial difficulty, the two main options available to it are:

- Administration. This aims to rescue the company so that it may continue trading as a going concern.

- Liquidation. This winds up the company, thus bringing its life to an end.

A voluntary liquidation occurs where the members pass a resolution to go into liquidation. The type of resolution needed depends on the circumstances:

- Where the period fixed for the duration of the company expires or an event occurs upon which the articles provide that a company should be wound up, an **ordinary resolution** must be passed.

- A **special resolution** must be passed if the company is being wound up for any other reason.

There are two types of voluntary liquidation:

- A members' voluntary liquidation is used where the company is solvent.

- A creditors' voluntary liquidation is used where the company is insolvent.

Members' voluntary winding up

> WINDING UP COMMENCES FROM THE PASSING OF THE APPROPRIATE RESOLUTION (S86 IA 1986).

> THE DIRECTORS MAKE A **DECLARATION OF SOLVENCY** UNDER S 89 IA 1986 STATING THAT THEY ARE OF THE OPINION THAT THE COMPANY WILL BE ABLE TO PAY ITS DEBTS WITHIN 12 MONTHS. IT IS A CRIMINAL OFFENCE TO MAKE A FALSE DECLARATION.

> THE MEMBERS **APPOINT A NAMED INSOLVENCY PRACTITIONER AS LIQUIDATOR** (S91 IA 1986).

> THE LIQUIDATOR IS RESPONSIBLE FOR REALISING THE ASSETS AND DISTRIBUTING THE PROCEEDS.

> THE LIQUIDATOR PRESENTS HIS REPORT TO A **FINAL MEETING** OF THE MEMBERS (S93 IA 1986).

> THE LIQUIDATOR **INFORMS THE REGISTRAR** OF THE FINAL MEETING AND SUBMITS A COPY OF HIS REPORT (S94(3) IA 1986).

> THE REGISTRAR REGISTERS THE REPORT AND THE COMPANY IS **DISSOLVED** 3 MONTHS LATER.

Creditors' voluntary winding up

WINDING UP COMMENCES FROM THE PASSING OF THE APPROPRIATE RESOLUTION (S86 IA 1986).

THERE IS NO DECLARATION OF SOLVENCY AS THE COMPANY IS INSOLVENT. A **MEETING OF CREDITORS MUST BE HELD WITHIN 14 DAYS** OF THE RESOLUTION TO LIQUIDATE (S98 IA 1986). THE DIRECTORS MUST SUBMIT A **STATEMENT OF THE COMPANY'S AFFAIRS** (S99 IA 1986).

BOTH THE MEMBERS AND THE CREDITORS HAVE THE RIGHT TO **APPOINT A NAMED INSOLVENCY PRACTITIONER AS LIQUIDATOR** (S100 IA 1986). THE CREDITORS' NOMINEE PREVAILS UNLESS THEY HAVE NOT MADE THEIR APPOINTMENT (S100(2)). THE MEMBERS AND CREDITORS MAY APPOINT UP TO FIVE PERSONS TO SERVE ON A **LIQUIDATION COMMITTEE** (S101 IA 1986).

THE LIQUIDATOR IS RESPONSIBLE FOR REALISING THE ASSETS AND DISTRIBUTING THE PROCEEDS.

THE LIQUIDATOR PRESENTS HIS REPORT TO THE **FINAL MEETINGS** OF MEMBERS AND CREDITORS (S105(2) IA 1986).

THE LIQUIDATOR **INFORMS THE REGISTRAR** OF THE FINAL MEETING(S) AND SUBMITS A COPY OF HIS REPORT (S106(3) IA 1986).

THE REGISTRAR REGISTERS THE REPORT AND THE COMPANY IS **DISSOLVED**.

Converting a members' voluntary liquidation into a creditors' voluntary liquidation

If the liquidator discovers that the company's debts will not be paid in full within the time specified in the declaration of solvency, he must convert the members' voluntary liquidation into a creditors' voluntary liquidation. This is done by convening a meeting of the company's creditors.

At the meeting the liquidator must:

- lay before the creditors a statement of affairs

- invite the creditors to appoint a different insolvency practitioner as liquidator

- invite the creditors to appoint a liquidation committee.

Test your understanding 1

Compare and contrast the characteristics of a members' voluntary winding up and a creditors' voluntary winding up.

2 Compulsory liquidation

Grounds for winding up: s122 IA 1986

A compulsory winding up commences when a petition for a winding up order is presented to the court. The possible grounds for the petition are set out in s122 IA 1986:

- The company has passed a special resolution to be wound up by the court.

- A public company has not been issued with a trading certificate within a year of incorporation.

- The company has not commenced business within a year of being incorporated or has suspended its business for over a year.

- The company is unable to pay its debts. A company is deemed to be unable to pay its debts where a creditor who is owed at least £750 has served a written demand for payment and the company has failed to pay the sum due within three weeks.

- It is just and equitable to wind up the company. However, the court will not make an order under this ground if some other more reasonable remedy is available.

Petitioners

The following persons may petition the court for a compulsory liquidation:

- the company itself

- the Official Receiver, who is a civil servant in The Insolvency Service and is an officer of the Court

- the Department for Business, Innovation and Skills

- a contributory. This is any person who is liable to contribute to the assets of the company when it is being wound up. (The contributory must prove that the company is solvent).

- a creditor who is owed at least £750.

Effect of winding up

The winding-up petition has the following effects:

- All actions for the recovery of debt against the company are stopped.

- Any floating charges crystallise.

- Any legal proceedings against the company are halted, and none may start unless leave is granted from the court.

- The company ceases to carry on business except where it is necessary to complete the winding up, e.g. to complete work-in-progress.

- The powers of the directors cease, although the directors remain in office.

- The employees are automatically made redundant, but the liquidator can re-employ them to help him complete the winding up.

Subsequent procedures

> ON THE MAKING OF THE WINDING-UP ORDER, THE OFFICIAL RECEIVER BECOMES LIQUIDATOR (S136(2) IA 1986).

⋮

> WITHIN 12 WEEKS, THE OFFICIAL RECEIVER WILL SUMMON MEETINGS OF THE CREDITORS AND CONTRIBUTORIES IN ORDER TO APPOINT A LICENSED INSOLVENCY PRACTITIONER TO TAKE OVER THE JOB OF LIQUIDATOR AND TO APPOINT A LIQUIDATION COMMITTEE (S136(5)(A) IA 1986).

⋮

> THE LIQUIDATOR IS RESPONSIBLE FOR REALISING THE ASSETS AND DISTRIBUTING THE PROCEEDS (S143 IA 1986).

⋮

> THE LIQUIDATOR PRESENTS HIS REPORT TO **FINAL MEETINGS** OF THE MEMBERS AND CREDITORS (S146 IA 1986).

⋮

> THE LIQUIDATOR **INFORMS THE REGISTRAR** OF THE FINAL MEETING(S) AND SUBMITS A COPY OF HIS REPORT.

⋮

> THE REGISTRAR REGISTERS THE REPORT AND THE COMPANY IS **DISSOLVED** 3 MONTHS LATER.

Test your understanding 2

Fill in the gaps in the following sentences:

The possible grounds for a compulsory liquidation petition are set out in .... :

A   The company has passed a .... resolution to be wound up by the court.

B   A .... company has not been issued with a trading certificate within .... of incorporation.

C   A creditor who is owed at least .... has served a written demand for payment and the company has failed to pay the sum due within ....

D   It is .... to wind up the company.

Application of assets

The liquidator must repay debts in the following order:

- fixed charge-holders.

- expenses of liquidation.

- preferential creditors
    - wages or salaries due in the four months preceding the commencement of winding up (maximum £800 per employee)
    - all accrued holiday pay.

    All preferential creditors rank equally amongst themselves.

- floating charge-holders.

- unsecured creditors – rank equally amongst themselves. The Enterprise Act 2002 introduced into the Insolvency Act 1986 a ring-fencing mechanism where part of assets which are subject to a floating charge are available to unsecured creditors. The amount ring-fenced is 50% of the first £10,000, plus 20% of the rest up to a maximum ring-fenced fund of £600,000.

- post-liquidation interest.

- members – declared but unpaid dividends.

- members – return of capital (in accordance with class rights).

- any surplus to be distributed to members.

Test your understanding 3

Sharepak Ltd is being wound-up. Rank the following persons in the order in which they will be paid by the liquidator:

Preference shareholders.

Mrs Patel – an employee who is owed holiday pay of £1,000.

Barlloyd Bank – which has a charge over all the company's current assets.

Midwest Bank – which has a charge on the company's headquarters.

HMRC – which is owed corporation tax of £15,000.

Ordinary shareholders .

3 Administration

Purpose

Administration involves the appointment of an insolvency practitioner, known as an administrator, to manage the affairs, business and property of a company. It was first introduced by Schedule 16 IA 1986, but has subsequently been amended by the Enterprise Act 2002.

Administration is often used as an alternative to putting a company into liquidation, e.g. to:

- rescue a company in financial difficulty with the aim of allowing it to continue as a going concern
- achieve a better result for the creditors than would be likely if the company were to be wound up
- realise property to pay one or more secured or preferential creditors.

Who can appoint an administrator?

An administrator can be appointed by any of the following persons:

- the court in response to a petition by, e.g. a creditor, the directors or the company itself
- the holder of a qualifying floating charge over the company's assets
- the company or its directors provided that winding up has not already begun.

The court will only agree to appoint an administrator if it is satisfied that:

- the company is or is likely to become unable to pay its debts, and
- the administration order is likely to achieve its objectives

Consequences of administration

The appointment of an administrator has the following effects:

- the rights of creditors to enforce any security over the company's assets are suspended
- any petition for winding up is dismissed
- no resolution may be passed to wind up the company
- the directors still continue in office, but their powers are suspended.

Carrying out the administration

The administrator has a number of tasks:

- He is the company's agent, but must act in the best interests of all the company's creditors.
- He has wide powers to manage the business and property of the company, including the power to bring and defend legal proceedings, sell assets and borrow money.
- He has the power to remove and replace directors and employees. If an employee's contract is not adopted by the administrator within 14 days, that employee is made redundant.
- He must draw up a statement of his proposals, which must be approved at a meeting of creditors within eight weeks of the commencement of administration.
- If the meeting does not approve the proposals, the court may dismiss the administrator or make such provisions as it sees fit.
- If the meeting approves the proposals, the administrator can carry them out.

Ending the administration

The administration will end when it is completed or when the administrator is discharged by the court:

- The administration must normally be completed within 12 months of the date on which it commenced. However, this term can be extended with the consent of the court or the secured creditors.

- The administrator may apply to the court for discharge at any time. He must make an application when the purpose of the order has been achieved. He must also notify the registrar and all of the creditors.

4 Chapter summary

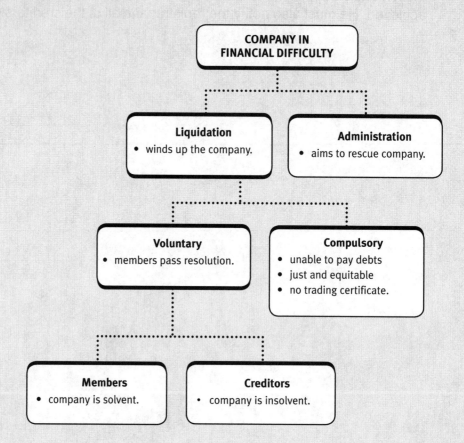

COMPANY IN FINANCIAL DIFFICULTY

Liquidation
- winds up the company.

Administration
- aims to rescue company.

Voluntary
- members pass resolution.

Compulsory
- unable to pay debts
- just and equitable
- no trading certificate.

Members
- company is solvent.

Creditors
- company is insolvent.

Test your understanding answers

Test your understanding 1

A voluntary winding up takes place when the company resolves by special resolution to be wound up for any cause whatsoever: S84 Insolvency Act 1986.

In both cases of voluntary winding up the passing of the resolution, which must be advertised within 14 days in the London Gazette, has the following consequences:

I   The winding up commences from the time of the passing of the resolution.

II   The company ceases to carry on business, except in so far as is necessary for its beneficial winding up.

III All transfers of shares, except those made with the concurrence of the liquidator, are void.

In the case of a members' voluntary winding up, the directors make a declaration of solvency stating that after full inquiry into the company's affairs they are of the opinion that the company will be able to pay its debts within 12 months of the commencement of the winding up. In a creditors' voluntary winding up, such a declaration is not possible owing to the circumstances leading to the winding up. In a members' voluntary winding up, the liquidator is appointed by the members and is accountable to them. In a creditors' voluntary winding up, both members and creditors have the right to nominate a liquidator and, in the event of dispute, subject to the right of appeal to the courts, the creditors' nominee prevails. Here the liquidator is primarily accountable to the creditors.

In a creditors' voluntary winding up, the resolution is followed by a creditors' meeting where it is possible for a liquidation committee to be appointed. Such meetings form no part of a members' voluntary winding up.

Test your understanding 2

The possible grounds for a compulsory liquidation petition are set out in s122 IA 1986:

A   The company has passed a special resolution to be wound up by the court.

B   A public company has not been issued with a trading certificate within a year of incorporation.

C   A creditor who is owed at least £750 has served a written demand for payment and the company has failed to pay the sum due within three weeks

D   It is just and equitable to wind up the company.

Test your understanding 3

The liquidator will repay in the following order:

Midwest Bank – the charge on the company's headquarters is a fixed charge.

Mrs Patel – employees who are owed holiday pay are classed as preferential creditors.

Barlloyd Bank – the charge over all the company's current assets is a floating charge.

HMRC – the Enterprise Act 2002 removed HMRC from the category of preferential creditors. They now rank as unsecured creditors.

Preference shareholders.

Ordinary shareholders – the ordinary shareholders will share in any surplus assets.

12

Corporate governance

Chapter learning objectives

Upon completion of this chapter you will be able to:

- explain the idea of corporate governance
- recognise the extra-legal codes of corporate governance
- identify and explain the legal regulation of corporate governance.

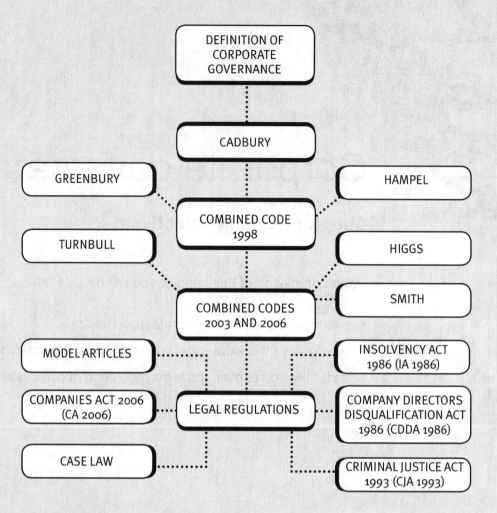

1 Introduction

Definition

Corporate governance is the system by which companies are directed and controlled.

It covers topics such as:

- how power is divided between the board and the shareholders
- the accountability of the board to the members
- the rules and procedures for making decisions
- the provision of controls for companies.

Corporate governance provides the structure through which the company's objectives are met, the means of attaining those objectives and monitoring performance.

Interaction of ethics, governance and company law

	Compliance requirements	Penalties
Law	The law must always be obeyed.	Penalties for infringement of the law may be civil or criminal. Civil remedies may allow the company to recover funds from directors who breach their legal obligations. A fine and/or imprisonment might result from certain criminal infringements.
Corporate governance	The stock exchange rules require listed companies to comply with the Combined Code (see below), it imposes disclosure requirements. If a listed company does not comply, it must specify the provisions with which it has not complied, and give reasons for its non-compliance. Unlisted companies are under no obligation to comply, although it is considered best practice to do so.	There are no formal penalties for non-compliance. However, the company may suffer loss of reputation and receive bad publicity.
Ethics	It is said that ethics begin where the law ends. If an action is legal, individuals generally have freedom of choice as to their conduct. However, good ethical behaviour may be above that demanded by the law. Accountants are expected to follow the code of ethics published by their professional body.	An individual who behaves unethically may suffer loss of reputation, dismissal from their job and sanctions may possibly be imposed by their professional body.

Expandable text

The need for corporate governance

During the late 1980s a number of large UK public companies failed, some of them as a result of large-scale fraud by their directors.

These failures reduced public confidence in financial reporting and auditing. Many people believed that company directors regarded accounting standards as a set of rules to be circumvented and 'creative accounting' was implicated in several company liquidations:

- Directors were pressurising auditors to accept the use of 'creative accounting' schemes. As the auditors often received extra remuneration from the company for consultancy work, disagreement with the directors in the audit process could result in the loss of this additional income. This situation often compromised the auditors' independence.

- There was no clear framework for ensuring that directors reviewed internal controls in their companies.

- There was a perceived lack of accountability for excessive directors' remuneration.

A need to strengthen the systems of corporate governance used by UK companies was perceived. This need led to the establishment of the Cadbury Committee, which is considered in the next section.

Test your understanding 1

Which one of the following is correct?

A   It is a criminal offence for listed companies to fail to comply with the Combined Code.

B   A listed public company has complied with the Combined Code if it produces a report explaining why it has not complied with its recommendations.

C   The Combined Code has no status and may be ignored by all companies.

D   A public company may be sued for breach of statutory duty if it fails to comply with the Combined Code.

2 The history of corporate governance in the UK

Expandable text

The Cadbury Committee

Set up by	The Financial Reporting Council (FRC), the London Stock Exchange and the accountancy profession.
Objective	To help raise the standards of corporate governance and the level of confidence in financial reporting and auditing by setting out clearly the respective responsibilities of those involved and what was expected of them.
Publication	A **Code of Best Practice (1992)** was designed to achieve the necessary high standards of corporate behaviour.
Recommended	• It is desirable to separate the role of chief executive and chairman. • The board should include sufficient non-executive directors (NEDs) for their views to carry significant weight. • An audit committee should be appointed to review the financial statements before their submission to the full board. • A remuneration committee consisting wholly or mainly of NEDs should set the remuneration of executive directors. • The imposition of a three-year maximum term on executive directors' service contracts.
Outcome	The Stock Exchange required all listed companies to state whether or not they had complied with the Code and to give reasons for any areas of non-compliance. It also required the company's statement of compliance to be reviewed by the auditors before publication.

The Greenbury Report

Set up by	The CBI in 1995.
Objective	To draw up guidelines on directors' remuneration, which was perceived to be excessive and did not seem to be linked to company performance.
Publication	A code of best practice in determining and accounting for directors' remuneration.
Outcome	All listed companies registered in the UK were required to comply with the Code. Their annual reports had to include a statement about their directors' remuneration. Any areas of non-compliance had to be explained and justified.

The Hampel Report

Issued	January 1998.
Objective	To restrict the regulatory burden facing companies and substitute broad principles (rather than detailed regulations) where practicable.
Summary	A board must not approach the various corporate governance requirements in a compliance mentality: the so-called 'tick-box' approach. Good corporate governance is not achieved by satisfying a checklist. Directors must comply with the substance as well as the letter of all best practice pronouncements.
Outcome	After publishing its report, the Hampel Committee drew up a single Combined Code of Best Practice, incorporating the Cadbury, Greenbury and Hampel recommendations.

The 1998 Combined Code

Objective	To combine the accepted principles and best practice guidelines of Cadbury, Greenbury and Hampel into a single code.
Outcome	The Stock Exchange Listing Rules require a listed company in the UK to include the following in its annual report and accounts: • A narrative statement of **how it has applied the principles** set out in the Combined Code, providing explanation which enables its shareholders to evaluate how the principles have been applied. • A statement as to **whether or not it has complied** throughout the accounting period with the Combined Code provisions. If it has not complied, it must specify the provisions with which it has not complied, and give **reasons for any non-compliance**. This approach to compliance is known as 'comply or explain'.

The Turnbull Report

Issued	In 1999 by the ICAEW.
Objective	To give additional guidance to listed companies on how to implement the provisions of the Combined Code dealing with internal control, and board responsibility.
Summary	• The board should look forward and not just consider past performance. • Companies should keep their shareholders informed about risks. • Directors should be aware that the company must continually adapt to its changing environment. • Risks should be reviewed regularly.
Outcome	The Turnbull Guidance is appended to the 2003 Combined Code.

The Higgs Report

Issued	2003.
Objective	To develop guidelines for making NEDs more effective.
Outcome	Most of the report's recommendations were either written into the 2003 Combined Code or included in the best practice guidelines that are appended to it.

The Smith Report

Issued	2003.
Objective	To give guidance to company boards in making suitable arrangements for their audit committees and to assist directors serving on audit committees in carrying out their role.
Outcome	The report's recommendations are appended to the 2003 Combined Code.

Expandable text

The role of the NEDs

At the time of the Cadbury Report, there was a history in the UK of public companies being dominated by an all-powerful chief-executive/chairman. In addition, NEDs, where they existed at all, were often heavily outnumbered by executive directors.

The Cadbury Report recommended the separation of the roles of chief executive and chairman, although it did not state that the same person could never be both. The role of the chief executive is to take charge of the executive management and the company's business operations; the role of the chairman is to manage the board of directors.

Cadbury recommended that there should be sufficient independent NEDs for their views to carry sufficient weight. As their independence might be put at risk if they had to rely on the chairman or chief executive for their appointment, Cadbury recommended that initial interviews should be conducted through a nominations committee.

The role of the NEDs is to bring judgement and experience to the board that the executive directors might lack. In contrast to the executive directors, NEDs do not usually have a full-time relationship with the company. They are not employees and only receive directors' fees. They are expected to exert a measure of control over the executive directors to ensure that they run the company in the company's best interests (rather than their own). They should scrutinise the performance of management in meeting agreed goals and objectives and monitor the reporting of performance.

They are also responsible for determining appropriate levels of remuneration for the executive directors.

Note that as far as company law is concerned, there is no distinction between executive directors and NEDs. Both are subject to the same controls and liabilities.

3 The Combined Code on Corporate Governance

History

The Combined Code on Corporate Governance was first issued in 1998. It consisted of principles and provisions (best practice).

A revised version of the Code was issued in 2003. This revised Code consisted of main principles, supporting principles and provisions (practical requirements).

The most recent version, which applies to reporting years beginning on or after 1 November 2006, was issued by the Financial Reporting Council in June 2006. None of the main principles have been changed. There were a few minor changes, which are outlined later.

Contents

The Code is divided into two sections:

- Section one is for companies
- Section two is for institutional shareholders.

The section for companies is subdivided into four areas:

- directors
- directors' remuneration
- accountability and audit
- relations with shareholders.

The Code has three appendices:

- the Turnbull Guidance on internal audit
- the Smith Guidance on audit committees
- the Higgs Guidance on best practice.

The main principles of each section are outlined below.

Directors

(1) Every company should be headed by an effective board, which is collectively responsible for the success of the company.

(2) There should be a clear division of responsibilities at the head of the company between the running of the board and the executive responsibility for the running of the company's business. No one individual should have unfettered powers of decision.

(3) The board should include a balance of executive directors and NEDs (and in particular independent NEDs), such that no individual or small group of individuals can dominate the board's decision taking.

(4) There should be a formal, rigorous and transparent procedure for the appointment of new directors to the board.

(5) The board should be supplied in a timely manner with information in a form and of a quality appropriate to enable it to discharge its duties. All directors should receive induction on joining the board and should regularly update and refresh their skills and knowledge.

(6) The board should undertake a formal and rigorous annual evaluation of its own performance and that of its committees and individual directors.

(7) All directors should be submitted for re-election at regular intervals, subject to continued satisfactory performance. The board should ensure planned and progressive refreshing of the board.

Directors' remuneration

(1) Levels of remuneration should be sufficient to attract, retain and motivate directors of the quality required to run the company successfully, but a company should avoid paying more than is necessary for this purpose. A significant proportion of executive directors' remuneration should be structured so as to link rewards to corporate and individual performance.

(2) There should be a formal and transparent procedure for developing policy on executive remuneration and for fixing the remuneration packages of individual directors. No director should be involved in deciding his or her own remuneration.

The Code provides that service contracts and notice periods should not exceed one year.

Accountability and audit

(1) The board should present a balanced and understandable assessment of the company's position and prospects.

(2) The board should maintain a sound system of internal control to safeguard shareholders' investment and the company's assets.

(3) The board should establish formal and transparent arrangements for considering how they should apply the financial reporting and internal control principles and for maintaining an appropriate relationship with the company's auditors.

The Code provides that the board should establish an audit committee of at least three (or in the case of smaller companies two) members, who should all be independent non-executive directors. The board should satisfy itself that at least one member of the audit committee has recent and relevant financial experience.

The committee should meet at least three times during the year at times coinciding with key dates within the financial reporting and audit cycle.

Relations with shareholders

(1) There should be a dialogue with shareholders based on the mutual understanding of objectives. The board as a whole has responsibility for ensuring that a satisfactory dialogue with shareholders takes place.

(2) The board should use the annual general meeting (AGM) to communicate with investors and to encourage their participation.

Institutional shareholders

(1) Institutional shareholders should enter into a dialogue with companies based on the mutual understanding of objectives.

(2) When evaluating companies' governance arrangements, particularly those relating to board structure and composition, institutional shareholders should give due weight to all relevant factors drawn to their attention.

(3) Institutional shareholders have a responsibility to make considered use of their votes.

The 2006 Combined Code

The FRC issued a new version of the code on 27 June 2006. The new version contains a few changes, e.g.:

- The restriction on a company chairman serving on a remuneration committee has been relaxed. However, it is still recommended that the chairman should not chair the committee.

- A 'vote withheld' option should be included on proxy forms so that investors can indicate reservations about resolutions that they do not wish to vote against.

- A recommendation that companies publish on their website the details of proxies lodged at a general meeting where votes are taken on a show of hands.

Both the 2003 and 2006 versions of the Combined Code are available online at www.frc.org.uk/corporate/combinedcode.cfm

Rules-based versus principles-based approaches to governance

The Combined Code is a set of principles, rather than a set of rules. It requires directors to describe in their own words the way in which they have applied the general principles of corporate governance.

A principles-based approach to governance has the following advantages and disadvantages.

Advantages

- Because the directors report on the actual circumstances of their own company, the report should be more meaningful than one based on specific detailed requirements.

- A code of practice can be changed much more easily than statutory requirements. This means that the Combined Code can be updated to respond to changing conditions and changing expectations of shareholders and others.

- A principles-based approach encourages the directors to follow the spirit of the Code; whereas a rules-based approach may result in a tick-boxes mentality. This means that under a rules-based approach the directors may follow the letter of the rules, rather than their spirit.

Disadvantages

- A principles-based approach tends to result in general, meaningless statements.

- It may be difficult for the directors to see whether they have met the specific requirements of the Code.

Test your understanding 2

A   **Define the term 'corporate governance'. (Your answer must not exceed 15 words.)**

B   **Which three reports are appended to the current Combined Code?**

C   **Complete the gaps. The following persons cannot be regarded as independent:**

- anyone who has been an employee of the company in the previous ......years.

- anyone who has had a material business relationship with the company in the previous ......years.

- anyone who has served on the board for more than ......years.

D   **Complete the following sentence in no more than 20 words:**

The Stock Exchange rules require listed companies to comply with the Combined Code. If it does not comply, the company must...

4 The legal regulation of corporate governance

Introduction

The legislation covering corporate governance has been covered in earlier chapters. The following table gives you an indication of where to find the relevant provisions:

Model articles	Set out the internal constitution of the company, e.g. allowing the company and/or the board to negotiate directors' service contracts.
CA 2006	Provides the main framework for the legislation affecting companies. Specifies that a director's service contract cannot exceed two years unless first approved by the members. Specifies the duties that directors owe to their companies.
IA 1986	Established liability for wrongful and fraudulent trading. Permits the liquidator to set aside transactions at an undervalue or where the company has given a preference.

CDDA 1986	Allows the court to disqualify someone from being a director if they: • have persistently breached the companies legislation • are found to be unfit, or • are convicted of an indictable offence in connection with the promotion, formation, management or liquidation of a company.
CJA 1993	Contains the legislation on insider dealing.

The Sarbanes-Oxley Act 2002

The Sarbanes-Oxley Act 2002 is a US law that applies to all companies (including foreign companies) that have a listing on the US stock exchange.

It was introduced in the wake of corporate scandals such as the unexpected collapse of Enron and WorldCom.

The US approach to corporate governance is a statutory rules-based one. This differs from the UK where it is principles-based with an emphasis on voluntary compliance. The Surbanes-Oxley Act requires all companies with a listing in the US to include in their annual report a certificate vouching for the accuracy of the financial statements. This certificate must be signed by the company's principal executive officer and principal financial officer.

Test your understanding 3

A   **What is the maximum permitted length of a director's service contract according to:**

    I   the Companies Act 2006

    II   the Combined Code?

B   **To which companies does the Sarbanes-Oxley Act apply?**

KAPLAN PUBLISHING

5 Chapter summary

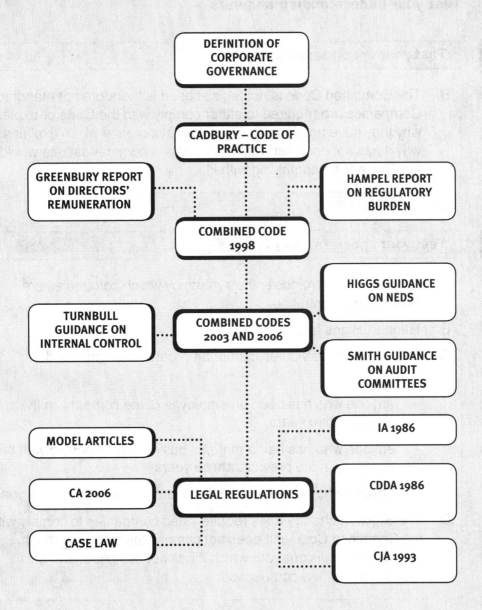

Test your understanding answers

Test your understanding 1

B   The Combined Code is not legislation. It is therefore not mandatory. Companies are required to either comply with the Code or explain why they have not done so. Therefore a company which explains why it has not complied with the Code's recommendations would nonetheless be complying with it!

Test your understanding 2

A   Corporate governance is the system by which companies are directed and controlled.

B   Turnbull, Higgs and Smith.

C   The following individuals cannot be regarded as independent:

–   anyone who has been an employee of the company in the previous **five** years

–   anyone who has had a material business relationship with the company in the previous **three** years

–   anyone who has served on the board for more than **nine** years.

D   The Stock Exchange rules require listed companies to comply with the Combined Code. If it does not comply, the company must specify the provisions with which it has not complied, and give reasons for its non-compliance

Test your understanding 3

A   The maximum permitted length of a director's service contract is:

I   two years according to the Companies Act 2006

II   one year according to the Combined Code.

B   The Sarbanes-Oxley Act applies to all companies (including foreign companies) that have a listing on the US stock exchange.

Fraudulent behaviour

Chapter learning objectives

Upon completion of this chapter you will be able to:

- recognise the nature and legal control over insider dealing
- recognise the nature and legal control over money laundering
- discuss potential criminal activity in the operation, management and winding up of companies
- distinguish between fraudulent and wrongful trading.

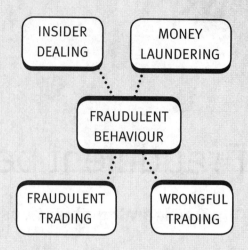

1 Insider dealing

The value of a share reflects the profitability and future prospects of a company. This type of information is usually only available to a prospective purchaser after it has been made available publicly. However, if a prospective purchaser could gain access to such information before it was made public, he could anticipate which way the price was likely to move and thereby make a profit. This is known as 'insider dealing'. Insider dealing has been made a criminal offence as it is perceived to undermine the integrity of the stock market.

Legislation

Insider dealing is a crime under part V of the Criminal Justice Act 1993.

The offences

The Criminal Justice Act 1993 sets out the three distinct offences in s52.

An individual will be guilty of insider dealing if they have information as an insider and:

- they deal in price-affected securities on the basis of that information
- they encourage another person to deal in price-affected securities in relation to that information
- they disclose the information to anyone other than in the proper performance of their employment, office or profession.

Dealing

Dealing is defined in s55 as acquiring or disposing of securities, whether as a principal or agent, or agreeing to acquire securities.

Inside information

S56 defines inside information as information which:

- relates to particular securities or to a particular issuer of securities
- is specific or precise
- has not been made public
- if made public would be likely to have a significant effect on the price.

Insider

S57 states that a person has information as an insider only if they know that it is inside information and they have it from an inside source.

A person has information from an inside source if:

- he has it through being a director, employee or shareholder of an issuer of securities
- he has it through having access to information by virtue of his employment, office or profession.

Consequences

On summary conviction an individual found guilty of insider dealing is liable to a fine not exceeding the statutory maximum and/or a maximum of six months imprisonment.

On indictment the penalty is an unlimited fine and/or a maximum of seven years imprisonment.

If the individual concerned is a director, he is in breach of his fiduciary duty and may be liable to account to the company for any profit made.

Test your understanding 1

(1) **Which statute contains the legislation on insider dealing?**

(2) **What are the three sub-categories of the offence of insider dealing?**

(3) **What are the three general defences to a charge of insider dealing?**

2 Money laundering

Definition

Money laundering is the process by which the proceeds of crime are converted into assets which appear to have a legal rather than an illegal source. The aim of disguising the source of the property is to allow the holder to enjoy it free from suspicion as to its source.

Legislation

Money laundering is primarily regulated by the Proceeds of Crime Act 2002.

The legislation imposes some important obligations upon professionals, such as accountants, auditors and legal advisers. These obligations require such professionals to report money laundering to the authorities and to have systems in place to train staff and keep records.

The three phases

Money laundering usually comprises three distinct phases:

- placement – the initial disposal of the proceeds of criminal activity into an apparently legitimate business activity or property

- layering – the transfer of money from business to business, or place to place, in order to conceal its initial source

- integration – the culmination of the previous procedures through which the money takes on the appearance of coming from a legitimate source.

The offences

The Proceeds of Crime Act 2002 created three categories of criminal offence: laundering, failure to report, and tipping off.

Laundering

It is an offence to conceal, disguise, convert, transfer, or remove criminal property from England, Wales, Scotland or Northern Ireland: s327 Proceeds of Crime Act 2002.

Concealing or disguising criminal property includes concealing or disguising its nature, source, location, disposition, movement or ownership, or any rights connected with it.

'Criminal property' is defined as property which the alleged offender knows (or suspects) constitutes or represents benefit from any criminal conduct.

'Criminal conduct' is defined as conduct that:

- constitutes an offence in any part of the UK
- would constitute an offence in any part of the UK if it occurred there.

Failure to report

Under s330 individuals carrying on a 'relevant business' may be guilty of an offence of failing to disclose knowledge or suspicion of money laundering where they know or suspect, or have reasonable grounds for knowing or suspecting, that another person is engaged in laundering the proceeds of crime.

This offence only relates to individuals, such as accountants, who are acting in the course of business in the regulated sector.

Any individual who is covered by s330 is required to make disclosure to a nominated money laundering reporting officer within their organisation, or directly to the Serious Organised Crime Agency (SOCA), as soon as is practicable.

Tipping off

Section 333 states that it is an offence to make a disclosure likely to prejudice a money laundering investigation. It therefore covers the situation where an accountant informs a client that a report has been submitted to SOCA.

Penalties

The maximum penalty for the s327 offence of money laundering is 14 years' imprisonment.

Failure to report and tipping off are punishable on conviction by a maximum of five years' imprisonment and/or a fine.

> **Test your understanding 2**
>
> (1) **Which Act contains the legislation on money laundering?**
>
> (2) **To which organisation must you report suspicions of money laundering?**
>
> (3) **Which of the three money laundering offences only applies to individuals, such as accountants, who are in business in the regulated sector?**
>
> (4) **What is meant by the term 'money laundering'?**

3 Potential criminal activity in the operation, management and winding up of companies

Introduction

There are a number of criminal offences that could be undertaken by individuals concerned in the operation, management or winding up of a company. Many of these points have been covered in earlier chapters and so are only dealt with in outline here.

Failure to file accounts or annual returns

Failure to deliver accounts or annual returns on time is a criminal offence. All the directors of a company in default could be prosecuted. If convicted, a director could end up with a criminal record and a fine of up to £5,000 for each offence.

Providing misleading information to an auditor

Under s499 CA 2006, an auditor is entitled to require from the company's officers and employees such information and explanation as he thinks necessary for the performance of his duties as auditor. It is a criminal offence for an officer of the company to:

- provide misleading, false or deceptive information or explanations, or
- fail to provide information or explanations required by the auditor.

An individual can defend such as charge if he can prove that it was not reasonably practicable to provide the information or explanations required.

Business Names Act 1985

It is a criminal offence to use a business name that requires prior approval, if that approval has not been obtained.

It is also a criminal offence to fail to disclose the business details that the Act requires. These details include stating the company's corporate name and address for the service of documents.

Company Directors Disqualification Act 1986 (CDDA 1986)

Under s13 CDDA 1986, any person who acts in contravention of a disqualification order (or while an undischarged bankrupt) is guilty of an offence. The maximum penalty is:

- two years' imprisonment and/or a fine on conviction on indictment
- up to six months' imprisonment and/or a fine not exceeding the statutory maximum on a summary conviction.

S15 CDDA 1986, provides that anyone who is involved in the management of a company while disqualified, or who acts on the instructions of someone who is disqualified, shall be personally liable for the company's debts incurred during the time they acted.

Phoenix companies

S216 and s217 Insolvency Act 1986 (IA 1986) are aimed at so-called 'phoenix companies'. They apply where a person was a director or shadow director of a company at any time in the period of 12 months ending with the day before the company went into liquidation.

The provisions apply for the five years following liquidation. They prevent the person being a director of a company with a similar name, or a name which suggests an association with the previous company, without leave of the court.

It is a criminal offence to contravene the provisions, punishable by imprisonment and/or a fine. In addition, the director will be personally liable for any debts of the new company which are incurred when he was involved in its management.

The Fraud Act 2006

The Fraud Act 2006 radically changed the law of criminal fraud.

Before the Fraud Act came into force, the statutory fraud offences under the Theft Act 1978 were based on deception. They included:

- Obtaining property by deception.
- Obtaining a money transfer by deception.
- Obtaining a pecuniary advantage by deception.
- Obtaining services by deception.

The Fraud Act swept all of the old statutory deception offences away. Instead a new offence of fraud has been defined as follows:

- The defendant must have been dishonest, and have intended to make a gain or to cause a loss to another; and
- The defendant must carry out one of these acts:

- s2: fraud by making a false or misleading representation, this being where any person makes "any representation as to fact or law ... express or implied" which they know to be untrue or misleading.

- s3: fraud by failing to disclose information whereby a person fails to disclose any information to a third party when they are under a legal duty to disclose such information.

- s4: fraud by abuse of position where a person occupies a position where they are expected to safeguard the financial interests of another person, and abuses that position; this includes cases where the abuse consisted of an omission rather than an overt act.

The new offence of fraud is intended to be wide and also flexible. There is no reliance on the concept of "deception". It does not matter whether the false information actually deceives anyone, it is the misleading intention which counts.

4 Transactions at an undervalue and preference

A liquidator may apply to the court to set aside company transactions at an undervalue (s238 Insolvency Act 1986) or where the company gives a preference (s239 Insolvency Act 1986).

Undervalue

A company enters into a transaction at an undervalue if the company makes a gift or otherwise enters into a transaction on terms that the company receives not consideration or insufficient consideration.

The transaction would not be set aside if it was entered into in good faith on the reasonable belief that it would benefit the company.

Preferences

A company gives a preference if it does anything to put a creditor in a better position in the event of the company's insolvent liquidation than they would otherwise be.

The court will not make an order unless the company was influenced by a desire to prefer the creditor. Therefore, a payment or charge created in favour of a creditor who is threatening legal proceedings might be a defence. However, if the preference was given to a connected person it is presumed that the company was influenced by its desire to give a preference.

5 Fraudulent and wrongful trading

Fraudulent trading

Fraudulent trading occurs where the company's business is carried on with intent to defraud creditors or for any fraudulent purpose.

Fraudulent trading can give rise to:

- civil liability under s213 Insolvency Act 1986 if the company is in the course of being wound up

- criminal liability under s993 CA06 whether or not the company is in the course of being wound up.

It is necessary to establish **dishonest intent.** In **Re William C Leith Bros (1932)** it was said that if the directors carry on the business and cause the company to incur further debts at a time when they know that there is no reasonable prospect of those debts being paid this is a proper inference of dishonesty. The court also added that if the directors honestly believed the debts would eventually be paid there would be no intent to defraud.

R v Grantham (1984)

Facts: The directors ordered a consignment of potatoes on a month's credit at a time when they knew that payment would not be forthcoming at the end of the month when it was due.

Held: The directors were convicted of fraudulent trading.

The second point required to establish liability is that the person concerned shall be **knowingly a party** to the fraudulent trading.

In **Re Maidstone Buildings (1971)** it was established that a person is not 'party' merely by reason of knowledge. They must take some active step, such as the ordering of goods.

Fraudulent trading can give rise to the following consequences:

- The court can order the individual to contribute to the company's assets.

- If a director, they may be disqualified for 15 years under CDDA86.

- If found guilty of the criminal offence, the individual can be fined and/or imprisoned for up to 10 years.

Wrongful trading

Wrongful trading occurs where on a winding-up it appears to the court that the company has gone into insolvent liquidation and, before the start of winding up, the director knew or ought to have known that there was **no reasonable prospect that the company would avoid going into insolvent liquidation:** S214 Insolvency Act 1986.

The provision of 'wrongful trading' contained in S214 IA86 is designed to remove one of the difficult obstacles to the establishment of being party to fraudulent trading – namely proving dishonesty. **It applies only to directors and shadow directors.**

The director is expected to reach those conclusions and take such steps as a reasonably diligent person would take. The legislation also expects such a director to:

- have the general knowledge, skill and experience which may reasonably be expected of a person carrying out the same functions as were carried out by that director (i.e. this is an objective test)

- use the general knowledge, skill and experience he himself has (i.e. this is a subjective test).

When considering the director's functions, the court will have regard not only to those functions he carried out but also to those entrusted to him. This means that the director could be made liable for those actions he should have carried out but failed to.

Re Produce Marketing Consortium Ltd (No 2) (1989)

Facts: The company, after trading successfully for nine years, built up an overdraft, had a continuing trading loss and had an excess of liabilities over assets. In February 1987 the directors recognised that liquidation was inevitable but carried on trading until October 1987, arguing that this period of trading minimised the loss to creditors by allowing an orderly disposal, for value, of the company's goods.

Held: The court required them to contribute £75,000 to the assets of the company (equating to the net debts incurred during the wrongful trading period) on the grounds that:

- they would have known that liquidation was inevitable in July 1986 had the company produced timely internal accounts and this therefore marked the beginning of the period from which they should have been minimising losses to creditors

- while trading on to dispose of assets might sometimes be justifiable, the directors had done no more than dispose of assets and so had failed to take every step to minimise losses.

Wrongful trading can give rise to the following consequences:

- a liquidator may apply to the court for an order that the director should make such contribution to the company's assets as the court thinks fit, thereby increasing the assets available for distribution to the creditors

- They may be disqualified for 15 years under CDDA86.

Test your understanding 3

Explain the main differences between a director fraudulently trading and wrongfully trading.

(Your answer must not exceed 40 words.)

Chapter summary

Insider dealing
- dealing in price-affected securities
- encouraging another to deal
- disclosing information.

Money laundering
- laundering
- failure to report
- tipping off.

Fraudulent behaviour

Fraudulent trading
- business carried on with intent to defraud
- criminal offence.

Wrongful trading
- no reasonable prospect of avoiding insolvent liquidation.

Test your understanding answers

Test your understanding 1

(1) Criminal Justice Act 1993.

(2) Dealing in securities.

Encouraging another person to deal.

Disclosing information.

(3) Did not expect the dealing to result in a profit.

Believed the information had been disclosed.

Would have done what he did even without the information.

Test your understanding 2

(1) The Proceeds of Crime Act 2002.

(2) Serious Organised Crime Agency

(3) Failure to report.

(4) Money laundering is the process by which the proceeds of crime are converted into assets which appear to have a legal rather than an illegal source. The aim of disguising the source of the property is to allow the holder to enjoy it free from suspicion as to its source.

Test your understanding 3

Fraudulent trading is trading with intent to defraud creditors and is a criminal offence. Wrongful trading occurs when it was known or ought to have been known that insolvency was unavoidable, and is not a criminal offence.

KAPLAN PUBLISHING

Questions & Answers

1 English legal system

Question 1

Describe the first instance jurisdiction of the civil courts and explain the system of appeals in civil cases.

(10 marks)

Question 2

Explain the rules and presumptions used by the courts in interpreting statutes.

(10 marks)

2 Contract law

Question 1

In relation to contract law distinguish between offers and invitations to treat and explain why it is important to make such a distinction.

(Adapted from ACCA June 2004)

(10 marks)

Question 2

Hilary advertised a printing press in a specialist trade journal for £15,000. Eleanor wrote to Hilary offering to buy it for £10,000. Hilary replied by return of post saying she would accept £13,000. When she heard nothing further from Eleanor, Hilary wrote again saying she would accept £10,000.

Hilary wrote to Amy offering for sale an office computer for £1,000. The morning that she received the letter Amy wrote to Hilary agreeing to buy at the asking price. After she had posted the letter, but before it was delivered, Amy changed her mind and sent Hilary a fax asking her to ignore the letter when it arrived.

Required:

Advise Hilary as to whether binding contracts exist between herself and:

A   Eleanor

B   Amy.

(Adapted from ACCA June 1997)

(10 marks)

Question 3

Explain the meaning of the following:

A   the principle that consideration must be sufficient but need not be adequate

B   the principle that consideration may be executed or executory, but must not be past.

(10 marks)

Question 4

Raymond runs a small consultancy business, of which he is the sole proprietor, specialising in personal taxation advice. He entered into a contract with Samantha, a struggling artist, under which he agreed to prepare some draft business accounts for her, covering the last three years, for the sum of £800. Raymond completed the work but Samantha told him she could only afford to pay £200 for the work. After a bitter argument Raymond reluctantly accepted a cheque for £200 from Samantha, which was stated to be in full and final settlement of the debt.

Shortly afterwards Samantha's paintings began to realise very high prices and Raymond has just read in a newspaper that her latest work has been sold for £20,000. He now wishes to claim the balance of £600 from Samantha and approaches you for advice.

Advise Raymond.

(Adapted from ACCA June 1996)

(10 marks)

Question 5

Grace, an accountant, works as a sole practitioner. She does not employ any staff. Grace has recently won a lucrative contract from Expansion Ltd to undertake all the company's payroll work. The initial period is for six months, renewable thereafter on a 12-monthly basis as long as the work done by Grace is satisfactory.

In order to undertake the work for Expansion Ltd, Grace hires a powerful desktop computer together with dedicated software from Office Supplies Ltd. Grace signed a written hire contract with Office Supplies Ltd but she did not read it. It contained a clause stating that 'Office Supplies Ltd are not liable for any financial losses or other losses, however caused, occasioned by using hardware or software products supplied by the company'.

Neither the computer nor the software operated correctly because of negligent design and manufacture by the company and as a result Grace failed to make proper National Insurance deductions for the employees of Expansion Ltd. Expansion Ltd consequently refused to renew the contract with Grace and she suffered considerable loss in her profits as a result.

Office Supplies Ltd admits that it has been negligent but denies any liability to Grace on the basis of the exclusion clause in the contract.

Advise Grace.

(Adapted from ACCA Dec 1994)

(10 marks)

Question 6 - Fixed Test 1

Describe briefly the main rules that govern:

A   the incorporation of exemption clauses into contracts

B   the interpretation of exemption clauses in contracts.

(10 marks)

Question 7

State and explain the remedies available for breach of contract.

(Adapted from ACCA Dec 2004)

(10 marks)

3 The law of torts

Question 1

Albert wishes to rent a flat. He views 116 High Street and applies to be a tenant. He fills out a form giving his accountant's details and the landlord, Brad, applies to the accountant for a reference relating to Albert's financial situation. The accountant, Charles, confuses Albert with another client and does not bother to check the file properly. He replies to Brad that Albert is an excellent client with high income and capital and recommends him as a tenant.

In fact had he looked at the correct file, he would have seen that Albert was continuously in overdraft and had been in serious debt with various banks on and off for several years. The reference was supplied with the words: 'This firm will not accept any liability for inaccuracy contained in this reference or any loss incurred as a consequence'.

Some months later, Albert disappears having taken the flat on and run up several thousand pounds' worth of rent arrears.

Required:

Advise Brad as to whether he can recover his losses from Charles.

(10 marks)

Question 2

Mary is made redundant after working seventeen years as a nurse with Barnett Hospital. She receives a large sum of money by way of redundancy payment.

Soon afterwards she is offered, subject to satisfactory references, a highly paid position with Comfort Home. The job offer is subsequently withdrawn and, when Mary makes further enquiries, she is given a copy of a reference supplied by Barnett Hospital which criticises her lack of commitment. When Mary confronts the hospital with the reference, they apologise profusely and point out that they had confused her with another employee with the same surname who was recently sacked for incompetence. Barnett Hospital informs Comfort Home and supplies a new reference but, by then, it is too late as Comfort Home have filled the vacancy with the second choice candidate.

Mary decides to invest her redundancy money into two companies. Shares in her ex- primary school, which is now offering private education, are purchased on the advice of Joe an investment advisor and old friend that Mary met for a drink. The share price falls dramatically after allegations that directors of the company are under investigation for fraud and bribery.

Mary also purchase shares in MGS.com, a newly floated company on the alternative investments market. The shares had been recommended in an article which Mary had downloaded from the Internet. The article had been written by Thomas, an investment guru, well known for being a regular guest on television chat shows and for having made several million pounds out of investments in internet companies. The article fails to mention the highly speculative nature of investment in such companies and the fact that, in most cases, what is being purchased is an idea rather than a proven record of performance. Six months later, Mary finds out the MGS.com shares are worthless.

Required:

Advise Mary whether she can recover her losses from:

A   Barnett Hospital

B   Joe

C   Thomas.

(10 marks)

4 Employment law

Question 1

Carol ran a business in Glasgow which specialised in producing computer software programmes. Dan and Eve both worked for Carol for a period of three years. They were both described as self-employed and both paid tax as self-employed persons. Carol provided all of their specialist computer equipment. Dan was required to work solely on the projects Carol provided, and he had to attend at her premises every day from 9am till 5pm. Eve usually worked at home and was allowed to work on other projects. Eve could even arrange for her work for Carol to be done by someone else if she was too busy to do it personally. When Carol lost her most important contract, which Dan had been working on, she decided to relocate the business to be closer to her one remaining large contract in London some 500 miles away. As a result she told Dan and Eve that there would be no more work for them.

Required:

Explain to Dan and Eve:

A   how the courts decide whether someone is self-employed or is an employee

B   into which category they are likely to fall.

(Adapted from ACCA June 2000)

(10 marks)

Question 2

In July 20X5, Norman applied for, and obtained, the post of marketing consultant with Allpass Ltd, based at their Manchester office. In August 20X7, Allpass Ltd told Norman that, because of a reduction of work in Manchester, from November 20X7 he was to be transferred to its Bristol office, some 200 miles away from Manchester. Norman refused to accept the transfer, arguing that he was employed to work in Manchester, and on 1 October 20X7 Norman wrote to Allpass Ltd, terminating his contract with the company.

Norman now wishes to pursue an unfair dismissal claim against Allpass Ltd.

Required:

Advise Norman on the following matters:

A   the significance of the fact that Norman terminated his contract with Allpass Ltd

B   his likely chances of success in a claim for unfair dismissal.

(Adapted from ACCA Dec 1997)

(10 marks)

5 Agency law

Question 1

Explain the difference between agency of necessity and agency by ratification.

(10 Marks)

6 Partnerships

Question 1

Clare, Dan and Eve formed a partnership 10 years ago. Two years ago the partnership employed Frank as its manager and last year Dan retired from the partnership. Eve and Clare subsequently left much of the day-to-day work to Frank who has let it be known generally that he has become a partner, although he has not. In January of this year Frank entered into a large contract with a longstanding customer, Greg, who had dealt with the partnership for some five years.

Greg believed Frank's claim that he was a partner in the business.

This contract has gone badly wrong leaving the partnership still owing £50,000 to Greg and unfortunately the business assets will only cover the first £25,000 of the total debt.

Required:

Consider and explain the potential liabilities of Dan, Clare, Eve and Frank.

(10 marks)

Question 2

Detail the grounds upon which a partnership can be terminated.

(10 marks)

7 Corporations and legal personality

Question 1

Explain what legal limitations there are on the names that may be adopted by companies, paying particular regard to the tort of 'passing off'.

(10 marks)

Question 2

Explain the meaning and effect of a company's articles of association, paying particular attention to the following issues:

A   The operation of the model articles of association.

(2 marks)

B   The effect of the articles on both members and non-members.

(4 marks)

C   The procedure for altering the articles of association.

(4 marks)

(Total: 10 marks)

Question 3 - Fixed Test 2

Fran, Gail, Hannah and Ian have just been made redundant and have received payments of £50,000 each. They were highly skilled workers and believe that they could carry on their own business successfully.

Required:

Explain four advantages of the registered company over the partnership as a form of business organisation and advise them as to which form of business best suits their situation.

You are not required to consider the Limited Liability Partnership.

(10 marks)

8 Capital and financing

Question 1

The board of Wealthy plc is considering lending a substantial sum of money to Hardup plc. As part of the consideration for the loan, Hardup plc has offered a debenture containing a floating charge over the assets and undertaking of the company. To help the board of Wealthy plc reach a final decision regarding the loan, you have been asked to provide certain information concerning the transaction.

Required:

A   Explain what is meant by a 'floating charge'.

B   Explain whether the floating charge will provide adequate security for Wealthy plc.

C   What initial steps should Wealthy plc take to ensure that the assets and undertaking of Hardup plc are not already the subject of a floating charge and how does it ensure that its own charge is a valid security?

(10 marks)

Question 2

LCP Ltd has three shareholders, Lola, Charlie and Pat, who are also the company's directors. Pat wishes to retire from the business and to sell his shareholding to LCP Ltd itself.

Required:

Explain the extent to which company law allows LCP Ltd to purchase Pat's shares.

(10 marks)

9 Directors

Question 1

Julie was appointed director of ABC Ltd in 20X5. Her service contract provided that she should hold office for five years and this term was also stated in the articles of association of ABC Ltd.

The other directors have now decided that Julie should be removed from her directorship. They tabled a resolution that Julie be removed from office and it was duly passed. Julie attended the meeting and made a statement that she intended to take legal advice as she believed she could not be removed in breach of the articles of association and of her service contract. The directors of ABC Ltd have asked for your advice.

Required:

Advise the directors, explaining whether the shareholders had the authority to pass the resolution and suggesting what legal redress Julie might have.

(10 marks)

Question 2

Len is a director of Mod plc, but he also owns a majority interest in Nim Ltd.

Last year Mod plc entered into a contract to buy new machinery from Nim Ltd. Len attended the board meeting that approved the contract and voted in favour of it, without revealing any link with Nim Ltd.

At the same meeting the board of Mod plc decided not to pursue the development of a new product that had been offered to them by its inventor. Len, however, liked the new product and arranged for it to be produced by Nim Ltd. It has proved to be a great success and Nim Ltd has made a great deal of money from its production.

Required:

Owen is a shareholder in Mod plc and has found out about Len's links with Nim Ltd. He seeks your advice on whether any action can be taken against Len in relation to either:

A   the purchase of the machinery from Nim Ltd, or

B   the development of the new product by Nim Ltd.

(Adapted from ACCA June 2000 examination)

(10 marks)

Question 3 - Fixed Test 3

GLM plc's articles of association contain the following regulation:

'No single director is empowered to enter into contracts on behalf of the company in excess of £250,000 without written authorisation by the chairman of the board of directors.'

Matthew, the managing director, has recently committed the company to a contract with PQR Ltd for the supply of equipment valued at £300,000. PQR Ltd demanded a copy of GLM plc's articles and asked Matthew whether he had obtained the consent of the chairman. Matthew stated that he had, which was untrue.

Required:

Explain whether the board of GLM plc can avoid the contract.

(10 marks)

10 Corporate administration

Question 1

A   What are the statutory requirements for companies to hold annual general meetings?

(3 marks)

B   What is a written resolution? When can it be used by a private company?

(7 marks)

(Total: 10 marks)

11 Insolvency

Question 1

In relation to company law explain:

A   the meaning of winding up

(3 marks)

B   the procedures involved in:
  I   a members' voluntary winding up

(3 marks)

  II   a creditors' voluntary winding up.

(4 marks)

(Total: 10 marks)

12 Corporate governance

Question 1

A   Who are non-executive directors? Explain whether they play a useful role in company boards.

(5 marks)

B   What guidance does the Higgs review give on the independence of NEDs?

(2 marks)

C   Outline the advantages and disadvantages of the system of self regulation introduced by the Combined Code.

(3 marks)

(Total: 10 marks)

13 Fraudulent behaviour

Question 1

Susan is a secretary working in her firm's corporate department. She overhears a senior lawyer in her firm taking a telephone call from the chair of AIM plc during the course of which she learns that a take-over bid for the share capital of AIM plc is to be announced by HIT plc the following week. She tells her father, Joseph, that evening about what she heard. Joseph is a stockbroker and the next day he buys up traded option on the market to acquire AIM shares for £1 each. On Monday the following week, HIT plc makes a public bid for AIM plc and AIM shares rises to £5 each. Joseph exercises his options over AIM plc shares and immediately resells them for £5 each, netting a profit of £4 per share.

Required:

Discuss whether Susan and Joseph have committed insider dealing.

(10 marks)

Question 2

Dome plc is listed on the stock exchange. Ewan works for Dome plc as an accountant. Whilst drawing up the annual accounts, Ewan notices that Dome plc's profits are better than anyone could have expected. As a consequence of this knowledge, he buys shares in Dome plc before the good results are announced. He makes a substantial profit on the share dealing. Ewan also tells his friend Frank about the results before they are announced. Frank also buys shares in Dome plc.

Required:

Have either Ewan or Frank done anything illegal and, if so, how is their action regulated?

(10 marks)

Test your understanding answers

Question 1

Civil courts

County court

County courts deal with the majority of the country's civil litigation. Jurisdiction includes contract and tort claims and undefended matrimonial cases.

The small claims track is for cases where the amount involved does not exceed £5,000, or if the parties agree to the procedure. The procedure is cheaper, quicker and more informal than a County court hearing.

The fast track is for cases under £15,000. Complex cases, and any cases over £15,000, are dealt with under the multitrack system.

High Court

The High Court has three divisions. The Chancery Division first instance jurisdiction covers bankruptcy, company matters, landlord and tenant, mortgages, probate, patents and copyright.

The Family Division first instance jurisdiction covers the whole range of family matters including validity of marriages, divorce, legitimacy, adoption, guardianship, wardship and disputes concerning the matrimonial home.

The first instance business of the Queen's Bench Division is wide but mainly covers contract and tort actions. Jurisdiction over commercial matters is exercised by a Commercial Court. The Division also has an Admiralty Court which deals with claims for damage, loss of life, or personal injury arising out of collisions at sea, claims for loss or damage to goods carried in a ship, and disputes concerning the ownership or possession of ships.

Appeal

Appeal from the County court and High Court generally lies to the Court of Appeal (Civil Division) with a further and final appeal with leave to the House of Lords.

Exceptionally, appeal from the matrimonial and insolvency jurisdictions of the County court lies to the Divisional Courts of Family and Chancery respectively with a further and final appeal with leave to the House of Lords.

Exceptionally appeal may be made with leave direct from the first instance jurisdiction of the High Court to the House of Lords. This 'leapfrog' appeal is rare. It is only permitted on a point of law of general importance on which there is a pre-existing binding Court of Appeal precedent such that the result of an appeal to the Court of Appeal is a foregone conclusion and therefore a needless expenditure of time and money, or where the case involves a point of statutory interpretation.

Question 2

Rules and presumptions

Judges use a number of rules and presumptions to help them decide the meaning of the words of a statute.

There are three main rules of statutory interpretation.

The literal rule

Under this rule, the judge is required to consider what the legislation actually says rather than considering what it might mean. In order to achieve this end, the judge should give the words in the legislation their literal meaning; that is their plain, ordinary everyday meaning, even if the effect of this is to produce what might be considered an otherwise unjust or undesirable outcome. In **Fisher v Bell (1961)** the court chose to follow the contract law literal interpretation of the meaning of the word 'offer' in the Act in question and declined to consider the usual non-legal interpretation of the word.

The golden rule

This rule is applied in circumstances where the application of the literal rule is likely to result in what appears to the court to be an obviously absurd result. It should be emphasised, however, that the court is not at liberty to ignore, or replace, legislative provisions simply on the basis that it considers them absurd. It must find genuine difficulties before it declines to use the literal rule in favour of the golden rule. As examples, there may be two apparently contradictory meanings of a particular word used in the statute, or the provision may simply be ambiguous in its effect. In such situations, the golden rule operates to ensure that preference is given to the meaning that does not result in the provision being an absurdity. Thus in **Adler v George (1964)**, the defendant was found guilty, under the Official Secrets Act 1920, with obstruction 'in the vicinity' of a prohibited area, although she had actually carried out the obstruction 'inside' the area.

The mischief rule

This rule permits the court to go behind the actual wording of a statute in order to consider the problem that the statute is supposed to remedy.

In its traditional expression, the mischief rule is limited by being restricted to using previous common law rules in order to decide the operation of contemporary legislation. Thus in **Heydon's case (1584)** it was stated that in making use of the mischief rule, the court should consider the following four things:

I   What was the common law before the passing of the statute?

II   What was the mischief which the common law did not adequately deal with?

III   What remedy for that mischief had Parliament intended to provide?

IV   What was the reason for Parliament adopting that remedy?

Use of the mischief rule may be seen in **Corkery v Carpenter (1950)**, in which a man was found guilty of being drunk in charge of a carriage although he was in fact only in charge of a bicycle.

In addition to the rules of interpretation, the courts may also make use of certain presumptions. As with all presumptions they are rebuttable and may be expressly overridden by the clear expression of such an intention in the statute under consideration. The presumptions operate:

I   against the alteration of the common law

II   in favour of the requirement that mens rea be a constituent in any criminal offence

III   against retrospective application

IV   against the deprivation of an individual's liberty, property or rights

V   against application to the Crown

VI   against breaking international law

VII   in favour of words taking their meaning from the context in which they are used. This general presumption appears as three distinct sub-rules. The noscitur a sociis rule is applied where statutory provisions include a list of examples of what is covered by the legislation. It is presumed that the words used have a related meaning and are to be interpreted in relation to each other. The eiusdem generis rule applies in situations where general words are appended to the end of a list of specific examples. The presumption is that the general words have to be interpreted in line with the prior restrictive examples **(Powell v Kempton Park Racecourse Co (1899))**. The expressio unius exclusio alterius rule simply means that where a statute seeks to establish a list of what is covered by its provisions, then anything not expressly included in that list is specifically excluded.

The above should be read within the context of HRA 1998, which requires all legislation to be construed in such a way as, if at all possible, to bring it within the ambit of the European Convention on Human Rights.

Question 1

Offer

An offer sets out the terms upon which an individual is willing to enter into a binding contractual relationship with another person. It is a promise to be bound on particular terms, which is capable of acceptance.

Offers, once accepted, may be legally enforced but not all statements will amount to an offer. It is important, therefore, to be able to distinguish what the law will treat as an offer from other statements which will not form the basis of an enforceable contract.

An offer must be capable of acceptance. It must therefore not be too vague. In **Carlill v Carbolic Smoke Ball Co (1893)** it was held that an offer could be made to the whole world and could be accepted and made binding through the conduct of the offeree.

Invitation to treat

However, most difficulties arise in relation to invitations to treat. These are distinct from offers in that they are invitations to others to make offers. The person to whom the invitation to treat is made becomes the actual offeror, and the maker of the invitation becomes the offeree. An essential consequence of this distinction is that the person extending the invitation to treat is not bound to accept any offers subsequently made to them.

The following are examples of common situations involving invitations to treat:

I **The display of goods in a shop window**. In **Fisher v Bell (1960)** a shopkeeper was prosecuted for offering offensive weapons for sale, by having flick-knives on display in his window. It was held that the shopkeeper was not guilty as the display in the shop window was not an offer for sale but only an invitation to treat.

II **The display of goods on the shelf of a self-service shop.** In **Pharmaceutical Society of Great Britain v Boots Cash Chemists (Southern) (1953)**, the defendants were charged with breaking a law which provided that certain drugs could only be sold under the supervision of a qualified pharmacist. They had placed the drugs on open display in their self-service store and, although a qualified person was stationed at the cash desk, it was alleged that the contract of sale had been formed when the customer removed the goods from the shelf. It was held that Boots were not guilty. The display of goods on the shelf was only an invitation to treat. In law, the customer offered to buy the goods at the cash desk where the pharmacist was stationed.

III **A public advertisement**. In **Partridge v Crittenden (1968)** a person was charged with 'offering' a wild bird for sale contrary to the Protection of Birds Act 1954, after he had placed an advertisement relating to the sale of such birds in a magazine. It was held that he could not be guilty of offering the bird for sale as the advertisement amounted to no more than an invitation to treat.

This should be contrasted with **Carlill v Carbolic Smoke Ball Co (1893)**, where the relevant newspaper advertisement was held to be an offer. The difference is due to the intention of the advertiser and the fact that the contract envisaged in **Carlill** is a unilateral contract and not a bilateral contract. In other situations where a unilateral contract is envisaged (the 'reward' cases), advertisements are treated as offers.

IV **Tenders**. A tender is regarded as the offer which the person or body seeking the goods or services is free to accept or not.

V **A share prospectus**. Such a document is merely an invitation to treat, inviting people to make offers to subscribe for shares in a company.

Importance of the distinction

The distinction is important in order to decide when the contract comes into existence. If the statement is merely an invitation to treat, both an offer and an acceptance are required in order to bring the contract into existence. However, if the statement is an offer, only an acceptance is required in order to bring the contract into existence.

Question 2

A   Eleanor

An offer is a definite and unequivocal statement of willingness to be bound by contract on specified terms without further negotiations. An offer can be contrasted with an invitation to treat, which is an invitation to the other party to make an offer.

Generally, advertisements are invitations to treat, not offers – **Partridge v Crittenden (1968)**. Exceptionally, advertisements are offers where no further negotiations are intended – **Carlill v Carbolic Smoke Ball Co (1893)**.

Here, Hilary's advertisement is an invitation to treat. Eleanor's reply is an offer.

Acceptance is the absolute (unconditional) and unqualified assent to all the terms of the offer. A counter-offer is an offer made in response to an offer – **Hyde v Wrench (1840)**.

Hilary's reply by return of post is not an acceptance: it is a counteroffer because it attempts to negotiate the price up to £13,000. A counter-offer terminates the original offer; therefore Eleanor's £10,000 offer no longer exists. Accordingly, when Hilary writes again saying she would accept £10,000, this is not an acceptance, it is a fresh offer which Eleanor then rejects.

In conclusion Hilary is advised that no binding contract exists with Eleanor.

B   Amy

Hilary's initial letter is an offer. Amy's letter replying is an acceptance. Once an acceptance has been made a contract comes into being. Therefore it is not possible to 'revoke' an acceptance: any such attempt is a breach of contract.

In general, acceptance is effective once it has been communicated to (i.e. received by) the offeror – **Entores v Miles Far East Corporation (1955)**. However, under the postal rule, a posted acceptance is effective when the letter is posted, not when it is received.

The postal rule only applies provided:

(1) the letter is properly stamped and addressed, and

(2) it is put into the hands of the postal authorities, and

(3) it is reasonable to use the post as a means of communication, in the sense that the post would be within the contemplation of the parties.

If the postal rule applies, acceptance will be effective when the letter is posted. Assuming the letter was properly stamped and addressed, the only issue is whether it was reasonable to use the post. As Hilary used the post for her offer it is strongly arguable that it was reasonable for Amy to reply by post.

In conclusion, a contract existed between Hilary and Amy from the moment Amy posted her acceptance. Her later fax cannot revoke it.

Question 3

Consideration principles

A   In considering the validity of a contract, the courts are generally unconcerned as to whether the parties to the contract have made a good or a bad bargain – that is regarded as a matter for the parties themselves and is not an issue on which the courts will interfere.

However, although consideration need not be adequate, it must be sufficient – in other words, it must have some value in the eyes of the law. There are a number of situations where consideration has been held to be insufficient:

I   The case of **Collins v Godefroy (1831)** established that the performance of an existing statutory duty is not sufficient consideration to establish a contract.

II   The performance an existing contractual duty is also not sufficient: **Stilk v Myrick (1809)**.

III   By contrast, however, performance beyond that already legally required is capable of amounting to sufficient consideration: **Glasbrook Bros Ltd v Glamorgan County Council (1925)**.

B   One of the well-established principles of the law of contract is that while consideration may be executed or executory, it must not be past. Executory consideration in effect consists of a promise in return for a promise. Executed consideration is a promise in return for an act. Thus, if X promises to dig Y's garden, in return for Y's promise to pay X £50, there is a valid contract between them, with both parties having obligations to perform in the future. The consideration is executory. Once X has dug Y's garden, he is said to have provided executed consideration for Y's promise to pay him £50.

Past consideration is best described as consideration which has been performed before the parties involved have reached any agreement. The general principle is that past consideration is insufficient to support a valid contract. A good illustration is **Roscorla v Thomas (1842)** where, after the promisee had purchased a horse, the promisor promised that the horse was sound. When it transpired that the horse was not sound, it was held that the promisee could not enforce the promise, because all he could show was past consideration. A more modern example is **Re McArdle (1951)** where, after the promisee had spent money on improving a property, the promisors promised that they would reimburse her. The court held that the promisee was not entitled to the payment because the promise had been made after the work had been done.

There are some exceptions to the above principles. Thus, where the work has been carried out in the course of a business and it was assumed that the work would be paid for, the consideration will not be past.

An important common law exception arises where a past act has been done at the request of the promisor and both parties understood that the act was to be paid for. If the promisor subsequently promises a payment then it will be enforced by the courts.

Question 4

Raymond has agreed to accept £200 in settlement of a debt of £800. The question is whether Raymond can go back on that agreement and sue for the balance.

The rule in **Pinnel's case (1602)** states that 'payment of a smaller sum does not discharge a debt of a greater amount'. This is because the debtor has not given consideration for the creditor's agreement to accept the smaller amount – **Foakes v Beer (1884)**. Under the rule Raymond may go back on his agreement to accept £200 in full and final settlement and may sue Samantha for the outstanding balance of £600.

There are, however, four exceptions to the rule in **Pinnel's case (1602)**.

(1) Accord and satisfaction

Accord means agreement and must be freely entered into by the creditor for his benefit. In **D & C Builders v Rees (1966)** Mrs Rees owed a sum to the claimants in respect of some building work. Knowing that the claimants were in a parlous financial state, she put pressure on them to accept a smaller sum. Under protest the builders accepted the smaller sum. It was held that there was no true accord. Likewise here, Raymond 'after a bitter argument … reluctantly' accepted the £200.

Satisfaction means consideration. Thus if, e.g. the creditor agreed to accept payment of a smaller sum at a date earlier than the whole debt was due, this benefit would constitute consideration for his promise to accept the smaller amount. Other examples of consideration include the giving of an asset, the performance of a service, and different modes of payment – although in **D & C Builders v Rees (1966)** it was held that there is no distinction, for these purposes, between payment by cheque and payment by cash. Thus Samantha's payment of £200 by cheque confers no benefit when compared to £800 in cash. If the agreement to accept the smaller sum is by deed then it is binding on the creditor even though the debtor has given no satisfaction. Accordingly Raymond is advised that there is most probably no 'accord' and certainly no 'satisfaction' sufficient to prevent him from suing for the £600 balance.

(2) Part payment by a third party

If the part payment to the creditor is made not by the debtor but by some third party then the creditor cannot pursue the debtor for the balance. The given facts state that Samantha paid the £200, not someone else; so this exception does not apply.

(3) Composition with creditors

If the agreement with the creditor is part of a wider agreement between the debtor and his creditors, and all the creditors accept the debtor's proposals, they cannot later pursue the debtor for any shortfall. The given facts do not indicate that Samantha entered into such a composition; so this exception does not apply.

(4) Equitable doctrine of promissory estoppel

In certain circumstances, equity will stop a creditor from going back on his promise to accept a smaller amount. In **Central London Property Trust v High Trees House (1947)** it was established that the doctrine applies only where the creditor has waived his rights with the intention that the debtor will alter his [legal] position in reliance on the waiver and that as a result of such reliance it would in all the circumstances be just and equitable to hold the creditor to his word.

There are limitations to the doctrine:

- It does not apply to simple debtor-creditor situations as is Samantha and Raymond's situation – **Re Selectmove (1995)** where the Inland Revenue was not estopped from going back on its agreement to accept overdue tax by instalments. In contrast, in **Central London Property Trust v High Trees House (1947)** a landlord agreed to reduce the head rent so as to enable the tenant to sub-let at much lower rents during the war.

- It does not apply where the debtor has acted unfairly such as in **D & C Builders v Rees (1966)** where the creditor's promise was extracted under pressure. In contrast, in **Central London Property Trust v High Trees House (1947)** the landlord freely agreed to reduce the head rent. Raymond did not freely agree to waive the full amount.

In summary: Raymond is advised that none of the exceptions to the rule in **Pinnel's case (1602)** apply and he may therefore sue Samantha for the £600 balance.

Question 5

The issue here is the validity of Office Supplies Ltd's exemption clause. An exemption clause is a term in a contract which seeks to limit or exclude the liability of one of the parties in the event of a breach. Grace is advised that it will be valid at common law if the clause is incorporated into the contract and is drafted with words that are apt to cover the loss suffered; and it must not be rendered void by UCTA 1977.

Common law – incorporation into the contract

Clauses can be incorporated into a contract by signature, notice or a consistent course of dealing between the parties. There is no indication on the facts of the problem that there has been a prior course of dealing between Grace and Office Supplies Ltd. Neither is there any evidence that the clause has been incorporated by notice. The issue therefore is whether the clause has been incorporated by signature.

If a person signs a document he is bound by its terms even if he has not read it – **L'Estrange v Graucob Ltd (1934)**, unless there is a misrepresentation as to its contents – **Curtis v Chemical Cleaning and Dying Co (1951)**. This is so even if he is incapable of reading it – **Thompson v LMS Railway Co (1930)**. Any signature must be obtained before the making of the contract.

Applying the above to the facts, the clause is incorporated because Grace signed the contract containing the exemption clause.

Common law – the wording of the exemption clause

The second requirement of common law is that in order to be valid the clause must be worded so as to exclude the loss in question. If the wording of the clause is ambiguous, the courts will interpret it contra proferentem, i.e. in the way least favourable to the party seeking to rely on it.

Here the words of the clause 'any financial losses or other losses' are wide enough to cover Grace's losses. And although the clause did not specifically refer to negligence, the words 'however caused' are probably wide enough to cover negligence.

Statutory test

As this is a contract made in the course of business, UCTA 1977 applies. This provides that any exclusion of liability for death or personal injury caused by negligence is void. Thus Office Supplies Ltd's clause does not exempt it from liability for Grace's personal injuries and therefore she can sue for these losses.

Any exclusion of liability for loss other than death or personal injury caused by negligence is void unless it satisfies the reasonableness test. Thus Office Supplies Ltd can only rely on its exemption clause to protect it from liability for Grace's loss of profits if it can prove that the exemption is reasonable.

The court adjudges whether the exclusion clause is reasonable in the light of all the surrounding circumstances and in particular:

- the relative bargaining strength of the parties. The given facts suggest that Grace ('a sole practitioner') is a 'small man' and may well be in a weak bargaining position. No indication is given as to whether Office Supplies Ltd was in the strong position of being able to dictate its terms to Grace.

- whether the party seeking to rely on the clause offered an inducement to the other to get him to agree to it. No information is given on the matter.

- whether the other party knew or ought to have known of the existence and extent of the clause. This factor will operate in Office Supplies Ltd's favour since Grace had the opportunity to read the clear words on the contract she signed.

- the ability to insure. This factor would appear to be neutral since presumably both Office Supplies Ltd and Grace could insure.

On the bare facts given, it would appear that Office Supplies Ltd's exclusion clause with regard to Grace's loss of profits is reasonable. Grace is advised that she cannot sue for these losses.

Question 6 - Fixed Test 1

This question is a FIXED TEST. Please answer the question in full, without reference to an answer.

Then log-in to en-gage and answer fixed test 1 based on your full long-form answer

...or alternatively register using the information at the back of your Complete Text and then go to www.en-gage.co.uk

Question 7

The principle remedies for breach of contract are:

Damages

Every failure to perform a primary obligation is a breach of contract. The secondary obligation on the part of the contract-breaker to which it gives rise by implication of the common law is to pay monetary compensation to the other party for the loss sustained by him in consequence of the breach **(Photo Productions Ltd v Securicor Transport Ltd (1980))**.

Monetary compensation for breach of contract is known as damages. The estimation of what damages are to be paid by a party in breach of contract can be divided into two parts: remoteness and measure.

I   Remoteness of damage involves deciding how far down a chain of events a defendant is liable **(Hadley v Baxendale (1854)** and **Victoria Laundry Ltd v Newman Industries Ltd (1949))**.

II   Measure of damages. The object is not to punish the party in breach, so the amount of damages awarded can never be greater than the actual loss suffered. The aim is to put the injured party in the same position they would have been in had the contract been properly performed.

Specific performance

An order for specific performance requires the party in breach to complete their part of the contract.

I   Specific performance will only be granted in cases where the common law remedy of damages is inadequate. It is most commonly granted in cases involving the sale of land, where the subject matter of the contract is unique.

II   Specific performance will not be granted where the court cannot supervise its enforcement. For this reason it will not be available in respect of contracts of employment or personal service.

III   Specific performance, as an equitable remedy, will not be granted where the plaintiff has not acted properly on their part.

Injunction

This is also an equitable order of the court, which directs a person not to break their contract. An injunction will only be granted to enforce negative covenants within the agreement, and cannot be used to enforce positive obligations. However, it can have the effect of indirectly enforcing contracts for personal service **(Warner Brothers Pictures Inc v Nelson (1937))**.

Rescission

This equitable remedy entitles the innocent party to a voidable contract to treat it as if it had never been made and consequently to recover all money or assets that had previously been exchanged under the contract.

Question 1

This question concerns the potential liability for economic loss caused by negligent advice and information. It is more difficult to impose liability for negligent statements than for negligent actions: careless words can spread rapidly resulting in a proliferation of claims and potentially unlimited financial losses. Therefore, policy considerations have led to the introduction of rules which limit the class of potential claimants in such cases. The mere foresight of harm arising from negligent advice is insufficient to establish a duty of care.

Starting from the House of Lords' decision in **Hedley Byrne & Co Ltd v Heller & Partners Ltd (1964)** a duty of care arising from negligent misstatement can only be established if the following criteria apply:

A   There must have been a special relationship of close proximity between the claimant and the defendant.

B   It must have been reasonable for the claimant to rely on the defendant's statement.

C   It would be fair, just and reasonable in all circumstances for the courts to impose a duty of care. This requirement is heavily influenced by policy considerations.

Special relationship of close proximity

The existence of such a relationship is dependent upon a variety of factors. It has been suggested that a relationship `equivalent to contract' must exist between the claimant and the defendant before the defendant will be held liable to have voluntarily assumed responsibility to the claimant

In **Caparo Industries v Dickman**, Lord Oliver defined the range of persons to whom a duty is owed in terms of the purpose for which the statement is made:

(1)   The advice must be required for a purpose which is either specified in detail or described in general terms, and this purpose must be expressly or inferentially made known to the adviser when the advice is given.

It is arguable here that the information concerning Albert is very specific and Charles had voluntarily assumed responsibility to Brad in respect of the accuracy of this statement.

(2) The advisor must know (expressly or inferentially) that the advice will be communicated to the claimant, either specifically or to a member as an ascertained class in order that it should be used by the advisee for that purpose. It is submitted that Charles knew Brad would be relying on him.

(3) It must be expressly or inferentially known that the advice communicated is likely to be acted upon by the advisee for that purpose without independent inquiry.

(4) The advice must be acted upon by the advisee to his detriment. Brad did rely on Charles' statement to his detriment.

(5) It must have been reasonable for the claimant to rely on the defendant's statement.

In **Hedley Byrne**, the appellants were advertising agents, who had contracted to place advertisements for their client's (Easipower) products. As this involved giving Easipower credit, they asked the respondents, who were Easipower's bankers, for a reference as to the creditworthiness of Easipower. Heller gave favourable references (but stipulated that the information was given without responsibility on their part). Relying on this information, the claimants extended credit to Easipower and lost over £17,000 when the latter, soon after, went into liquidation. The claimants sued Easipower's bankers for negligence.

Held: The respondents' disclaimer was adequate to exclude the assumption by them of the legal duty of care. However, in the absence of the disclaimer, the circumstances would have given rise to a duty of care in spite of the absence of a contractual or fiduciary relationship. Thus, but for the disclaimer, the bank was liable on its misleading statement. Note: nowadays the disclaimer might be invalidated under Unfair Contract Terms Act 1977 (UCTA 1977).

In this scenario Charles had supplied the reference with a disclaimer. As such this disclaimer was adequate to exclude the assumption by him of the legal duty of care.

It is unlikely that Brad would succeed in an action against Charles. However, in the absence of the disclaimer, the circumstances would have given rise to a duty of care in spite of the absence of a contractual or fiduciary relationship.

Question 2

This question requires discussion of the legal requirements for negligence and proximity, then a discussion of whether there is a 'special relationship' involving an 'assumption of responsibility' as required in **Hedley Byrne & Company v Heller & Partners.**

Mary v Barnett Hospital

Can it be said that Barnett Hospital are in the business of providing references and are they aware that Comfort Home will act on it? Strictly speaking no, but it could be argued that it is part of an employer's function to provide references.

Can **Caparo** be applied?

- The advice is required for a purpose made known to the adviser, either actually or inferred by the circumstances;

- The adviser knows that his advice will be communicated to the recipient, either specifically or as a member of an ascertainable class; He knows that the advice is likely to be acted upon by the claimant without independent enquiry; and

- The advice is acted upon to the claimant's detriment.

Spring v Guardian Assurance – the decision here is directly applicable to the problem. The House of Lords felt that there was sufficient proximity between an ex-employer and ex-employee and that it was just, fair and reasonable to impose a duty.

Mary v Joe

Although Joe is an investment advisor, is he aware that Mary intends to act on his advice? Although as the advice has been given in a social setting, rather than a business setting, it could be argued that he assumed responsibility by claiming to know about investments.

It will also be necessary to test whether there has been reliance.

Were the shares bought solely on Joe's advice or were there sentimental reasons for choosing to purchase shares in her old school?

If Mary can get round the problems of the social setting and reliance, the fact that the advice was given face to face may support an argument that there is an assumption of responsibility on Joe's part.

Mary v Thomas

Again this would involve a discussion of whether there is 'special skill' and 'reasonable reliance'. It is unlikely that there is 'special skill' as Thomas is not in the business of giving investment advice, neither is he aware that Mary was seeking considered advice and intended to act on it. Further no duty would arise following the decision in **Caparo Industries v Dickman**. This now contains the general position on when a duty of care arises for misstatements. Lord Oliver stated that a duty will arise where:

- The advice is required for a purpose made known to the adviser, either actually or inferred by the circumstances;

- The adviser knows that his advice will be communicated to the recipient, either specifically or as a member of an ascertainable class; He knows that the advice is likely to be acted upon by the claimant without independent enquiry; and

- The advice is acted upon to the claimant's detriment.

Thomas knows nothing about Mary or the fact that Mary read his article with the intention of acting upon it. Given the number of individuals likely to read the article, it would also not be 'just, fair and reasonable' to impose a duty of care on Thomas in the circumstances.

Question 1

(Part A)

Employees are people working under a contract of service. Those who work under a contract for services are independent contractors. They are not employees, but are self-employed.

The courts have developed tests for distinguishing the employee from the self-employed.

The first test to be applied by the courts was known as the control test. The key element in this test is the degree of control exercised by one party over the other. The question to be determined is the degree to which the person who is using the other's services actually controls, not only what they do, but how they do it. An example of the use of this test can be seen in **Walker v Crystal Palace Football Club (1910)** in which it was held that a professional football player was an employee of his club, on the ground that he was subject to control in relation to his training discipline and method of payment.

The control test looks back to and reflects the previous master/servant relationship of employment, but its main shortcoming lies in its lack of any degree of subtlety. Highly-skilled professionals, such as surgeons, by necessity have a high level of control over how they perform their day-to-day work, and under the control test, they were deemed to be self-employed rather than employees. Consequently, patients who had suffered as a consequence of negligence would only be able to sue the doctor, rather than the health authority which used the surgeons' services. Such weakness in the control test led to the courts developing a more subtle test.

The integration test shifted the emphasis from the degree of control exercised over an individual to the extent to which the individual was integrated into the business of his putative employer. An example of the application of the integration test may be seen in **Whittaker v Minister of Pensions & National Insurance (1966)** in which the court found that the degree to which a circus trapeze artist was required to do other general tasks in relation to the operation of the circus in which she appeared, indicated that she was an employee rather than selfemployed. As a consequence, she was entitled to claim compensation for injuries sustained in the course of her employment. However, even the integration test was not without problems, as some employers attempted to give the impression of using a self-employed workforce whilst effectively still controlling what that workforce did.

The response on the part of the courts was the development of the multiple, or economic reality, test. Rather than relying on one single factor, this test uses a more general assessment of the circumstances of any particular case in order to decide whether someone is an employee. In so deciding, the courts will not be bound by how the parties themselves describe the relationship. Thus it is immaterial that the agreement between the parties states that someone is to be self-employed. If the indications are otherwise then the person will be recognised, and treated, as an employee **(Market Investigations Ltd v Minister of Social Security (1968))**.

The economic reality test was first established in **Ready Mixed Concrete (South East) Ltd v Minister of Pensions & National Insurance & Others (1968)** in which it was held that there were three conditions supporting the existence of a contract of employment:

I   the employee agrees to provide his own work and skill in return for a wage

II   the employee agrees, either expressly or implicitly, that he will be subject to a degree of control, exercisable by the employer

III   the other provisions of the contract are consistent with its being a contract of employment.

In deciding whether or not there is a contract of employment, the courts tend to focus on such issues as whether wages are paid regularly or by way of a single lump sum; whether the person receives holiday pay; and on who pays national insurance and income tax. However, there can be no definitive list of tests, as the whole point of the multiple test is that it examines all aspects of the situation in order to reach a determination. For example in **Nethermere (St Neots) Ltd v Taverna and Gardiner (1984)**, a group of home workers (people who carried out paid work in their own homes) were held to be employees on the grounds that they were subject to an irreducible minimum obligation to work for their employer.

(Part B)

Applying the economic reality test, it is more than likely that Dan would be treated as an employee, but Eve would be treated as self-employed. It is true that they were both described as self-employed, but it should be recognised that the label applied does not by itself define the relationship **(Market Investigations Ltd v Minister of Social Security (1968))**. Looking at the circumstances, it can be seen that the manner in which they paid tax might indicate that they were self-employed, but the fact that Carol provided them with their equipment suggests that they were employees. In the final analysis, the most significant factor would appear to be the degree to which Carol controlled them. Dan had to work for Carol only and on her premises, whereas Eve not only was allowed to work for others but, most importantly, she was also allowed to use others to do her work for Carol. This suggests clearly that Eve was not employed by Carol, although Dan was.

Question 2

A   The essential issue here is whether Norman is able to terminate his contract with Allpass Ltd, but nevertheless argue for the purposes of the legislation providing protection against unfair dismissal that he has been, in law, 'dismissed'.

The definition of dismissal is contained in s95 ERA 1996 which provides that an employee is treated as dismissed if:

I   the contract under which he is employed is terminated by the employer (whether with or without notice), or

II   he is employed under a contract for a fixed term and that term expires without being renewed under the same contract, or

III   the employee terminates the contract under which he is employed (with or without notice) in circumstances in which he is entitled to terminate it without notice by reason of the employer's conduct.

Since the decision in **Western Excavating (ECC) Ltd v Sharp (1978)** it has been clear that an employee can argue that he has been constructively dismissed, by virtue of s95(1)(c), in situations where the employer has breached the contract in such a way as to justify the employee in treating himself as discharged from future performance. On the facts of the problem, Norman will be able to regard himself as constructively dismissed if Allpass Ltd's actions in requiring him to work in Bristol rather than Manchester are a sufficiently serious breach of Norman's contract such as to entitle Norman to treat himself as discharged from future performance.

B   If the employment tribunal is satisfied that Norman was constructively dismissed from his employment, then Norman will be able to pursue an unfair dismissal claim. He has more than the necessary qualifying period of service – one year – but, in order for him to succeed, the employment tribunal will need to be satisfied that the employer's reasons underlying the dismissal were not such as to justify it, or that the employer had acted unreasonably in treating the reason/s as sufficient.

There are several categories of reasons which may be used by an employer to justify dismissal, but the one which is relevant in the present instance relates to redundancy: if an employer dismisses an employee for reasons of redundancy, then that may be a fair reason for dismissal (as long as the employer, in addition, acts reasonably). 'Redundancy' covers situations where the employer's requirement for work of a particular kind to be done in the place where the employee is employed has ceased or diminished. The facts of the problem make it clear that there has been such a diminution in the employer's requirements. The indications are that Norman's place of work is Manchester (as opposed, for example, to the whole of the UK). Prima facie, therefore, a redundancy situation has arisen. The essential question will be whether Allpass Ltd has acted reasonably.

Tribunals have not come too readily to the conclusion that dismissals based on redundancy are unfair, but this does not abrogate the responsibility on employers to act reasonably in dismissing for redundancy. The kinds of factors which are relevant are the period of warning of impending redundancy which has been given, whether objective criteria have been applied in selecting a person for redundancy and whether an employer has applied these fairly, whether there has been consultation with the employee and whether the employer has investigated whether it is possible to offer an employee alternative employment rather than dismiss him. Norman would need to be advised that his chances of success in an unfair dismissal action will depend on whether Allpass Ltd has considered such factors before deciding on Norman's relocation.

Question 1

Agency of necessity

A person who acts to save the property of another, or gives him some other form of assistance, may as a matter of law be regarded as an agent of necessity. For example, a person who goes to the aid of a ship at sea and saves life or property is entitled to a reward. The amount of the reward is at the discretion of the court. The doctrine of agency of necessity is confined to fairly narrow limits. In general three conditions must be satisfied.

I   There must be an emergency, making it necessary for the agent to act as he did. In **Pager v Blatspiel**, A bought skins as agent for P but was unable to send them to P because of prevailing war conditions. Since A was also unable to communicate with P, he sold the skins before the end of the war. It was held that A was not an agent of necessity, because he could have stored the skins until the end of the war. There was no real emergency.

II   It must be impossible to get instructions from the principal. In **Springer v Great Western Railway**, a consignment of fruit was found by the carrier to be going bad. The carrier sold the consignment locally instead of delivering it to its destination. It was held that the carrier was not an agent of necessity because he could have obtained new instructions from the owner of the fruit. He was therefore liable in damages to the owner.

III The agent must have acted in good faith, and in the interests of the principal. In **Great Northern Railway v Swaffield (1874)** a horse was sent by rail and on its arrival at its destination there was no one to collect it. GNR incurred the expense of stabling the horse for the night. It was held that GNR was an agent of necessity, who therefore had authority to incur the expense in question.

Agency of ratification

If a duly appointed agent exceeds his authority, or a person having no authority purports to act as agent, the principal is not bound. The principal may however adopt the contract at a later date, provided:

I   The agent named or otherwise identified his principal and the third party knew that the agent was contracting as agent. In **Keighly Maxsted v Durant**, A was authorised by P to buy wheat at a certain price. In excess of his authority, A bought from T at above that price. A professedly contracted in his own name, without disclosing the agency to T. The next day P purported to ratify. It was held that P could not ratify because A had neither named nor otherwise identified P and T did not know he was dealing with an agent.

II   The principal had contractual capacity at the date of both the contract and the ratification. If the principal is a company, this means it must have been incorporated at the time of the contract. In **Kelner v Baxter (1866)** P sold wine to D who purported to act as agent for a company which was about to be formed. When it was formed the company attempted to ratify the contract made by D. It was held that it could not do so, since it was not in existence when the contract was made.

III The principal had full knowledge of all material facts, or was prepared to ratify in any event. For example, in **Fitzmaurice v Bayley**, a principal in effect said to a third party – I don't know what my agent has agreed to do, but I must support him. It was held that he had ratified. Although he did not know that the agent had exceeded his authority, he had agreed to take the risk.

IV The principal must ratify the whole contract, not merely parts of it.

V The principal must ratify within a reasonable time.

VI The principal must communicate a sufficiently clear intention of ratifying, either by express words or by conduct.

A void or illegal contract cannot be ratified because it is of no legal effect from its inception.

It can therefore be seen that the main difference between creation of agency by ratification and creation by necessity is that agency of necessity is created by operation of law without the agreement of the principal, whereas agency by ratification can only be created with the knowledge and consent of the principal.

Question 1

Dan

The rules relating to the residual responsibility of retired partners for partnership debts depend on when the debts were contracted and the action taken by the former partner to announce their retirement from the business.

A retired partner remains liable for any debts or obligations incurred by the partnership prior to retirement. Thus the date of any contract determines responsibility: if the person was a partner when the contract was entered into, then they are responsible, even if the contract is completed after their retirement. It is possible for the retiring partner to be discharged from existing liability though as a consequence of a contract of novation.

Novation is essentially a tripartite contract involving the retiring partner, the remaining members of the continuing partnership and the existing creditors. Under such an agreement any liability of the retiring partner is passed to the remaining partners. As creditors effectively give up rights against the retiring partner, their approval is required. Such approval may be express or it may be implied from the course of dealing between the creditor and the firm.

Where someone deals with a partnership after a change in membership, they are entitled to treat all the apparent members of the old firm as still being members until they receive notice of any change in the membership.

In order to avoid liability for future contracts, a retiring partner must ensure that individual notice is given to existing customers of the partnership; and advertise the retirement in the London Gazette. This serves as general notice to people who were not customers of the firm prior to the partner's retirement, but knew that that person had been a partner in the business. Such an advert is effective whether or not it comes to the attention of third parties.

It follows from this that Dan could be liable for any debts towards the longstanding customer, Greg, unless he has taken steps to notify Greg of his retirement from the partnership, which does not appear likely.

Frank

Frank had let it be known generally that he was a partner and if, as would appear likely, the other partners knew about Frank's claim and did nothing to deny it, then they would be estopped subsequently from insisting on the true nature of affairs **(Freeman and Lockyer v Buckhurst Park Properties Ltd (1964))**. Frank would therefore be seen as a partner with the authority to bind the partnership (s.5 Partnership Act 1890). However, the partnership would be liable for the contracts even if the other partners were not aware of Frank's claim to be a partner. The question states that Eve and Clare left much of the day to day running of the business to Frank and it can be seen that, on that basis alone, he had the authority to manage the business irrespective of the question as to whether he was a member of the partnership or not. Third parties are entitled to assume that agents holding a particular position have all the powers that are usually provided to such an agent. This is referred to as implied actual authority and means that, without actual knowledge to the contrary, outsiders may safely assume that an agent has the usual authority that goes with their position **(Watteau v Fenwick (1893))**. Entering into ordinary trading contracts, such as the one with Greg, would come within Frank's implied actual authority as the business manager.

As for Frank's liability, anyone who represents themselves, or knowingly permits themselves to be represented, as a partner is liable to any person who gives the partnership credit on the basis of that representation. The partners would be estopped from denying Frank's membership if they knew of his claim to be a partner. Frank would also be estopped from denying that he was a partner. Frank therefore would also be liable for the debts.

Clare and Eve being active partners have full responsibility for the partnership debts.

Under s9 of the PA 1890, the liability of partners as regards debts or contracts is joint and several. The effect of joint liability used to be that, although the partners were collectively responsible, a person who took action against one of the partners could take no further action against the other partners, even if they had not recovered all that was owing to them. That situation was remedied by the Civil Liability (Contributions Act) 1978. This act effectively states that a judgment against one partner does not bar a subsequent action against the other partners. This means that as regards Greg's debt Clare, Dan, Eve and Frank are all personally responsible for any shortfall and he may take action against any one of them. The one against whom the action is taken will be able to claim a proportionate indemnity from the others.

Question 2

Grounds for dissolution

Partnerships are created by agreement and may be brought to an end in the same way. However, subject to any provision to the contrary in the partnership agreement, the PA 1890 provides for the dissolution of a partnership on the following grounds:

The expiry of a fixed term or the completion of a specified enterprise

It is possible for a partnership to be established for a stated period of time and at the end of that time the partnership will come to an end and the partnership will be dissolved. Alternatively it is possible for the partnership to be established in order to achieve a particular goal and again once that goal has been attained the partnership will come to an end.

The giving of notice

If the partnership is of indefinite duration, then it can be brought to an end by any one of the partners giving notice of an intention to dissolve the partnership.

The death or bankruptcy of any partner

As in English law the ordinary partnership has no legal personality in its own right, but merely exists as a collection of individuals, it is apparent that the death of a member will bring about the end of the partnership (n.b. this of course is not the case with limited partnerships formed under the Limited Liability Partnerships Act 2000 which does provide legal capacity to such partnerships formed under its provisions). The bankruptcy of a partner has the same effect.

Although the occurrence of either of these events will bring the original partnership to an end, it is usual for partnership agreements to provide for the continuation of the business under the control of the remaining/solvent partners who will constitute a new partnership.

Illegality

The occurrence of events making the continuation of the partnership illegal will bring it to an end. This is illustrated by the case of **Hudgell, Yeates and Co v Watson (1978)**. Practising solicitors are legally required to have a practice certificate. However, one of the members of a three-person partnership forgot to renew his practice certificate and thus was not legally entitled to act as a solicitor. It was held that the failure to renew the practice certificate brought the partnership to an end, although a new partnership continued between the other two members of the old partnership.

By court order

In addition to the provisions listed above, the court may, mainly by virtue of s35 of the PA 1890, order the dissolution of the partnership under the following circumstances:

I   Where a partner becomes a patient under the Mental Health Act 1893.

II   Where a partner suffers some other permanent incapacity.

        This provision is analogous to the previous one. It should be noted that it is for the other partners to apply for dissolution and that the incapacity alleged as the basis of dissolution must be permanent.

III   Where a partner engages in activity prejudicial to the business.

        Such activity may be directly related to the business, such as the misappropriation of funds. Alternatively, it may take place outside the business but operate to its detriment. An example might be a criminal conviction for fraud.

IV   Where a partner persistently breaches the partnership agreement.

        This provision also relates to conduct which makes it unreasonable for the other partners to carry on in business with the party at fault.

IV   Where a partner persistently breaches the partnership agreement.

        This provision also relates to conduct which makes it unreasonable for the other partners to carry on in business with the party at fault.

IV   Where the business can only be carried on at a loss.

This provision is a corollary of the very first section of the PA 1890 in which the pursuit of profit is part of the definition of the partnership form. If such profit cannot be achieved, then the partners are entitled to avoid loss by bringing the partnership to an end.

VI   Where it is just and equitable to do so.

The courts have wide discretion in relation to the implementation of this power. A similar provision operates within company legislation (s.122 Insolvency Act 1986) and the two provisions come together in the cases involving quasi-partnerships **(Re Yenidje Tobacco Co Ltd (1916) and Ebrahimi v Westbourne Galleries Ltd (1973))**.

Question 1

Except in relation to specifically exempted companies, such as those involved in charitable work, companies are required to indicate that they are operating on the basis of limited liability. Thus private companies are required to end their names, either with the word 'limited' or the abbreviation 'ltd', and public companies must end their names with the words 'public limited company' or the abbreviation 'plc'. Welsh companies may use the Welsh language equivalents (Companies Act (CA) 2006 ss58, 59 & 60).

Although there is no longer an official Business Names Registry, the Registrar of companies maintains a register of business names, and will refuse to register any company with a name that is the same as one already on that index (CA06 s66(1)). This control is less rigorous than that exercised under the previous legislation and has led to an increase in the use of the tort of 'passing off', as a means of protecting the goodwill attached to particular business names (see (b) below).

Certain categories of names are, subject to the decision of the Secretary of State, unacceptable per se, as follows:

- Names which in the opinion of the Secretary of State constitute an offence (s53(a)). As an example, it is illegal for non-designated businesses to claim to be banks, but the powers of the Secretary of State are wide enough to control names which might be considered as inciting race hatred.

- Names which in the opinion of the Secretary of State are offensive (s53(b)).

- Names which are likely to give the impression that the company is connected with either government or local government authorities (s54(1)).

- Names which include a word or expression specified under the Company and Business Names Regulations 1981 (s55(1)).

  This category requires the express approval of the Secretary of State for the use of any of the names or expressions contained on the list, and relates to areas which raise a matter of public concern in relation to their use.

Under s67 of the Companies Act 2006 the Secretary of State has power to require a company to alter its name under the following circumstances:

- Where it is the same as a name already on the Registrar's index of company names.

- Where it is 'too like' a name that is on that index.

The name of a company can always be changed by a special resolution of the company so long as it continues to comply with the above requirements (s77).

Although a company's name must not be the same as any already registered, the Business Names Act 1985 does not prevent one business from using the same, or a very similar, name as another business. However, the tort of passing off prevents one person from using any name which is likely to divert business their way by suggesting that the business is actually that of some other person or is connected in any way with that other business. It thus enables people to protect the goodwill they have built up in relation to their business activity. In **Ewing v Buttercup Margarine Co Ltd (1917)** the plaintiff successfully prevented the defendants from using a name that suggested a link with his existing dairy company.

Question 2

A   Model articles of association are prescribed by the Secretary of State, although companies may alter the models to suit their particular circumstances and requirements. It is usual for companies to draw up their own particular articles, but if they elect not to draw up their own, the model articles apply automatically. The model articles also apply to the extent that the company's articles have not expressly excluded their provisions. The model articles cover such matters as the issue and transfer of shares, the rights attaching to particular shares, the rules relating to the holding of meetings, the powers of directors, and the payment of dividends.

B   Section 33 of the Companies Act provides that the provisions of a company's constitution (i.e. its articles) 'bind the company and its members to the same extent as if there were covenants on the part of the company and each member to observe those provisions'. This section has three effects.

I   The documents establish a contract which binds each member to the company. Thus in **Hickman v Kent or Romney Marsh Sheep-Breeders' Association (1915),** the company was able to enforce an article against a member that provided that disputes involving the member and the company should go to arbitration.

II   The company is contractually bound to each of its members. On this basis in **Pender v Lushington (1877)** a member was able to sue in respect of the wrongful denial of his right to vote at a company meeting.

III   The articles constitute a contract between the members. In **Rayfield v Hands (1960)**, the articles of the company provided that, where shareholders wished to transfer their shares, they should inform the directors of the company, who were obliged to take the shares equally between them at fair value. When the directors refused to purchase the plaintiff's shares, the court held that the directors were bound as members by the articles and therefore had to comply with the procedure set out there.

Articles only operate as a contract in respect of membership rights and obligations. Consequently it has been held that, although members can enforce them, non-members, or members suing in some other capacity than that of a member, will not be able to enforce promises established in the company's articles. In **Eley v Positive Government Security Life Assurance Co (1876)**, the articles of a company stated that the plaintiff was to be appointed as the company's solicitor. It was held that Eley could not use the articles to establish a contract between himself and the company as those articles only created a contract between the company and its members. Although Eley was in fact a member, he was not suing in that capacity but in the capacity of solicitor, which was not a membership right.

C   Section 21 of the Companies Act 2006 allows companies to alter their articles by passing a special resolution. It is, however, possible to entrench certain provisions. This means that they can only be altered by following a specified procedure, such as obtaining unanimous consent: s22.

Any attempt in the articles to provide that a particular provision is unalterable is ineffective. The articles cannot be altered, however, in such a way as to conflict with any provision of the Companies Act. In particular, no member can be bound by any alteration to subscribe for more shares or increase their liability in any way (s25).

Any alteration must be made 'bona fide in the interest of the company as a whole', although the exact meaning of this phrase is not altogether clear. It is evident that it involves a subjective element in that those deciding the alteration must actually believe they are acting in the interest of the company. There is additionally, however, an objective element. In **Greenhalgh v Arderne Cinemas Ltd (1951)** it was stated that any alteration had to be in the interest of the 'individual hypothetical member'.

In **Brown v British Abrasive Wheel Co (1919)** an alteration to the articles of the company was proposed to give the majority shareholders the right to buy the shares of the minority. It was held that the alteration was invalid as it would benefit the majority shareholders rather than the company as a whole. However, in **Sidebottom v Kershaw Leese & Co (1920)**, an alteration to the articles gave the directors the power to require any shareholder, who entered into competition with the company, to transfer their shares to nominees of the directors at a fair price. It was held that under those circumstances the alteration was valid as it would benefit the company as a whole.

Question 3 - Fixed Test 2

This question is a **FIXED TEST. Please answer the question in full, without reference to an answer.**

Then log-in to en-gage and answer fixed test 1 based on your full long-form answer

...or alternatively register using the information at the back of your Complete Text and then go to www.en-gage.co.uk

Question 1

A   The judge in **Re Yorkshire Woolcombers' Association (1903)** stated that a floating charge has the following characteristics:

- it attaches to a class of asset, both present and future
- the assets within the class will be changing from time to time
- until some step is taken which crystallises the charge, the company remains free to deal with the assets in the ordinary course of business.

B   Floating charges have the following disadvantages which may mean that they provide inadequate security:

- Priorities: fixed charges take priority over floating charges even though they may have been created later.
- The company's freedom to deal with assets subject to a floating charge includes the ability of the company to dispose of the assets. This may mean that if a liquidation occurs there are few assets available to the floating chargee.
- On liquidation the claim of the floating chargee is subject to the prior claims of any fixed chargees on the same assets and the preferential creditors.

C   Wealthy should check the register of charges at Hardup plc's registered office and Companies House. In order to be valid, all charges must be registered at Companies House within 21 days of their creation. It is Hardup plc's duty to register the charge, but anyone interested (i.e. Wealthy plc) may affect the registration. If unregistered, the charge is void as against the liquidator, i.e. Wealthy plc becomes an unsecured creditor if Hardup plc goes into insolvent liquidation.

Question 2

As a general rule, a limited company cannot purchase its own shares because this would lead to a reduction of the company's share capital.

However, s690 CA 2006 allows a company to purchase its own shares subject to any restriction or prohibition in its articles. Therefore LCP Ltd's purchase of Pat's shares will be lawful if the following conditions are complied with.

(1) LCP Ltd's articles of association must not prohibit the purchase by the company of its own shares. If the articles need to be changed, this can be done by special resolution (75% majority), unless the provision is entrenched, in which case the specified procedure to change the articles must be followed.

(2) Pat's shares must be fully paid for.

(3) As the company is a private company, the purchase will be an off-market purchase. The contract for such a purchase must be authorised in advance by special resolution. Thus a draft contract between Pat and LCP Ltd detailing the purchase must be drawn up and approved by the members. Pat may not use his shares to vote on the resolution.

(4) The shares must be paid for and as a general rule the financing must come from distributable profits or from the proceeds of a fresh issue of shares made especially for the purpose. If financed out of distributable profits, a transfer must be made, of an amount equal to the nominal value of the purchased shares, from distributable profit to capital redemption reserve.

As LCP Ltd is a private company, it may finance the purchase out of capital to the extent that its distributable profits, together with the proceeds of any fresh issue, are insufficient. Such a capital payment is permissible if (i) the directors make a statutory declaration, backed by a special auditors' report, that LCP Ltd is able to pay its debts and will be so able for the next year, and (ii) a special resolution authorising the payment is passed. Objection can be made to the court by any creditor or member.

(5) Once the shares have been purchased they must be cancelled and a return detailing the purchase must be made to the registrar of companies.

Question 1

S168 CA 2006 states that a director can be removed from office at any time by ordinary resolution (i.e. only a simple majority is required). The resolution requires special notice (28 days) and Julie can require the company to circulate written representations to members. S168 therefore overrides the provision in ABC Ltd's articles and Julie's service contract. Provided the procedure was followed correctly, the members had the necessary authority to remove Julie.

As regards the provision in Julie's service contract, if the contract has been properly approved by the members, she will have an action against the company for breach of contract. However, if it has not been approved and the correct procedures under s168 have been carried out, the contract has been properly brought to an end and no action will lie for breach.

As regards the provision in the articles, s33 CA 2006 states that the articles are a contract between the company and its members in their capacity as members. The situation is similar to **Eley v Positive Government Security Life Assurance Co (1876)** in which it was held that a provision in the articles stating that Eley was to be the company's solicitor was not enforceable as it was not a right given to him as a member. Therefore, as Julie is affected by the breach of the articles in her capacity as a director, she cannot sue the company for breach of the articles.

Question 2

A   The purchase of the machinery from Nim Ltd

Through his majority interest in Nim Ltd, Len has an interest in the contract with Mod plc.

This means that he should have declared his interest to the board of Mod plc at the meeting at which the contract was discussed in order to comply with s175 CA 2006. He should not have voted at the board meeting at which the contract was approved, nor should he have been counted in any necessary quorum for the meeting. There is therefore a clear breach of duty by Len.

Accordingly, Owen is advised that Mod plc (rather than Owen personally) has grounds for an action against Len to make him account for any profit he made on the deal. It may also be possible to avoid the contract with Nim Ltd.

A company is a connected person of a director if the director controls more than 20% of its shares. Nim Ltd is therefore a connected person of Len. If the value of the machinery was more than £100,000, the contract was substantial and this means that it should have been put before the members of Mod plc so as to comply with s190 CA 2006. If s190 is applicable, breach of it renders the contract voidable. It also renders Len and Nim Ltd liable to account for any profit made or to indemnify Mod plc for any loss. Again, any such action must be brought by Mod plc, not Owen personally.

B   The development of the new product by Nim Ltd

Under s177 CA06, Len is under a statutory duty to declare his interest in any proposed transaction or arrangement. He should therefore have declared the extent and nature of his interest to the other directors. This declaration can be made in writing, at a board meeting or by a general notice that he has an interest in a third party.

The situation is similar to that in the case of **IDC v Cooley (1972)**, in which a director was made to account for the profit he made on a contract taken personally because the opportunity to take that contract arose through his directorship. It made no difference that the company would not have been offered the contract by the other party. However, the facts here are not the same as **IDC** in that here the board of Mod plc has decided not to develop the new product and therefore Mod plc is not actively pursuing the opportunity. In **Peso Silver Mines v Cropper (1965)** it was held that a director was not in breach of duty where he took an opportunity personally after it had been rejected in good faith by his board. The board of Mod plc has rejected the opportunity. The difficulty is whether or not this decision was reached in good faith. This will not be the case if Len attempted to persuade the board to reject the opportunity because he wished to take it personally, or, indeed, if he did not use his knowledge and experience for the benefit of Mod plc and thus failed to point out to the board why he liked the new product. If Len is accountable, any action to recover the profit must be brought by Mod plc, not Owen personally.

Question 3 - Fixed Test 3

This question is a **FIXED TEST**. Please answer the question in full, without reference to an answer.

Then log-in to en-gage and answer fixed test 1 based on your full long-form answer

...or alternatively register using the information at the back of your Complete Text and then go to www.en-gage.co.uk

Question 1

A Requirements for companies in respect of holding AGMs

S336 Companies Act 2006 requires every public company to hold an AGM within the six months following their financial year end.

If an AGM is not held in accordance with s336 CA06, the company and every officer in default are liable to a fine.

Private companies are not required to hold an AGM.

B Written resolution

A private company can use a written resolution to pass any type of resolution (ie, ordinary or special) which would otherwise need to be passed at a general or class meeting.

This is subject to two exceptions: removal of directors and removal of auditors – both require a meeting to be convened so that the person concerned can exercise his rights to attend and speak on the resolution.

The resolution is achieved once a copy has been signed by the requisite percentage of members who would be entitled to attend and vote at a meeting. The resolution takes effect from the date the last person signs.

A copy of the proposed written resolution must be forwarded to the company's auditor (if any). Failure to do so is a criminal offence, but failure does not affect the validity of the resolution.

All written resolutions must be recorded in the company's Register of written resolutions.

Question 1

A   One of the many consequences of incorporation is that a registered company becomes a legal entity in its own right having existence apart from its member shareholders. One of the attributes of this legal personality is that the company has not only separate, but perpetual existence, in that it continues irrespective of changes in its membership. Indeed the company can continue to exist where it has no members at all. Winding up, or liquidation, is the process whereby the life of the company is brought to an end and its assets realised and distributed to its members and/or creditors. The rules governing winding up are detailed in the provisions of the Insolvency Act 1986 (IA) and the exact nature of the procedure depends on the type of winding up involved, which in turn depends upon the solvency of the company at the time when liquidation commences. Winding up can be conducted on a voluntary basis, in which case the members of the company themselves determine that the time has come for it to come to an end. Alternatively the court may make an order that the company's life should come to an end. This question refers to the first of these alternatives, voluntary winding up.

A   Section 84 IA states that a company may be wound up voluntarily:

   I   when any period fixed for the duration of the company by the articles expires or any event occurs which shall, according to the articles, lead to its dissolution. Under such circumstances the winding up has to be approved by an ordinary resolution.

   II for any other reason whatsoever. Under these circumstances a special resolution is required to approve the winding up.

   In either case the winding up is deemed to have started on the date that the appropriate resolution was passed.

There are two distinct forms of voluntary liquidation:

I   Members' voluntary winding up

This takes place when the directors of the company are of the opinion that the company is solvent and is capable of paying off its creditors. The directors are required to make a formal declaration to the effect that they have investigated the affairs of the company and that in their opinion it will be able to pay its debts within 12 months of the start of liquidation. It is a criminal offence for directors to make a false declaration without reasonable grounds. On appointment, by an ordinary resolution of the company, the job of the liquidator is to wind up the affairs of the company, to realise the assets and distribute the proceeds to its creditors. On completion of this task the liquidator must present a report of the process to a final meeting of the shareholders. The liquidator then informs the Registrar of the holding of the final meeting and submits a copy of his report to it. The Registrar formally registers these reports and the company is deemed to be dissolved three months after that registration.

II   Creditors' voluntary winding up

This takes place when the company is insolvent when it is decided to wind it up. The essential difference between this and the former type of winding up is that, as the name implies, the creditors have an active role to play in overseeing the liquidation of the company. Firstly a meeting of the creditors must be called within 14 days of the resolution to liquidate the company at which the directors must submit a statement of the company's affairs. The creditors have the final say in who should be appointed as liquidator and may, if they elect, appoint a liquidation committee to work with the liquidator. On completion of the winding up the liquidator calls and submits his report to meetings of the members and creditors. The liquidator then informs the Companies' Registry of the holding of these final meetings and submits a copy of his report to it. The Registrar formally registers these reports and the company is deemed to be dissolved three months after that registration.

Question 1

A   The Cadbury Committee examined boardroom accountability issues and one of its solutions was the monitoring role of non-executives directors.

Cadbury recommended that there should be sufficient independent NEDs in number and quality to carry significant weight in board decisions. These NEDs should be independent of the company.

The NEDs should sit in sub-committees of the board to cover issues concerning appointments of directors, remuneration of directors and the audit process. The role of the NEDs is to bring judgement and experience to the board that the executive directors might lack. In contrast to executive directors, NEDs do not usually have a full time-relationship with the company. They are not employees and only receive directors' fees. They are expected to exert a measure of control over the executive directors to ensure that they run the company in the company's best interest. NEDs should scrutinise the performance of management in meeting goals and objectives, and monitor the reporting of performance. As far as company law is concerned there is no distinction between the executive directors and NEDs; both are subject to the same control and liabilities.

The following are evidence in favour of the presence of NEDs on boards.

There is evidence that non-executive directors perform an important corporate governance function. Without the monitoring function of NEDs, it would be more likely that executive directors would be able to manipulate their position by gaining complete control over their own remuneration packages and securing their jobs.

Without NEDs, executive directors can become excessively cohesive.

The addition of the NEDs brings new information and ideas and allows the entire board to make sound decisions.

NEDs provide an independent and fresh review of long term decisions, effectuate impartial, uncontaminated audits of managerial performance and counterbalance the influence of top management.

NED's independent influence has led to the removal of ineffective chief executives.

However, there is also a perception that the involvement of non-executive directors can damage corporate governance by reducing entrepreneurship in the business and weakening board unity.

This was certainly the view expressed by many board directors in their initial response to the Higgs recommendations to broaden the role and effectiveness of non-executive directors in the UK. Higgs recommended that a senior independent director should be identified and this senior NED should be available to shareholders if their concerns have not been met through normal channels of contact.

There was also potential for the appointment of non-executive directors to result in more cronyism and a more comfortable network of close ties and cosy relationships between the directors of leading companies.

Accusations were made that the new level of non-executive directors provides just more 'jobs for the boys' and the opportunity for even firmer golden handshakes than retiring directors receive already. Nonetheless despite these criticisms, the presence of independent non-executive directors is necessary to improve the quality of governance in listed companies.

B   The Higgs review has provided detailed guidance on the role of the NEDs.

It specified the number of independent NEDs on a main board and crucially gives a good definition of independence.

Below are the key recommendations of Higgs to ensure the independence of NEDs.

(1) At least half the board, excluding the chairman, should be independent NEDs.

(2) Higgs sets out a definition of independence. A NED is considered independent when the board determines that the director is independent in character and judgement and there are no relationships or circumstances which could affect, or appear to affect, the director's judgment. Such relationships and circumstances arise where the director is or has been an employee of the company, has or had a business relationship with the company, is being paid by the company other than a director's fee and certain other payments; has family ties to the company or its employees; holds cross-directorships or has significant links with other directors through involvement in other companies or bodies; represents a significant shareholder, has served on the board for 10 years.

(3) The board should identify in its annual report the NEDs it determines to be independent. The board should state its reasons if a director is considered independent notwithstanding the existence of relationships or circumstances which may appear relevant to its determination.

Higgs contribution is significant. Its key weakness is perhaps companies get to say who is independent or not according to the Higgs criteria without additional external scrutiny.

C   The Combined Code is a set of principles, rather than a set of rules. It requires the directors to describe in their own words the way in which they have applied the general principles of corporate governance.

Self-regulation: advantages

– Legislation may be too rigid and difficult to change to keep pace with corporate change. A 'one size fits all' piece of legislation may be based on the 'lowest common denominator' and hinder rather than improve good governance because of the diversity amongst corporations.

– The present system is flexible and provides for responsiveness to change. This means that the Combined Code can be updated to respond to changing conditions and changing expectations of shareholders and others.

– Because the directors report on the actual circumstances of their own company, the report should be more meaningful than one based on specific detailed requirements.

– A principles-based approach encourages the directors to follow the spirit of the Code; whereas a rules-based approach may result in tick-box mentality. This means that, under a rules-based approach, the directors may follow the letter of the rules rather than their spirit.

Self-regulation: disadvantages

– Bias – favouring the interest of members at the expense of other interests.

– Prevents coherent reforms by government as self-regulatory practices will have developed and been relied upon.

– Enforcement problems – insufficient investigatory and enforcement powers and difficulties of co-ordination.

Question 1

Under the Criminal Justice Act (CJA) 1993, insider dealing involves the deliberate exploitation of unpublished price sensitive information obtained through a privileged relationship to make a profit by dealing in securities of a company when the price of the securities would be altered if the information were to be disclosed.

Is Susan an insider?

Susan will be an insider if she has information which she knows is inside information and that she knows it is from an inside source: Section 57 CJA 1993. This is a subjective belief and understanding. Anyone can be an insider, but the information must come direct from a director of the issuer. Susan heard the information during the course of her employment and from the way in which the question is phrased she is aware that the information is coming from the Chairman of HIT plc.

Is this insider information?

Section 56(1) CJA 1993 describes what constitutes inside information.

It has to relate to particular securities or to a particular issuer of securities.

It is specific or precise. The rumour which Susan has is that there is to be a takeover bid and this is specific information under this section. This is not a rumour or casual information.

It has not been made public. Section 58 states publication means the information is provided to investors or is to be found in public records. The facts here indicate that this information has not been made public.

If made public would be likely to have a significant effect on the price. This condition is satisfied in our present scenario.

The offence in section 52 is dealing with the price-affected securities in a prohibited way. This means dealing with the securities yourself, encouraging another to deal in the securities or disclosing information other than in the proper course of employment.

In considering whether Susan has encouraged Joseph to deal with the securities, it makes no difference whether she stands to make any gain from the deal. We are not told what Susan said to James, so it is difficult to conclude that Susan had encouraged Joseph to deal in the shares. However, in the facts it would appear that Susan will be guilty of insider dealing as she disclosed the information otherwise than in the proper performance of her employment and in this situation it is irrelevant whether Susan intends Joseph to act on the information or suspects that he might.

Defences

Under s53 CJA 1993, Susan will have a defence if she can show that:

(1) She did not expect the dealing in the shares to result in a profit (or the avoidance of a loss) attributable to the fact that the information in question was price sensitive. It is probably difficult to prove in this situation.

(2) She believed on reasonable grounds that the information had been widely disclosed.

Joseph

Joseph has received the information and knows that it is inside information. He will be an insider by virtue of being tipped off by Susan and so will fall under section 57(2)(b) CJA 1993.

He has dealt with securities which are price-affected securities and so has committed an offence under s52(1) CJA 1993.

Defences

The only possible defence is under Sched 1, para 2(1) which provides that a person who has market information as an insider has a defence if he can show that it was reasonable for them to have acted as they did despite being in possession of the information as an insider.

However para 2(2) states account must be taken of the circumstances and capacity in which the individual first had the information so it looks as though there will be no defence for Joseph.

Question 2

The stock market value of shares in a company fluctuates in relation to the underlying performance of the company and the expectations of investors. Amongst other things, good company results will lead to an increase in the value of the shares. Since share prices fluctuate on the stock market, the possibility arises for individuals to make large profits, or losses, by speculating in shares. It can also provide people with the opportunity to take advantage of their close relationship with particular companies in order to make profits from illegal share dealing. Such illegal trading in shares, known as insider dealing, occurs when someone trades on the basis of price sensitive information before the general public has access to that information. Insider dealing is governed by Part V of the Criminal Justice Act 1993.

Section 52 of the Criminal Justice Act 1993 states that an individual, who has information as an insider, is guilty of insider dealing if he deals in securities that are price-affected securities in relation to the information. An individual is also guilty of an offence if he encourages others to deal in securities that are linked with this information, or if he discloses the information otherwise than in the proper performance of his employment, office or profession.

Section 56 makes it clear that securities are price-affected in relation to inside information if the information, when made public, would be likely to have a significant effect on the price of those securities.

Section 57 defines an insider as a person who knows that he has inside information and knows that he has the information from an inside source. This section also states that inside source refers to information acquired through being a director, employee or shareholder of an issuer of securities, or having access to information by virtue of his employment. Additionally, individuals who acquire their information from those primary insiders (those previously mentioned) are also insiders.

There are a number of defences to a charge of insider dealing. For example, s53 makes it clear that no person can be so charged if he did not expect the dealing to result in any profit or the avoidance of any loss.

On summary conviction an individual found guilty of insider dealing is liable to a fine not exceeding the statutory maximum and/or a maximum of six months' imprisonment. On indictment the penalty is an unlimited fine and/or a maximum of seven years' imprisonment. There is also the possibility that the person who benefits from the information, which belongs to the company, will be required to account to the company for any profit made. This would certainly be the case with regard to directors who engaged in insider dealing, as they would have breached their duty to the company.

Applying the law to the situation in the question, it can be seen that, as an employee of Dome plc, Ewan is an insider under s57, and the information he has is certain to affect the price of the company's shares. It therefore follows that when he buys the shares in Dome plc, Ewan is liable to a charge of insider dealing under s52(1) of the Criminal Justice Act 1993. Ewan is also liable for the separate offence, under s52(2), of disclosing the information to Frank otherwise than in the proper performance of his employment.

Because he received the information from an insider, Frank is treated as an insider under s57 and is liable for trading on the basis of the information under s52.

Index

Index

Index

Index